RAFLE
Research Academy for Foreign Language Examinations
朗阁海外考试研究中心
Since 1999

朗阁IELTS应试系列

雅思精品系列教程

CW01651492

中心

xaminations

IELTS

雅思精品写作

王华 张月 曹美玲 编著

上海交通大學出版社
SHANGHAI JIAO TONG UNIVERSITY PRESS

内容提要

本书的目标读者是雅思备考考生，也可供雅思写作老师上课所用。本书共分10章，第一章重点介绍了雅思写作基本信息和评分标准解读。第二章至第四章讲述了雅思写作小作文的几种类型：静态图、动态图、地图和流程图。第五章至第八章按照话题划分，将大作文分为教育类、科技类、媒体类等几大版块，每个版块里分别融入了具体话题及思考角度，话题词汇及相关句型翻译、段落写作及论证方式的具体讲解。最后两章重点讲解了G类书信写作。

图书在版编目(CIP)数据

雅思精品写作／王华，张月，曹美玲编著. —上海：
上海交通大学出版社，2017（2018重印）
ISBN 978-7-313-15956-4

Ⅰ.①雅… Ⅱ.①王… ②张… ③曹… Ⅲ.①
IELTS-写作-自学参考资料 Ⅳ.①H315

中国版本图书馆CIP数据核字(2016)第256562号

雅思精品写作

编　　著：王　华　张　月　曹美玲
出版发行：上海交通大学出版社　　地　　址：上海市番禺路951号
邮政编码：200030　　电　　话：021-64071208
出 版 人：谈毅
印　　制：常熟市文化印刷有限公司　　经　　销：全国新华书店
开　　本：787mm×1092mm　1/16　　印　　张：15.5
字　　数：354千字
版　　次：2017年1月第1版　　印　　次：2018年1月第3次印刷
书　　号：ISBN 978-7-313-15956-4/H
定　　价：49.00元

总　序

朗阁海外考试研究中心（Research Academy for Foreign Language Examinations，简称RAFLE）成立于1999年，是朗阁教育集团旗下的专业学术机构，是针对各类海外语言考试及教学进行系统性研究的专业研发机构。RAFLE研发团队拥有上百位资深中外研究人员，他们遍布全国36个大中型城市，并长期活跃在雅思、新托福、SAT、ACT、GRE、GMAT、TOEFL Junior、SSAT等各大教学领域，对提升朗阁教育集团整体教学水平和研发实力起着重要的作用。

雅思精品阶段系列丛书是由朗阁海外考试研究中心的资深研究员老师通过多年一线教学经验的总结，结合雅思考试的最新趋势所创作出的一套适合雅思考生备考的实用系列教材。该套教材旨在帮助中国考生熟悉、适应和从容应对雅思考试中各种题型的特点，了解和熟悉最新雅思考试的趋势和难点，掌握并灵活运用必要的考试技巧，提高应试能力。书中的内容讲练结合，难度贴近考试，适合具有大二、大三英语程度，已通过大学英语四级考试，英语基础较为扎实，但对雅思缺乏明确认识的考生。学习完该系列教程及相关课程，考生可以达到雅思6分及以上水平。

本系列丛书由朗阁海外考试研究中心教材编写团队共同制作完成。编写团队深谙雅思官方的出题思路，对教材的定位、全书的框架结构、重点难点、题目、解析及答案、精品系列与其他系列教材之间的通路等各个方面都进行了深入细致的探讨。教材从拟写草稿到初稿，再到后面的二稿和定稿，编写团队的老师们经过反复推敲，最终确定了最适合最实用的版本。

本书在使用的过程中，学生可以根据教材的章节顺序进行学习，也可根据自己的实际情况进行调整：

雅思精品系列的听力书，针对雅思听力题型多样性的特点和难点，以雅思听力题型为主线，对各题型的题型特点与核心技巧进行全面深入的总结和剖析，并基于研发中心对于雅思听力考试长期不懈的追踪，为考生抽丝剥茧，整理出最精准、最高效的解题方法步骤。

考生只要按照书中的要求训练和备考，一定可以融会贯通、取得优异的听力成绩，同时大大提升自身的听力能力。

阅读书由十个章节组成。第一章是雅思阅读简介。其中讲解了雅思阅读的题型介绍和技巧汇总，而且列出了相关的技能提高小贴士。第二章到第九章是雅思阅读题型技能训练，分析了雅思主流题型的题目特点和应试技巧，并辅以相关的文章训练，使学生掌握所有题型的应试方法。第十章是雅思阅读测试（学术类和普通培训类）。这章中的所有文章和题型设置，均参照最新雅思阅读考试的特点，从文章和题目的难度到各种题型所占比例，完全符合雅思考试的特点，尽可能还原雅思阅读考试的特点，而且考虑到学生类和普通培训类考生的不同需求，我们编排了两类练习。

写作对 A 类考生来说，建议大小作文交叉着学习。小作文练习熟练度很重要，但是四种类型一起学，难免效率会低下，所以建议交叉学。对 G 类考生来说，建议将 70% 的时间花在大作文方面，信件类文章相对简单，但要熟悉常用表达。

口语教材涵盖了雅思口语几乎所有的常考话题。针对每一类话题，本书中都有相应的高分范文和解析，并配有相应的练习题、小贴士和话题词汇。此外，本书还配有雅思口语的评分标准，以及 6.5 分水平的考生案例，供同学们参考。同学们可以根据目录来查找相应的雅思口语话题。朗读高分范文，并在老师的指导下分析范文。然后完成练习题，并背诵话题词汇。

本系列教材的主要编写者有：贾若寒、曹燕、王华、张月、梁一晓、赵瑜斌、曹美玲、活玮靖、李赫。在此谨向各位老师致以最衷心的感谢！

朗阁海外考试研究中心

2016.10.9

目　　录

Chapter 1 Introduction to IELTS Writing

雅思写作简介

Section 1 Basic Information

Part 1 关键数据

Task 1	20 minutes	150 words
Task 2	40 minutes	250 words

Part 2 分数换算

雅思大小作文(Task 1 和 Task 2)均有四项评分标准,每个标准的分数段都在 0 ~9 之间,每篇作文的最终得分是四个标准得分的平均值,最终的作文得分是大小作文得分分别乘以自己的权重(分别是 2/3 和 1/3)再相加的结果。例如,你的小作文得分是 5.5 分,大作文得分是 6 分,那么你的最终分数是

$$5.5 \times 1/3 + 6 \times 2/3 = 5.815(6)$$

Part 3 注意事项

EXAMINER'S USE ONLY

EXAMINER 2
TASK 2

TR		CC		LR		GRA	

UNDERLENGTH		NO OF WORDS		PENALTY	
OFF TOPIC		MEMORISED		ILLEGIBLE	

EXAMINER 1
TASK 2

TR		CC		LR		GRA	

UNDERLENGTH		NO OF WORDS		PENALTY	
OFF TOPIC		MEMORISED		ILLEGIBLE	

通过上图得知,考官在评卷时的参考依据,除了左边的四项评分标准(这在 Section 2 会重点讲解),右边方框中的一些关键词也值得注意。例如:

- Under length/No. of Words/Penalty：表明考官是有可能记录你的作文字数的，如果达不到最低标准则会扣分。
- Off-topic：文章写跑题了要扣分。
- Memorized：文章有背诵模板的迹象要扣分。
- Illegible：字迹不清会扣分。

Part 4 考试内容

A 类(学术类)小作文：数据图和非数据图。如：

Bar（静态图）

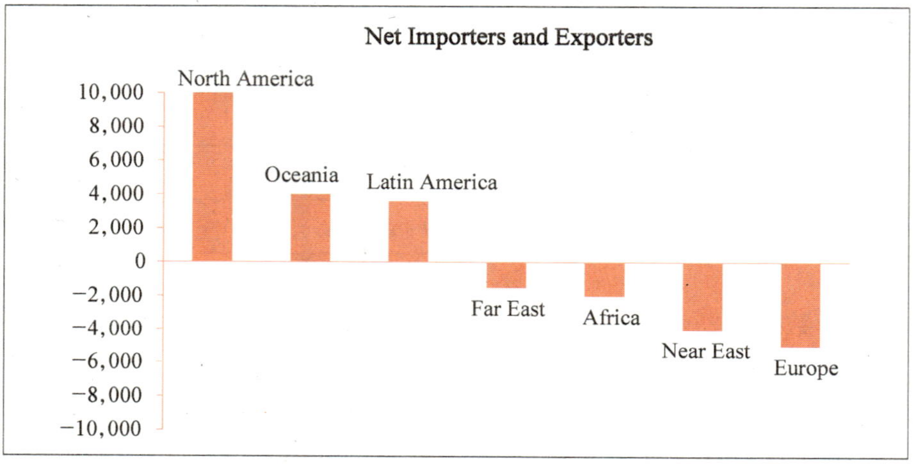

Pie（静态图）

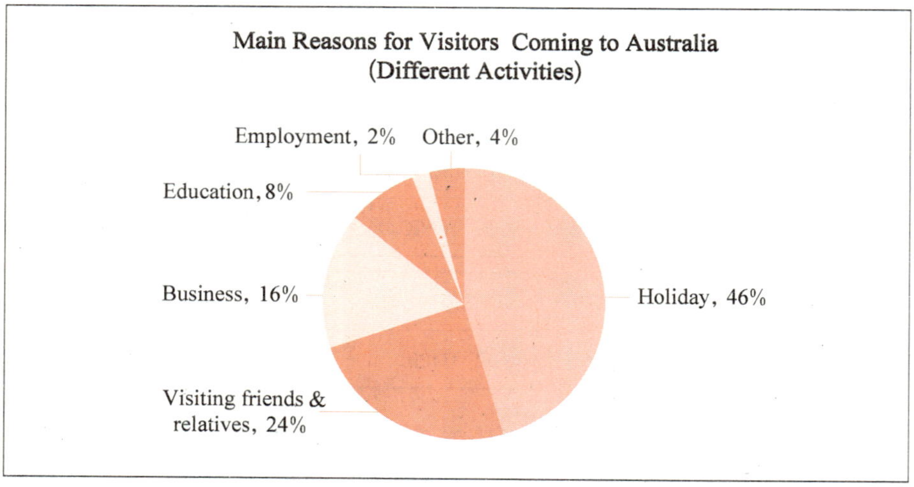

Line（动态图）

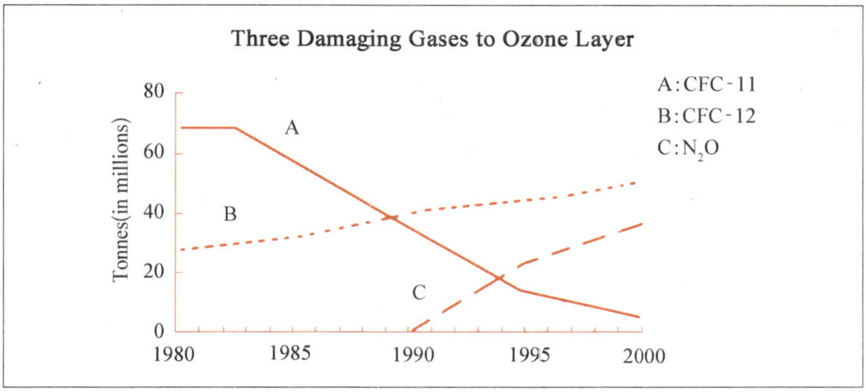

Table（动态图）

	1991	2001
	Australian Dollar Per Month	
Food	155	160
Electricity and Water	75	120
Clothing	30	20
Housing	95	100
Transport	70	45
Other goods and services*	250	270
Total	675	715

Map

area: 5,200 m^2 area: 6,800 m^2

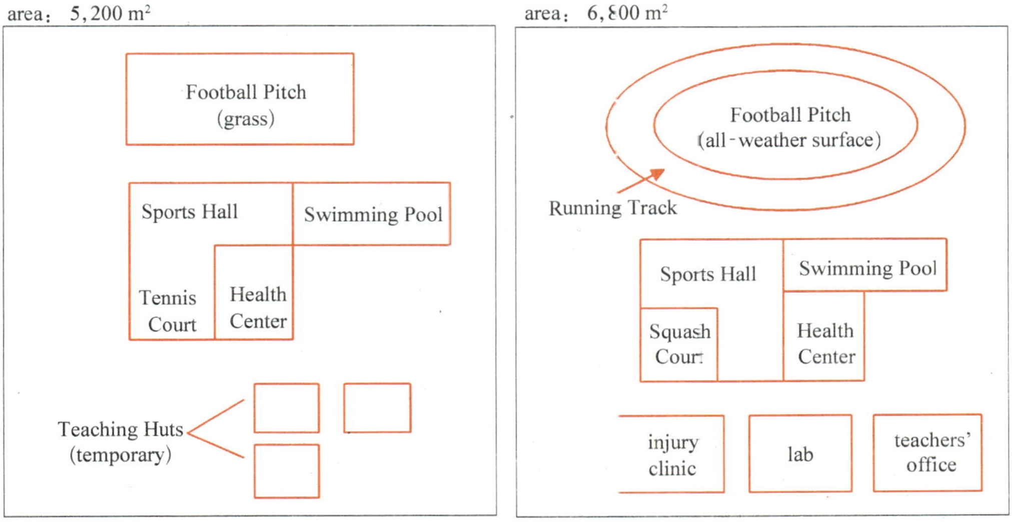

2007 Present day

Flow-chart

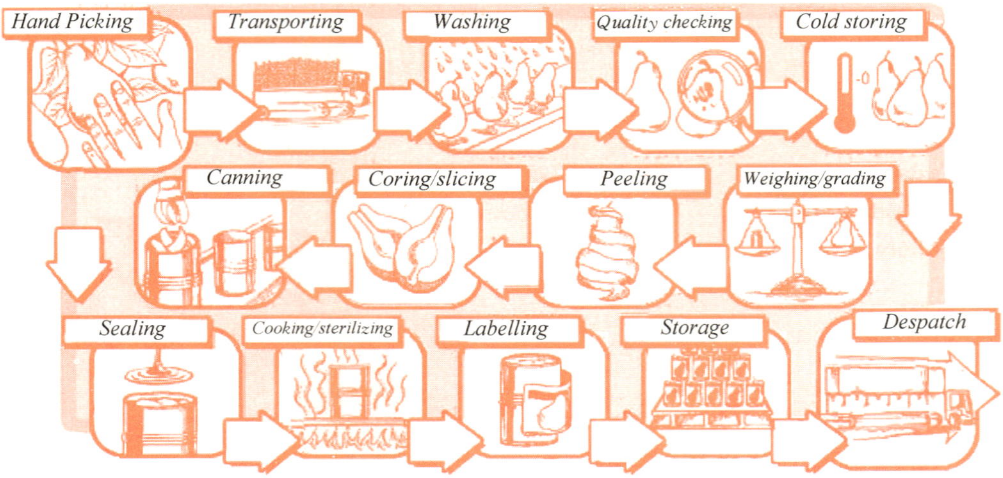

G 类(移民类)小作文:书信类,包括投诉信、咨询信、申请信、道歉信、友情信、推荐信等。如:

You will move to a new city for one-year work. Your friend said that he would help you find the accommodation. Write a letter to your friend. In your letter,

(1) give thanks to your friend;

(2) explain which district you would like to live in;

(3) describe what type of room you would like to rent.

A/G 类大作文:按话题分,包括教育类、科技类、政府类、媒体广告类、环境类、文化旅游类、社会类、犯罪法律类等;按问题形式分,包括观点类、report 问题及两者的结合。如:

(1) Differences between countries have become less evident, so we can enjoy the same films, brands and TV programs. Do you think the disadvantages of this outweigh the advantages? (全球化类,观点-利弊讨论)

(2) The government money should be invested in teaching science rather than other subjects so as to help a country make progress and develop. To what extent do you agree? (政府/教育类,观点-单边提问)

(3) Human activities have negative effects on plant and animal species. Some people think it is too late to do anything about this problem. Others believe effective measures can be taken to improve this situation. Discuss both views and give your opinion. (动植物类,观点-双边讨论)

(4) Nowadays, the increase in the production of consumer goods has caused great damage to the natural environment. What are the causes? What can be done to solve it? (环境类,report -原因 + 解决方案)

(5) Nowadays, children spend more time playing computer games than doing sports. Why? Is it a positive or negative trend? (科技类,report + 观点)

Section 2 Scoring Criteria

评分标准分为以下四条

- Task Achievement（T1）/Task Response（T2）（任务的完成/对任务的回应）
- Coherence & Cohesion（连贯与衔接）
- Lexical Resource（词汇资源）
- Grammatical Range & Accuracy（语法多样性及准确性）

Part 1 Task Achievement/Task Response

Task Achievement（TA）

在 TA 部分，要做到体现图表作文的 overview 和 key features。

例：

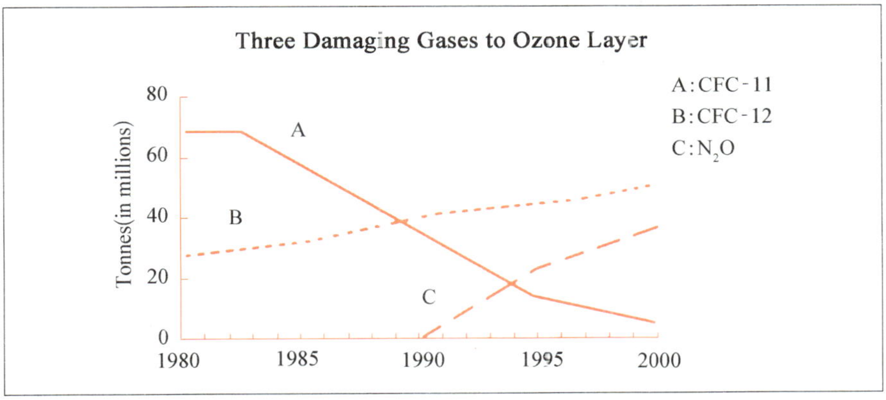

Overview：A 曲线是下降的，而 B 和 C 曲线是上升的。

Key features：起点、终点、交叉点、最高点、最低点所代表的意义。

练习 1：你能辨别出下图的 overview 和 key features 吗？

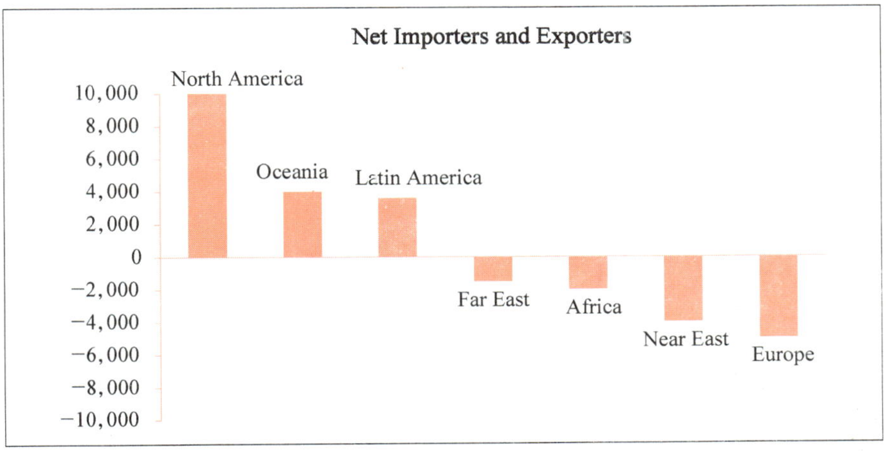

Overview: ____________________

Key features: ____________________

____

Task Response (TR)

在TR部分,要注意审题,作文必须要能够回应题目中所有的关键词,同时也要注意问题的重心,不能偏题。

例:

Some think that cultural traditions will be destroyed when they are used as money-making machines aimed at tourists. Other people think that it is the only way to save such traditions in the world. Discuss both views and give your own opinion.

关键词: will be destroyed, money making, the only way

Which one of the following should we focus on in our essay?

A. We should not use cultural traditions as money-making machines.

B. How to prevent tourists from destroying cultural traditions?

C. Whether the destruction of cultural traditions will happen?

Answer: C

练习2: 你能辨别出以下考题的关键词吗?

Some people believe countries have moral obligation to help each other, while others worry about the aid money cannot get to the poor of this world. Discuss both views and give your own opinion.

关键词: ____________________

Part 2 Coherence & Cohesion

顾名思义,Coherence & Cohesion (CC)是指文章的每个部分之间是自然地衔接在一起,让读者不必费劲地去思考你到底想要表达什么。在这个部分,至少要掌握以下三个要点。

1. a range of cohesive devices

要掌握各种形式的衔接手段。例如:

(1) 表因果: because, due to, therefore

(2) 表转折: although, but, however

(3) 表递进: also, moreover, furthermore

(4) 表类比: like, similarly, in the same way

(5) 表对比: unlike, by contrast, on the contrary

(6) 表举例: like, such as, for instance

(7) 表强调: indeed, above all, in fact

（8）表解释：that is to say，in other words，namely
（9）表条件：if，provided that，as long as
（10）表目的：in order that，so as to，for the purpose of
（11）表总结：to sum up，in short，on the whole

练习 1：你能想出更多的衔接词吗？请针对以上 11 种逻辑关系再分别给出 3 个。

（1）表因果：________________
（2）表转折：________________
（3）表递进：________________
（4）表类比：________________
（5）表对比：________________
（6）表举例：________________
（7）表强调：________________
（8）表解释：________________
（9）表条件：________________
（10）表目的：________________
（11）表总结：________________

此外，还要了解同类衔接词怎么用，建议首先按意思来分，再按词性来分。例如表转折的衔接词按意思分，有表“虽然”的，也有表“但是”的。在表“虽然”的单词中有连词，如 although，though，while，也有介词，如 despite，regardless of，in spite of，这样就表示用法不一样了。前者接完整的句子，后者只能接名词和动名词。

练习 2：请将以下单词填入表格的适当位置，并翻译以下句子。

since，thanks to，accordingly，result from，due to，be attributable to，because，so，therefore，as a result of，due to，lead to，as，be credited to，so that，as a consequence，result in

	conj.	prep.	adv.	verb phrase
cause				
effect				

（1）由于空气污染严重，最近人们出门都戴口罩。（accordingly）

____

（2）由于人口激增，地球上的自然资源已经急剧地减少了。（due to）

____

（3）由于擅长处理人际关系，他很快就被提拔到人事经理这个职位。（result in）

____

（4）由于有可能遇到交通堵塞，我提前了1个小时出发。（so）

____

2. Referencing

在写作中要注意指代，以避免重复。指代一般有以下四种：

人称代词	指示代词	地点副词	时间副词
he, she, they, him, her, ours, etc.	this, that, these, those, the former, the latter, etc.	here, there	now, then, afterwards, sooner, earlier, etc.

3. Substitution

替代和指代有类似的功能，都是为了避免重复，使行文更流畅。常用的替代方式有以下四种：

同义替换	词性变化	上下义	反义替换
teenagers	a very important book	tiger	reduce road accidents
adolescents	a book of great importance	predator	increase road safety

练习3：请试着用以上方法来替换下列表达式。

（1）children

（2）develop economy

（3）do not waste energy

（4）a remote place

Part 3 Lexical Resource

在词汇部分，必须要掌握最基础的拼写和词性变化。

练习1：请用括号中所给的正确形式来填写。

（1）We appreciated the ________ of the idea. （novel）

（2）He was ________ of his rich colleague. （envy）

（3）Children can become very ________ when they are unwell. （irritability）

（4）We have to ________ our campaign against smoking. （intense）

(5) The sudden arrival of a storm caused the ________ of a number of flights. (cancel)

(6) Until the police complete the ________ the accused will not be released on bail. (investigate)

(7) My grandmother takes great ________ in feeding stray dogs. (please)

(8) We had a ________ vacation in Miami. (memory)

(9) The woman ________ at the death of her husband. (grieve)

(10) The circus artist performed many dangerous tricks while walking ________ on a rope. (precarious)

其次,要注意搭配或惯用法。

练习2:请改正一下表达式中的错误。

(1) do contributions to

(2) make progress about

(3) I remember obviously that

(4) The lions are shouting.

Part 4 Grammatical Range and Accuracy

此项评分标准考察写句子的能力。它体现在两点上:多样性和准确性。

1. 多样性

语法的多样性取决于句子类型的丰富性,能否熟练使用不同的句型。

如:随着20世纪末科技的繁荣,人们开始广泛使用电脑。

A. With the prosperity in science and technology in the late 20th century, the computers were widely applied.

B. The late 20th century witnessed the prosperity in science and technology, thus giving rise to the wide application of computers.

C. It was the prosperity in science and technology in the late 20th century that gave rise to the wide application of computers.

with结构状语前置、witness句型、强调句型分别应用在以上三句话中,相同意思用不同的句型来表达,使文章句型更加丰富。

此外,句子的多样性和丰富性还可通过句子种类表现,文章需要简单句和复杂句结合使用。考生要掌握几种在考试中常用的复杂句的用法,如定语从句、状语从句及名词性从句。请看下面的例子:

In the same year, a road was constructed linking the residences and the river, and a bridge could be seen over the river.

若用定语从句表示:

In the same year, a road was constructed linking the residences and the river over which a bridge could be seen.

使用了从句后句子更加简洁。

2. 准确性

语法的准确性指对语法的掌握能力，如句子结构、主谓一致、单复数、时态、语态以及标点符号等。以下几类是中国学生在写作中出现比较频繁的语法错误。

(1) There is a river run from the north to the south.

is 和 run 两个谓语不应同时出现，此句改为：

A river runs from the north to the south.

(2) Travel around the world in the gap year enriches the students' life experience.

experience 作为可数名词用时，解释为“经历”；作为不可数名词用时，解释为“经验”，此句改为：

Travel around the world in the gap year enriches the students' life experiences.

(3) Mobile phones have instead of the letters.

instead of 不能当作谓语用，此句改为：

Mobile phones have replaced the letters.

(4) Most of the people go to work by bus, others would like to choose subway.

逗号没有连接句子的功能，所以必须加连词，此句改为：

Most of the people go to work by bus, while others would like to choose subway.

(5) The ways we evaluate teachers is difficult to change.

ways 与 is 主谓不一致，此句改为：

The ways we evaluate teachers are difficult to change.

(6) In the present society, people tended to take private cars rather than public transport.

present 与 tended 时态不一致，此句改为：

In the present society, people tend to take private cars rather than public transport.

语法错误会在不同程度上影响考官对文章的评价，从而导致扣分。

通过以上对雅思写作评分标准的具体分析，可以清楚地发现，考生只有从结构、内容和语言等多方面下功夫，才能最终提高雅思写作成绩。

Section 3 Sample Answers

1. Examiner's Answer（选自剑桥真题 10）

You should spend about 40 minutes on this task.

Present a written argument or case to an educated reader with no specialist knowledge of the following topic.

It is important for children to learn the difference between right and wrong at an early age. Punishment is necessary to help them learn this distinction.

To what extent do you agree or disagree with this opinion?

What sort of punishment should parents and teachers be allowed to use to teach good behaviour to children?

Give reasons for your answer and include any relevant examples from your own knowledge or experience.

Write at least 250 words.

One important stage in a child's growth is certainly the development of a conscience, which is linked to the ability to tell right from wrong. This skill comes with time and good parenting, and my firm conviction is that punishment does not have much of a role to play in this. Therefore I have to disagree almost entirely with the given statement.

To some extent the question depends on the age of the child. To punish a very young child is both wrong and foolish, as an infant will not understand what is happening or why he or she is being punished. Once the age of reason is reached however, a child can be rewarded for good behaviour and discouraged from bad. This kind but firm approach will achieve more than harsh punishments, which might entail many negative consequences unintended by the parents.

To help a child learn the difference between right and wrong, teachers and parents should firstly provide good role modelling in their own behaviour. After that, if sanctions are needed, the punishment should not be of a physical nature, as that merely sends the message that it is acceptable for larger people to hit smaller ones — an outcome which may well result in the child starting to bully others. Nor should the punishment be in any way cruel.

Rather, teachers and parents can use a variety of methods to discipline their young charges, such as detention, withdrawal of privileges, and time-out. Making the punishment fit the crime is a useful notion, which would see children being made to pick up rubbish they have dropped, clean up graffiti they have drawn, or apologise to someone they have hurt. In these ways responsibility is developed in the child, which leads to much better future behaviour than does punishment.

2. 8 分范文(选自剑桥真题 9)

You should spend about 40 minutes on this task.

Write about the following topic:

Some people believe that unpaid community service should be a compulsory part of high school programmes (for example working for a charity, improving the neighbourhood or teaching sports to younger children).

To what extent do you agree or disagree?

Give reasons for your answer and include any relevant examples from your own knowledge or experience.

Write at least 250 words.

It has been suggested that high school students should be involved in unpaid community services as a compulsory part of high school programmes. Most of the colleges are already providing opportunities to gain work experience, however these are not compulsory. In my opinion, sending students to work in community services is a good idea as it can provide them with many lots of valuable skills.

Life skills are very important and by doing voluntary work, students can learn how to communicate with others and work in a team but also how to manage their time and improve their organizational skills. Nowadays, unfortunately, teenagers do not have many after-school activities. After-school clubs are no longer that popular and students mostly go home and sit in front of the TV, browse internet or play video games.

By giving them compulsory work activities with charitable or community organizations, they will be encouraged to do something more creative. Skills gained through compulsory work will not only be an asset on their CV but also increase their employability. Students will also gain more respect towards work and money as they will realise that it is not that easy to earn them and hopefully will learn to spend them in a more practical way.

Healthy life balance and exercise are strongly promoted by the NHS, and therefore any kind of spare time charity work will prevent from sitting and doing nothing. It could also possibly reduce the crime level in the high school age group. If students have activities to do, they will not be bored and come up with silly ideas which can be dangerous for them or their surroundings.

In conclusion, I think this is a very good idea, and I hope this programme will be put into action for high schools/colleges shortly.

Examiner's Comment:

TR: The answer addresses all parts of the prompt sufficiently, focusing on the benefits for students rather than society. A number of relevant, extended and supported ideas are used to produce a well-developed response to the question. However, some ideas, for example the reference to the crime level, are not fully extended.

CC: The ideas are logically ordered and cohesion is consistently well managed. Paragraphing is used appropriately, and progression between paragraphs is managed with some sophistication.

LR: A wide range of vocabulary is used to articulate meanings precisely, with skillful use of uncommon lexis, and very few inappropriacies.

GRA: The range of grammatical structures used is also wide, with only occasional minor errors.

3. 7分范文(选自剑桥真题11)

You should spend about 40 minutes on this task.

Write about the following topic:

Some people say that the only reason for learning a foreign language is in order to travel or to work in a foreign country. Others say that these are not the only reasons why someone should learn a foreign language.

Discuss both these views and give your own opinion.

Give reasons for your answer and include any relevant examples from your own knowledge or experience.

Write at least 250 words.

Many may say, and I agree, that today's society has most erased all its boarders and soon will become limitless in what concerns travelling for both work and pleasure. Therefore, if this is to happen, then learning a new language is necessary.

Nowadays, learning a new language for the purpose of working in other countries seems to become more and more popular. Adults in need of money or, why not, recognision are trying to pursue their happiness far away from home. Also, the hey days of employees looking only for capable people have gone. It seems that today's employers are looking not only for multi-skilled employees, but they also want people who know more than their mother tongue. Sooner or later, those who omitted learning more are prone to become jobless.

However, to my mind, a new language shouldn't be learned just for travelling or working in a foreign country. A foreign language should help the learner broaden his mind. By this I mean that the new language should and will allow us to understand more about the world itself, and maybe our ancestors' ways of thinking and acting. Needless to say, knowing another language will help us when it comes to understanding the human race, because language is the first poem of a country.

All of this being said, I believe that learning a different language should not only be satisfying our physical needs, like money, but also our moral needs, because never before had such a big thirst for knowledge been display.

Examiner's Comment:

TR: All parts of the prompt are addressed and a clear position is presented throughout the response. Main ideas are extended and supported.

CC: Ideas are logically organised and there is a clear progression throughout the response. A range of cohesive devices is used flexibly, while each paragraph has a clear central topic which is developed.

LR: The lexical resource is sufficient to allow some flexibility and precision and although there are a few spelling errors, these do not detract from the overall clarity of the response.

GRA: A variety of complex structures is used with some flexibility and accuracy. Grammar and punctuation are well controlled and error-free sentences are frequent.

4. 6.5 分范文(选自剑桥真题 8)

You should spend about 40 minutes on this task.

Write about the following topic:

In some countries the average weight of people is increasing and their levels of health and fitness are decreasing.

What do you think are the causes of these problems and what measures could be taken to solve them?

Give reasons for your answer and include any relevant examples from your own knowledge or experience.

Write at least 250 words.

In some countries the average weight of people is increasing and their levels of health and fitness are decreasing. I think that the cause of these problems are due to unhealthy lifestyle and the lack of exercise.

Nowadays, people are getting more and more lazy. They want convenience in everything. When they come home from work, they will have microwaved dinner or fast food so that they do not have to take the trouble to prepare a meal or wash up after dinner. The introduction of fast food is also the main cause of unhealthy living. People are opting a fast food restaurant meal rather than a simple homecooked meal but think of all the calories you are swallowing. The oil they used to fry your fries. It is literally black. Eating too much fast food will also lead to health problems. Sugary drinks, pacheted chips, candies and chocolate are also some of the causes that contributes to unhealthy lifestyle. Heavy consumption can lead to weight gain and diabeties.

I think that the main cause is the lack of exercise. As you grow older, your metabolism rate drops. Even if you are eating the same amount as before, you will still gain weight. The one and only situation to this is exercise. The recommended exercise per day is at least 30 minutes of brisk walking. This target can be easily achieved if people do not drive to work. They can take a bus or a train and drip one stop earlier than walk to the office. Every little bit counts when you comes home from work, you can play with your kids or bring the dog for a walk. Anything to get your attention away from the couch. More exercise will suppress your cravings for sugary stuffs.

People should also balance their diet. For example, by eating more vegetables and fruits. Eat less meat and drink plenty of water throughout the day. Organise the time with your family to take a walk outdoors to enjoy the sceneries rather than cooping yourself in the house. This is healthy living for the body, heart and the soul. It is also less likely to fall sick if you do plenty of exercise as your body is strong enough to fight off illness and disease.

Examiner's Comment:

TR: This script answers both parts of the task and presents a dear opinion on the issues. There are relevant main ideas, although the supporting examples are sometimes less appropriate.

CC: The answer is organised with some good use of connectives and time-markers giving an overall progression to the argument. There are also mistakes, however, and some lack of linking between sentences. Paragraphing is used, but is not always logical, and the concluding paragraph is confused.

LR: The range of vocabulary is the best feature of this script, and includes some good use of natural expressions and idiomatic language. There is some inappropriate use of a less formal style at times, but control is generally good. There are few word choices that are inaccurate, and errors in word form and spelling are only occasional.

GRA: A variety of sentence forms is used with accuracy and fluency, but there are a lot of short, simple sentences that reduce the range of complex structures. There are grammatical errors and omissions, but these are not frequent.

5. 6分范文(选自剑桥真题5)

You should spend about 40 minutes on this task.

Write about the following topic:

Some people think that a sense of competition in children should be encouraged. Others believe that children who are taught to co-operate rather than compete become more useful adults.

Discuss both these views and give your own opinion.

Give reasons for your answer and include any relevant examples from your own knowledge or experience.

Write at least 250 words.

Nowadays, purpose of education being changed in Korea. There are some people who think that competition in children should be made, also others believe that children who are taught to co-operate as well as become more useful adults. There are advantages and disadvantages for both of the arguments.

To begin with, what is good if a sense of competition in children is made? They could develop themselves more and more as they learn and study a lot to win from the competition. To prove this, in Korea, it is popular — even common now — to have a tutor who come to student's house to teach extra pieces of study with paying a lot of money. They learn faster than what they learn at school. Furthermore, during the vacations, students study abroad to learn English for a month instead of revise school work. If they have experiments such as study abroad, it is one of the greatest plus point to go to the famous well-known high school. Moreover, there are four big school exams and two national examinations to test students' level of studies generally, only the highest 40% can go to the good quality high schools and colleges. Children learn as much as they can, to win the competition to obtain good quality schools.

On the other hand, as they are busy to enter the schools and study individually with their own tutors, there are problems. They become selfish. They become careless and don't help others a lot if it is about studies. There will be no co-operations for them. Then, why are these companies for many people to work in? Each of them are clever, however, there are weak parts and strong parts for each person. To co-operate is to improve this part. People talk and listen to what others thinking of and learn. That could also be a great opportunity to learn instead of learning alone with one teacher.

In conclusion, I strongly agree with that children should be taught to co-operate rather than compete. Nobody is perfect. People learn together, work together to develop each other. Therefore, I want parents and teachers to educate children concentrating on co-operation, not compete and ranking them.

Examiner's Comment:

TR: Although the answer considers the main issues in the question, it deals much more with the aspect of "competition" than it does with "co-operation". Some of the supporting examples are overdeveloped and divert the reader away from the argument. However, the main points are relevant and the writer's point of view is generally clear.

CC: The argument has a logical progression and there is some good use of linking expressions, though the use of rhetorical questions to signal topic changes is not very skilful. There are also examples of overusing markers, and of errors in referencing.

LR: The candidate tries to use a range of language, but there are regular errors in word choice and word form, and this occasionally causes problems for the reader.

GRA: Similarly, a range of structures is attempted, but not always with good control of punctuation or grammar. However, the meaning is generally clear.

6. 5.5 分范文(选自剑桥真题 11)

You should spend about 40 minutes on this task.

Write about the following topic:

Governments should spend money on railways rather than roads.
To what extent do you agree or disagree with this statement?

Give reasons for your answer and include any relevant examples from your own knowledge or experience.

Write at least 250 words.

In recent years, government focus on improving quality of life, that would bring a lot benefits for citizens such as, communication, transportation, health care. Some argument that built railways is more useful for local people than roads. In my opinion, it is a good idea that more than train station is built. There are some reasons.

First of all, it reduced pollution when more people give up driving to work in weekday. Nowaday, people spend a lot of time on the road in rush hours. At the same time, emissions of car bring a pollution in our environment. People easily get upset, if they got into traffic jam for long time. Research has shown that it is get more pollution of air that car stopped on the road without cutting power. Train station is a good way to make easy that train never could get into congestion and train is a public transport which is more helpful to reduce air pollution.

Secondly, it solved congestion on the road while many people commute by train, nearly years, a number of car is growing. So, a question that a number of car is over volume of road is following. This caused traffic jam have being horrible problem. However, the train will take more people to go to their destinations without waiting on road in rush hour. It is more convince for citizen.

Finally, taking public transport is cheaper than private viechle. People could save money to do others they interested.

Overall, government pay more money for building railway. It bring more it is a good decision that advantages than drawbacks.

Examiner's Comment:

TR: The candidate puts forward three reasons for why he agrees with the statement and develops/supports the first two of these. Further support and development would be necessary to achieve a higher score here.

CC: Organisation is evident, with some simple cohesive devices (sometimes used inaccurately) (*First of all*, *Nowaday*, *At the same time*, *Secondly*, *This*, *However*, *It*, *Finally*, *Overall*), and there are attempts to use paragraphs to present ideas.

LR: The range of lexis is generally adequate and appropriate (*pollution*, *driving to work*, *rush hours*, *emissions*, *environment*, *traffic jam*, *congestion*, *public transport*, *commute*, *destinations*, *advantages*, *drawbacks*) and although there are spelling errors, these do not usually impede communication.

GRA: The candidate attempts to use complex sentences (relative clauses, if clauses), but error levels are high and there are also quite frequent errors in punctuation.

7.5分范文(选自剑桥真题11)

You should spend about 40 minutes on this task.

Write about the following topic:

Some people claim that not enough of the waste from homes is recycled.

They say that the only way to increase recycling is for governments to make it a legal requirement.

To what extent do you think laws are needed to make people recycle more of their waste?

Give reasons for your answer and include any relevant examples from your own knowledge or experience.

Write at least 250 words.

Nowadays, more than million tons of wastes have been produced which from home every day and some people claim that not enough of the litters is recycled. Therefore, they think the governments should have a policy to increase recycling.

It is necessary to say that their governments should take action. For example, providing rubbish bag into each family so that separate a litter and make it to have value. Many waste, paper, box or steel from home can sale to governments or decrease council tax. Either, the government should provide junk bank that the citizen can deposit recycled waste an inverse to be some money.

Moreover, the government should have spot advertisement on television to motivate advantages of recycling. In Thailand, my country, we have "3R" advertisement standing. For reuse, reduce and recycle and easy example way to do in house such as using less plastics bag (reduce), reuse take away box or sale some paper.

In school teacher teach children how to recycle waste at home and go back to tell their parent and come back to report their teacher. There is one day a week in order that clean school together which help they have a good attitude in cleaning.

In conclusion, it should be good that the government make some law about waste tax and make people follow the law by give them back some money. Starting give education at school so that when they growth up the will do easier.

In my opinion, it is very easy to government to do as I mention above to reduce waste from homes such as "3R", junk bank, providing rubbish bins and teaching at school and it will be a good habit and good in long term.

Examiner's Comment:

TR: The candidate expresses a position, but only partially addresses the prompt (he or she considers ways in which people can be encouraged to recycle, rather than explicitly looking at the extent to which laws are required); however, ideas are relevant and are supported with clear examples.

CC: There is a clear overall progression and cohesive devices are used effectively, if somewhat mechanically (apart from *Either*). Paragraphing is just adequate.

LR: Lexical range is adequate for the task and there are attempts to use less common items (*policy*, *junk bank*, *citizen*, *deposit*), but there are errors in word formation (sale/sell, growth/grow up) and some errors in word choice cause difficulty for the reader (*inverse to be some money*, *motivate advantages of recycling*).

GRA: There are attempts to use complex sentence structures, but grammatical errors are frequent (*million tons of wastes have been being produced which from home everyday*, *easy example way to do in house. There is one day a week in order that clean school together which help they have ...*, *Starting give education*).

8. 4分范文(选自剑桥真题9)

You should spend about 40 minutes on this task.

Write about the following topic:

> ***Every year several languages die out. Some people think that this is not important because life will be easier if there are fewer languages in the world.***
>
> ***To what extent do you agree or disagree with this opinion?***

Give reasons for your answer and include any relevant examples from your own knowledge or experience.

Write at least 250 words.

I agree about this opinion.

Nowadays, Several languages die out. I think this situation is right. In the world. already have to much languages minimum 100 languages include small country. But we know just some languages, kind of English, French, Japanese, Chinese.

At this moment, we live in the world. So we need first language in the world. Therefore several languages need to die out.

Also, small country language is almost difficult to learn and not useful. so we don't need to learn this languages. Even if we learning this languages not using in the world. Just useful this country and we don't find small language education academy.

So I think small country languages make spend money and time also we need find first language using all of country. This is very important for all country of developing.

After when decide first language our communication will be more easier with another country people. Beside we don't need invest of another part kind of economic and culture developing by decrease education money.

According to this opinion.

Examiner's Comment:

TR: This answer expresses a position on the topic, but the ideas are not always clear because of repetition and a lack of development (the answer is unfinished and under length).

CC: The information is not organised coherently and it is difficult to follow a progression through the answer. Although some linking devices occur, substitution and referencing are not used, and connections between the ideas are unclear.

LR: The range of vocabulary is limited and repetitive, and inappropriate word choices, e. g. small country language; invest, make it difficult for the reader to follow the meaning.

GRA: There are some attempts to produce complex sentences and some grammatical structures are produced accurately, but frequent errors and omissions in basic sentence formation and in punctuation make the writing difficult to understand.

Section 4 Writing Procedures

本小节以雅思大作文为例,列出以下必要的写作步骤。

Step 1 审题

拿到雅思写作考题后,先认真把题目读上一到两遍,划出关键词,理解题目中句子的逻辑关系,看答题的重心在哪里。

Step 2 构思

紧紧围绕题目关键词进行思路的拓展,可以从不同的角度切入,同时也要多思考相关的理由、影响和例子。

Step 3 组织

将构思好的内容有序地整合起来,确定观点、段落划分、段内主题句和支持句。

Step 4 首段落写作

根据给出的雅思考题进行题目的改写,注意对关键词要进行替换,切不可原句抄下。同时要表明自己的立场。

Step 5 主体段写作

主体段一般分为两到三段,每段都必须围绕一个中心展开。段内要保证逻辑流畅,也要确保段落之间过渡自然。

Step 6　结尾段写作

对前几段的内容做一个总结,在语言上不要有重复。

Step 7　检查及修改

在时间宽余的情况下,要通篇检查一遍,看看有无犯简单的语法错误,如拼写、时态、单复数等,加以修改。

Chapter 2 Static Graphs

静态图

Section 1 A Quick Scan

什么是静态图?

静态图是不体现一定时间段内变化趋势的图表。它描述的往往是某一个特定年份或某个时间点的状态,甚至图表中根本不出现时间要素。静态图包括柱状图(bar)、表格(table)和饼状图(pie)。以下就是一些常见的静态图。

Bar

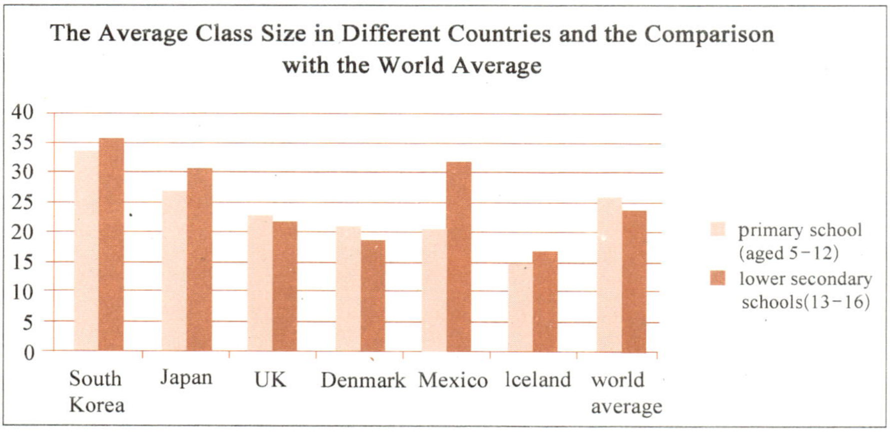

Table

Percentages of Student Employment

Students from	Permanent employment	Temporary employment	Overseas employment	Total employment
England	45%	18.7%	2.3%	66%
Wale	34.2%	26.3%	2.3%	62.8%
Scotland	34.4%	26.1%	2.9%	63.4%
Northern Ireland	35.8%	15.8%	5%	56.6%

Pie

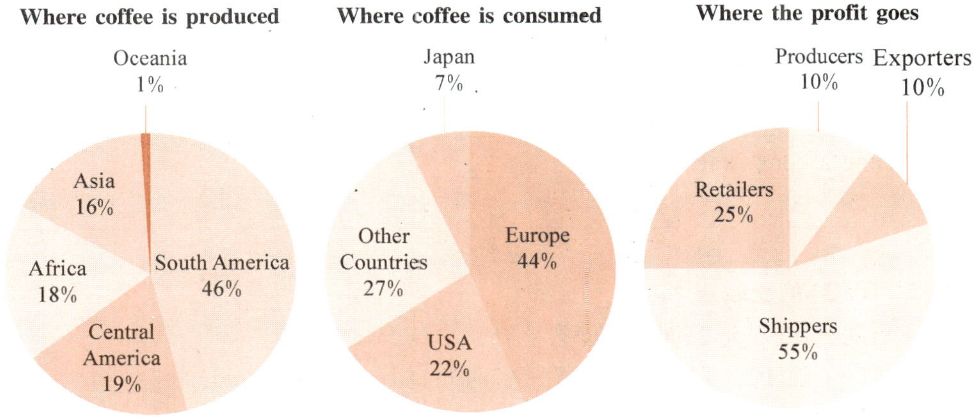

Section 2 Language Input

静态图不管是以柱状、表格还是饼的形式呈现,它们所用到的基本语言还是非常接近的,以对比较级的灵活应用为主,其他语言点包括对比结构、百分比表达、排序等等。

Part 1 than 结构

1. 主系表(SVP)的比较级

A is + 形容词比较级 + than B

注意:

1) A 和 B 的对称性

例: Shanghai's population is larger than Hangzhou. (×)

Shanghai's population is larger than that of Hangzhou. (√)

2) 注意主语和表语的搭配

例: His salary is more than his wife's. (×)

His salary is higher than his wife's. (√)

练习 1: 用 SVP 比较级写出以下句子。

例: the city/the countryside

The city is noisier than the countryside.

The countryside is quieter than the city.

The countryside is less noisy than the city.

1) learning grammar/learning vocabulary

____

2) travelling by plane/travelling by train

____

3）New York/Paris

4）boys/girls

5）reading a book/watching TV

---

2. 主谓宾（SVO）的比较级

1）主语间的比较（形容词的程度有差异）

A + 动词 +（冠词）+ 形容词比较级 + 名词 than B（do/does/did）

例：Shanghai has a **larger** population **than** Hangzhou（does）.

He earns a **higher** salary **than** his wife（does）.

2）数量或程度的比较

（1）主语间数量的比较

例：**More girls than boys** choose to learn dance in their free time.

（2）宾语间数量的比较

例：He eats **more fish than meat**.

Watching TV too much has **more negative effects than positive effects.**

（3）程度副词的比较

例：He likes reading a book **more than** watching TV in his spare time.

（在此句中，more 是副词，修饰 likes）

练习 2：请用任意方式（SVP 或 SVO/SV）来翻译以下句子。

（1）中国人对茶的消耗量大于美国人。

（2）男孩子在看体育节目上花的时间多于女孩子。

（3）在这个公司，拥有硕士学位的女性比有同样学位的男性多。

（4）女性在化妆品和服装上花的钱多于在电子产品上花的钱。

（5）日本男性工作的时间普遍比中国男性长。

---

3. 在比较级中加入程度副词

1）程度副词有哪些

· much · a lot · slightly · a bit · considerably · a little · far

请把以上的词填入下面的表格。

Showing small difference	Showing big difference

你能想到更多的词吗？可继续填入以上表格。

2）程度副词在句中的位置

（1）A is + 程度副词 + 形容词比较级 + than B

（2）A + 动词 +（冠词）+ 程度副词 + 形容词比较级 + 名词 than B（do/does/did）

例：Shanghai's population is considerably larger than that of Hangzhou.

He earns a slightly higher salary than his wife.

练习 3：根据以下图形组词成句，请用上程度副词。

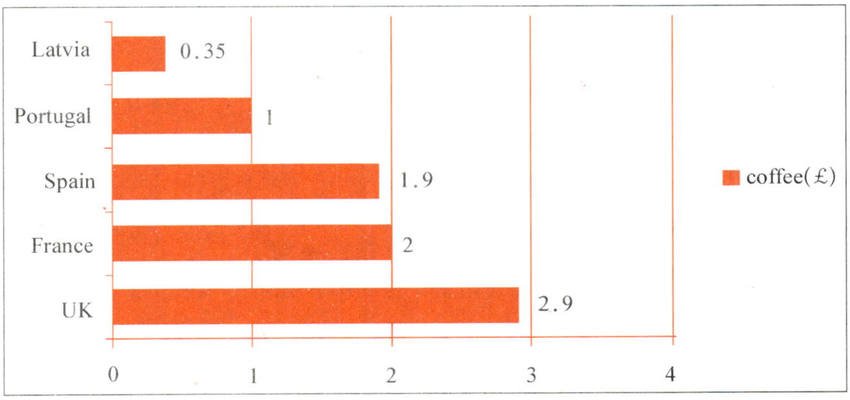

（1）Coffee in the UK/expensive/France

____

（2）The cost of a coffee in Spain/low/France

____

Part 2 as ... as 结构

1. 基本结构

A is + as + 形容词原级 + as B

A + 动词 + as + 形容词 + 名词 + as B

例：His spending on books is as high as mine.

He spends as much money on books as I (do).

注意：A 和 B 依旧需要保持对称，主语 A 和形容词搭配要一致

否定时，not 加在 is 后面

与 than 结构的转换

Her salary **is lower than** her husband's.

Her salary **is not as high as** her husband's.

练习 1：请用 not as ... as 结构来表达以下每组的意思。

（1）hamburgers £2/french fries £1.90

______

（2）Majorca 30 degrees/Castellon 35 degrees

______

（3）southern trains 125 mph/northern trains 100 mph

______

2. 倍数表达

A is + 倍数 + as + 形容词原级 + as B

A + 动词 + 倍数 + as + 形容词 + 名词 + as B

例：His salary is 3 times as high as his wife's.

He earns 3 times as much money as his wife.

3. 关于"大约"的表达

关于"大约"的常见表达有 about，almost，nearly，around，可以再增加两个：approximately，roughly。这些词在句子中都要放在倍数前面。

例：The amount of water consumed in my family **is approximately 4 times as large as** that in her family.

练习 2：翻译以下句子。

（1）爱踢足球的男生数量大约是五倍于女生数量。

______

（2）南美咖啡的产量大约是亚洲的三倍。

______

（3）船运公司所得利润是零售商的两倍多。

______

（4）拥有长期稳定的工作的人数是临时工作从业人数的三倍。

______

（5）英国居民花在食品方面的开销大约是娱乐方面的四倍。

______

Part 3 导入数据

（1）在描写两个事物的对比数据时，可以先只把一个事物说清楚，再将第二个事物的数据通过连词或介词的形式接在逗号后面。

A. Monster Hits Records sold 230,000 CDs in 1990, **while** Crooners plc sold 225,000.

B. Monster Hits Records sold 230,000 CDs in 1990, **as opposed to** Crooners plc. who sold 225,000.

A. A hundred couples chose the name James in 2000, **whereas** just 20 couples opted for the name Peter.

B. A hundred couples chose the name James in 2000, **compared to** 20 who opted for the name Peter.

请注意以上例句中衔接词的用法:

while, whereas: 连词,接句子

as opposed to, compared to: 介词短语,接名词

(2) 表述数据时,也可以用 respectively 这个词将两个数据串起来。

A. The number of visitors to Portugal was twice as high as that of visitors who went to Greece, **at** 500 and 250 **respectively**.

B. The number of visitors to Portugal and to Greece was 500 and 250 **respectively**.

C. The number of visitors to Portugal was twice as high as that of visitors who went to Greece (**500 and 250 respectively**).

请注意:

(1) respectively 表示"各自、分别"。

(2) 数据的引用有三种方式,一是与介词 at 搭配起补充说明作用;二是直接用于主干中;三是通过括号的方式来体现。

练习 1: 请用带 respectively 字样的句子来表述所给信息。

(1) house in Notting Hill average £500,000/house in Sloane Square average £620,000

(2) people aged 20 – 30 who like jazz 11%/people same age who like hip-hop 35%

(3) JFK Airport (March) 2.9 million users/Newark Airport (March) 1.9 million users

练习 2: 请根据所给图片任意写出 5 个带数据的句子。

Gold Medals, Beijing Olympics, 2008

China	62
USA	48
Russia	47
UK	42
France	83
Australia	21
Italy	19
Ethiopia	10
Japan	9
South Korea	5

(1) ______________________________

(2) ______________________________

(3) ______________________________

(4) ______________________________

(5) ______________________________

Part 4 抽象化表达 + 数据说明

有时通过数据可以得出两个比较的主体的性质,如数据大的可能表明更受欢迎、更重要、更成功等,可以用上 popular, prefer, favor, important, successful, 等词。

例如:

(1) Monster Hits Records sold 360,000 CDs in 1990, whereas Crooners plc. sold 225,000.

Monster Hits Records was more successful in 1990, with 360,000 CDs sold, compared to 225,000 for Crooners plc.

(2) A hundred couples chose the name James in 2000, while just 20 couples opted for the name Peter.

James was a more popular name in 2000, chosen by 100 couples, while the Peter was only used by 20 couples.

(3) It costs an average of £95 to spend a night in a hotel in Paris, as opposed to £150 in Zurich.

The price of a night in a hotel in Paris is more acceptable than in Zurich, averaging at £95 and £150 respectively.

注意:抽象类表达比较适合放在小作文概述或总结的地方使用。

Part 5 "占比"的基本结构

当出现百分比的图标时,需要用到"占据多少"等表达式。请看下面的饼图。

where coffee is consumed

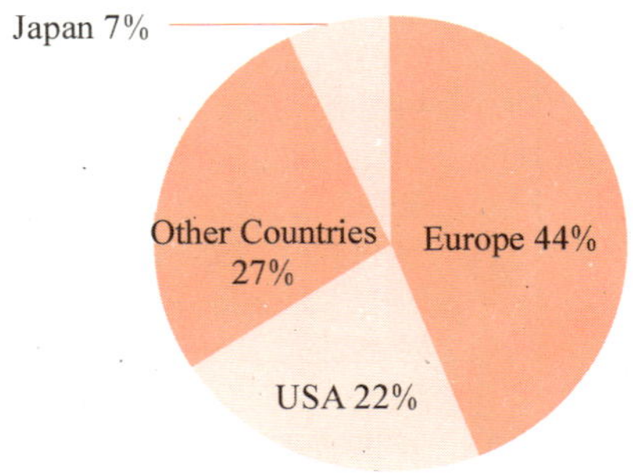

以 44% 为例,来写一下这样一个句子:

Europe's consumption of coffee **occupies** 44% of all.

（欧洲对咖啡的消费量占所有的 44%。）

此处，occupy 意为"占据"，还可以用 take up, represent, comprise, constitute, make up, comprise 等词来替换。

再来看一幅图：

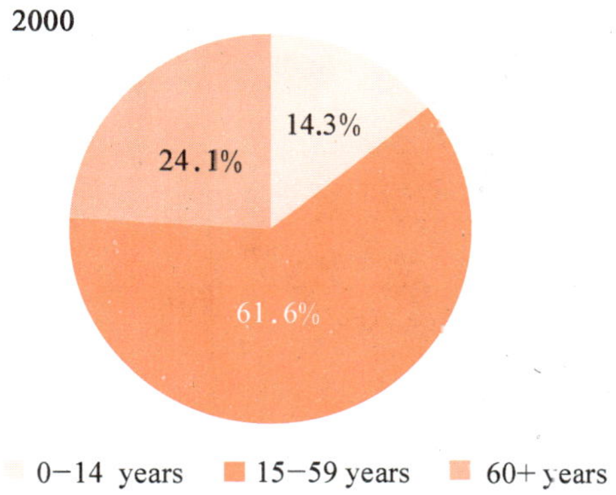

这幅图表示所有的人口被分为 1～14 岁的、15～59 岁的以及 60 岁以上的。

可以写成：

The total population **is divided into** people aged under 14, between 15 – 59 and above 60.

也可以说：

The total population **is composed of** people aged under 14, between 15 – 59 and above 60.

be composed of 表"由……组成"，此处可由 be made up of, comprise, be comprised of, consist of 等替换。

Part 6 百分比的替换

（1）百分比可以用分数来替换，请将以下两组进行配对：

a 50%　b 25%　c 75%　d 33.3%　e 40%　f 10%　g 66.6%

1 two-thirds　2 half　3 a/one quarter　4 two-fifths　5 three-quarters

6 a/one third　7 a/one tenth

a：_____　b：_____　c：_____　d：_____　e：_____　f：_____　g：_____

（2）另一种替换方法：

10% = a tenth of/one in ten/one out of ten/one out of every ten

请按以上方式对下面的百分比进行替换。

20%：________________________________

25%：________________________________

50%：________________________________

Part 7　三者或三者以上的排序

1. 看下图，你能写出几个表“排序”的句子。

Most popular leisure activities London, December 2008 Percentage of people who did this activity in the month of December
Sport/fitness activities: 62%
Play a team sport: 54%
Listen to music: 53%
Read: 46%
Use a computer/Internet: 38%
Travelling: 23%
Socializing: 20%
Shopping: 10%
Eating out: 8%
Play music: 2%

例：Sport was the most popular leisure activity.

实际跟“排序”有关的关键词有 come, rank, place, list, follow 等词，例如，表 Jack 在班级中的英文成绩排列第一，可以说：

Jack **comes/ranks first** in English study.

Jack is **in the first place** in English study.

练习 1：参照上图，请用以下关键词填空并口头练习句型。

list, one, place

- In first/second/last ___(1)___ was . . .
- Top/Bottom of the ___(2)___ was . . .
- The number-___(3)___. activity was . . .
- First/Last on the ___(4)___ was . . .
- Ranked in third ___(5)___ was . . .
- The most/second most/next most/least popular is/was . . .
- Next came . . .
- This was followed by . . .

2. 更灵活的表达法

在实际写作中，往往用一句话来体现三者或三者以上的排序关系，需要使用到更加灵活复杂的表达。假设顺序分别是 A、B、C，可以用以下两种方式来表达。

（1）（将 A 的数据表达清楚），**followed by B and then C**.

（2）（将 A 和 B 进行比较），**and C the least**.

例如：

Most popular leisure activities London, December 2008 Percentage of people who did this activity in the month of December
Sport/fitness activities: 62%
Play a team sport: 54%
Listen to music: 53%
Read: 46%
Use a computer/Internet: 38%
Travelling: 23%
Socializing: 20%
Shopping: 10%
Eating out: 3%
Play music: 2%

1) Sport was the most popular leisure activity, with 62% people participating in it, followed by playing a team sport and then listening to music.

2) Socializing was twice as popular as shopping, chosen by 20% and 10% people respectively, and playing music the least (only 2%).

练习 2：请自拟一个问卷调查，以了解班上同学最喜欢的科目，然后用不同的句型来汇报统计数据。

Section 3 Writing

实战演练：

The graph shows data about the average Saturday sales of two bakeries in London in 2010.

Summarize the information by selecting and reporting the main features, and make comparisons where relevant.

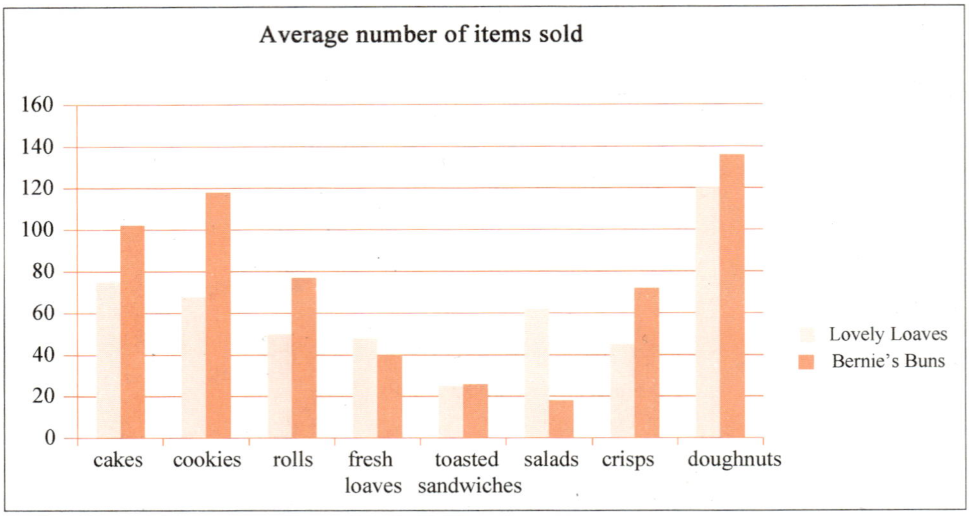

Part 1 图表分析

Key points:

(1) What elements are compared?

(2) What does the horizontal axis represent?

(3) What does the vertical axis represent?

(4) What are the noticeable features in the graph?

(5) What are the differences between the two bakeries?

(6) How would you group the different items if necessary?

(7) In what order would you describe the information?

(8) What will be the most frequently used word in your writing? And how would you replace it with other words or expressions?

Part 2 预热-单句练习

写句子是写文章的基础,在写小作文前,考生需要具备的基本能力就是对随意抽取出来的一个数据可以自由用英文来表达。

例如: Lovely Loaves, cakes 对应的是 75,可以写成:

On average, 75 cakes were sold by Lovely Loaves on Saturday.

The average number of the cakes sold by Lovely Loaves was 75.

练习 1: 根据 Section 2 所给图表,请任意选取 5 个数据进行单句练习。

(1) ____________________

(2) ____________________

(3) ____________________

(4) ____________________

(5) ______________________________

其次,还需要具备对任何一组数据进行比较的能力。

例如:cookies:Lovely Loaves vs Bernie's Buns,可以写成:

Nearly 120 cookies were sold by Bernie's Buns, far larger than the quantity by Lovely Loaves (around 68).

Bernie's Buns:crisps vs doughnuts,可以写成:

Doughnuts were the most popular item in Bernie's Buns, with nearly 140 sold on Saturday, approximately twice the number of crisps.

练习 2:根据 Section 2 所给图表,请任意选取 5 组数据进行单句练习。

(1) ______________________________

(2) ______________________________

(3) ______________________________

(4) ______________________________

(5) ______________________________

Part 3 思路梳理

小作文的写作一般包括三部分:题目改写、整体概述、重点特征描述。前两部分相对固定,重点特征描写的思路因人而异,可以有不同的角度和顺序,目的在于让读者通过你的文字描述对图表特征一目了然即可。

根据 Part 1 的分析,可以给出以下思路(当然,可以有更多其他思路)

1) 交代题目信息

2) 概述:Bernie's Buns 的销量高于 Lovely Loaves,在 6 个单品上卖得更多。整体来说,甜味食品更受欢迎。

3) Bernie's Buns 的销量:从高到低来描写

4) Lovely Loaves 的销量:从高到低来描写

练习:你有其他思路吗?请写在下面的横线上。

____

____

____

____

____

____

Part 4 首段落写作

首段落写作的关键是对题目中的关键词进行改写,或用自己的言语将图表的横坐标和纵坐标及所给图示的信息解释清楚。

原题：The graph shows data about the average Saturday sales of two bakeries in London in 2010.

几乎所有的题目开头都使用 The graph shows，对于 graph 和 show 这两个词有多种替换：

graph：chart，diagram

写作时可以更具体化，如 the bar chart given（所给的柱状图）

show：demonstrate，indicate，illustrate，reveal，compare，etc.

题目中的宾语往往是以名词词组形式呈现，不妨把它改成从句；反之，出现从句时，也可以将它改成名词词组（当然，这只是一种建议方式，也可以不改结构，只是进行词的同义替换）。这样，题目改写就显得比较容易了。如：

The bar chart given demonstrates how the average Saturday sales of 8 items differed in Lovely Loaves and Bernie's Buns in London in 2010.

在这一句中，添加了横坐标内容，即 8 items，也添加了两个图示，及 Lovely Loaves 和 Bernie's Buns，也是对原题中 two bakeries 的同义替换。

注意：主句的时态是一般现在时，从句里的时态要根据时间而定，接下来正文的写作中关于具体数据描述的时态也要依据时间而定。

练习：请对以下题目进行首段落写作。

（1）The table below shows the proportion of different categories of families living in poverty in Australia in 1999.（C4T1）

Family type	Proportion of people from each household type living in poverty
single aged person	6%（54,000）
aged couple	4%（48,000）
single，no children	19%（359,000）
couple，no children	7%（211,000）
sole parent	21%（232,000）
couple with children	12%（933,000）
all households	**11%（1,837,000）**

____

____

____

（2）The first chart below shows how energy is used in an average Australian household. The second chart shows the greenhouse gas emissions which result from this energy use.（C10T1）

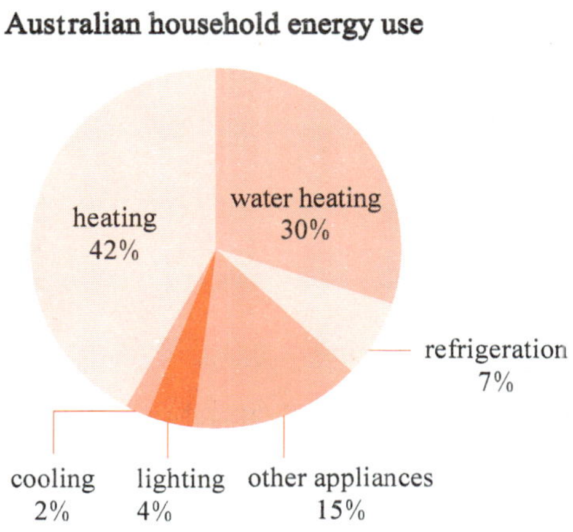

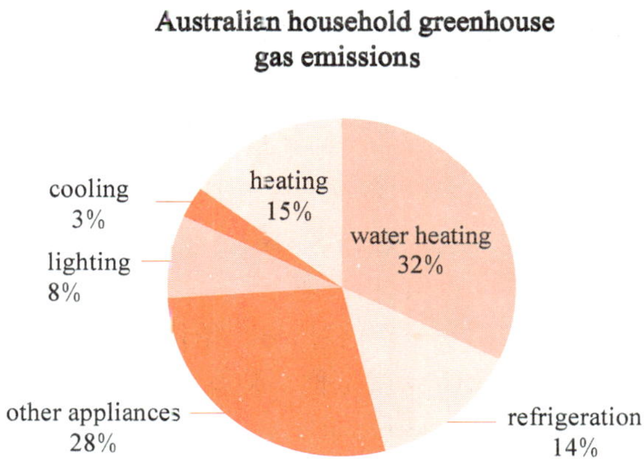

(3) The charts below show the results of a survey of adult education. The first chart shows the reasons why adults decide to study. The pie chart shows how people think the costs of adult education should be shared. (C1T1)

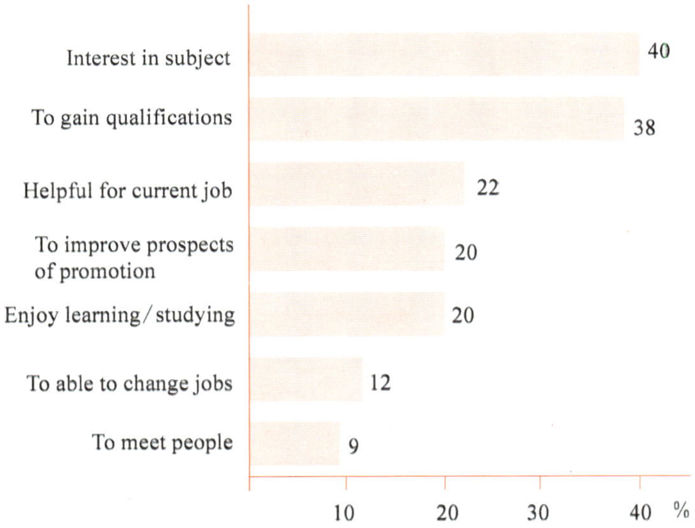

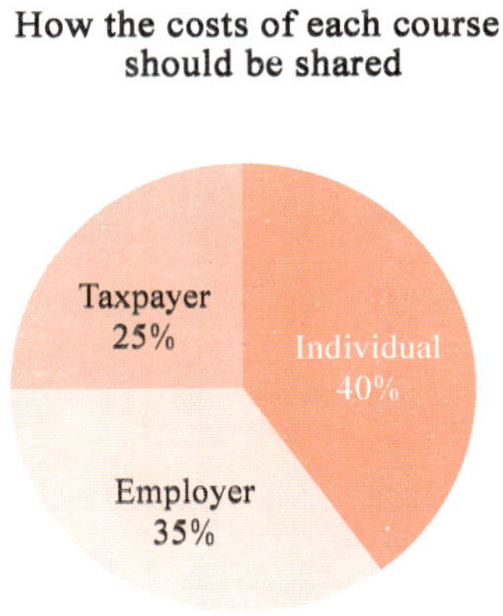

Part 5 概述(overview)

根据 Part 3 的思路梳理,发现概述部分包含两条信息:

(1) Bernie's Buns 的销量高于 Lovely Loaves,在 6 个单品上卖得更多。

(2) 整体来说,甜味食品更受欢迎。

有两种方式来处理这两条信息:

(1) 将两条信息在同一段内体现出来,那么总结段可省略。

(2) 先只写一条信息,另一条信息放在最后一段写。(更常见)

所谓 overview 就是你一眼就能看到的明显特征,注重于整体。在句型上,可以用上

It is clearly seen that . . .

As can be clearly seen, . . .

It is noticeable that . . .

等等。

Sample(第二种处理方式):

It can be seen that Bernie's Buns is busier, outselling Lovely Loaves in six out of eight items.

练习:请针对 Part 3 练习中的图表写出 overview。

Part 6 主体段写作

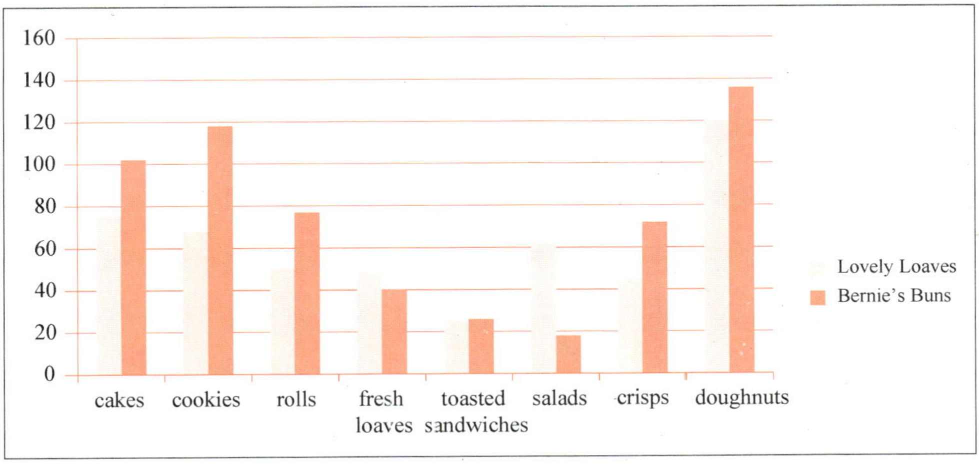

根据 Part 3 的思路分析，现给出关于 Bernie's Buns 的信息描写：

In terms of sales at Bernie's Buns(in terms of sth. 可以用来引入一个话题，比较合适放在段首), doughnuts came top of the list, with an average of around 135 sold on a Saturday (一般会先描述最大的那个数据，也是明显的特征。句型上 with 结构适合用来导入数据). Cookies and cakes were the next best sellers, with around 115 and 100 of these snacks sold respectively(类似的内容可并在一起写). Savoury foods are less popular with customers. (体现了比较关系，也体现了对要素的分类：甜味和咸味) Take toasted sandwiches and salads for example. Their sales only reached 25 and 18, ranking the last of all. (可以抓典型，无须列出所有数据)

练习：请自行描述 Lovely Loaves 的信息。

Part 7 结尾段写作

结尾段在形式上，可用 overall, in short, in summary, to sum up 等词来开头。内容上，对信息要点做个概述即可。此处的概述跟正文部分的概述可以加以一定的区分。如刚才的 overview 的 sample 中，我们考虑的是从两家店的角度去比较，那么结尾段就可以从出售物品的角度去做个整体的比较总结。

Sample

On the whole, savoury foods such as toasted sandwiches, salads and rolls are not as popular as sweet items like cakes and cookies.

Part 8 真题练习

(1) The charts below show the percentage of coffee production from different regions, of consumption in different regions and of the profits in different fields in 2014.

Summarize the information by selecting and reporting the main features, and make comparisons where relevant. (2016.01.23)

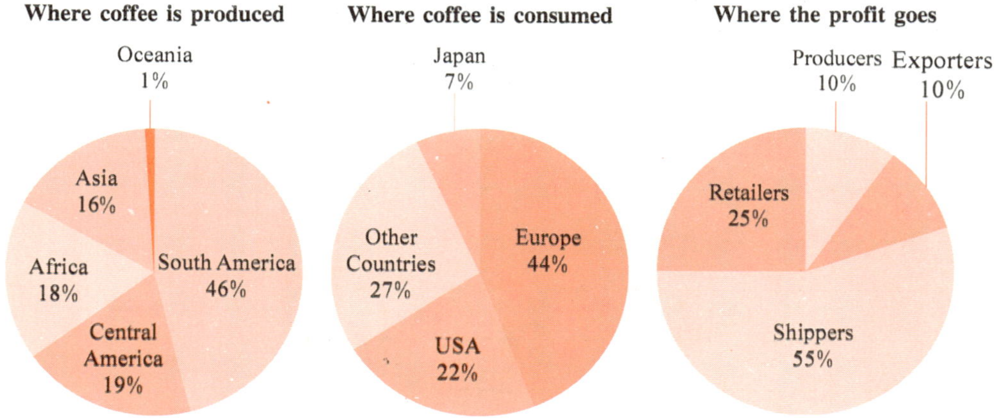

(2) The table below gives information about the employment of students from four countries in the UK after their first degree courses in 2001.

Summarize the information by selecting and reporting the main features, and make comparisons where relevant. (2016.03.12)

Students from	Permanent employment	Temporary employment	Overseas employment	Total employment
England	45%	18.7%	2.3%	66%
Wale	34.2%	26.3%	2.3%	62.8%
Scotland	34.4%	26.1%	2.9%	63.4%
Northern Ireland	35.8%	15.8%	5%	56.6%

(3) The chart below shows UK citizen's expenditure by different age groups on three categories in 2004.

Summarize the information by selecting and reporting the main features, and make comparisons where relevant. (2015.02.28)

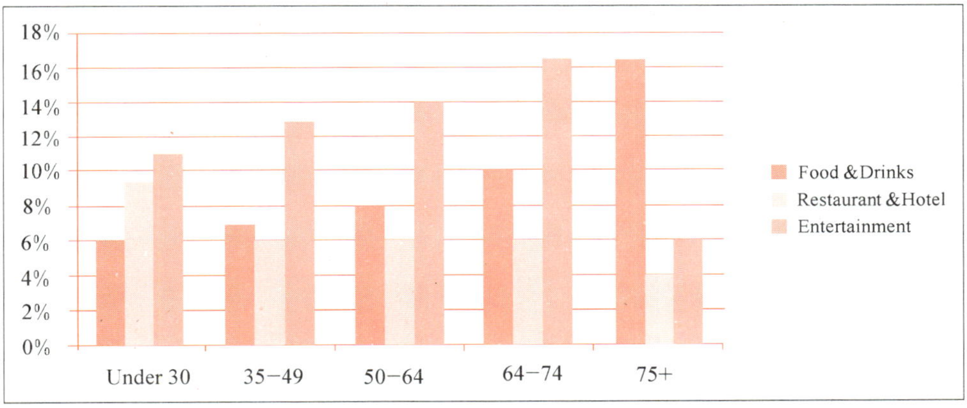

(4) The charts below show the number of working hours per week in the industrial sector in four European countries in 2002.

Summarize the information by selecting and reporting the main features, and make comparisons where relevant. (2015.03.28)

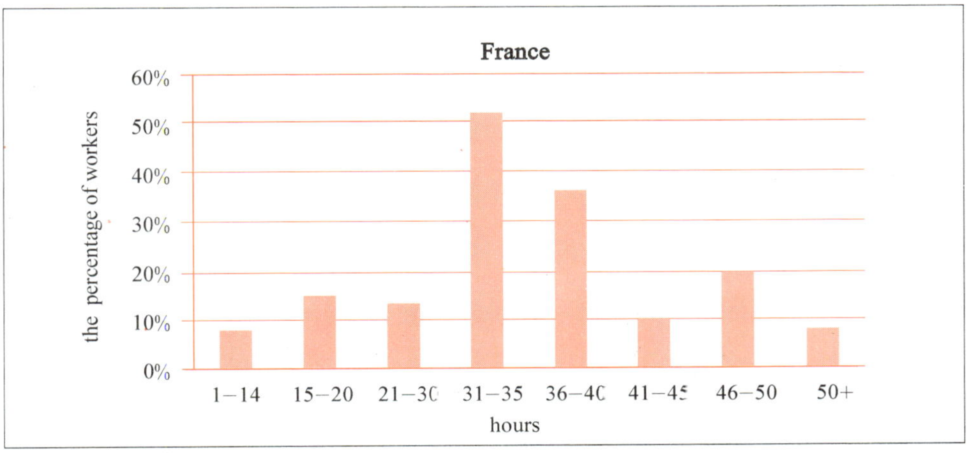

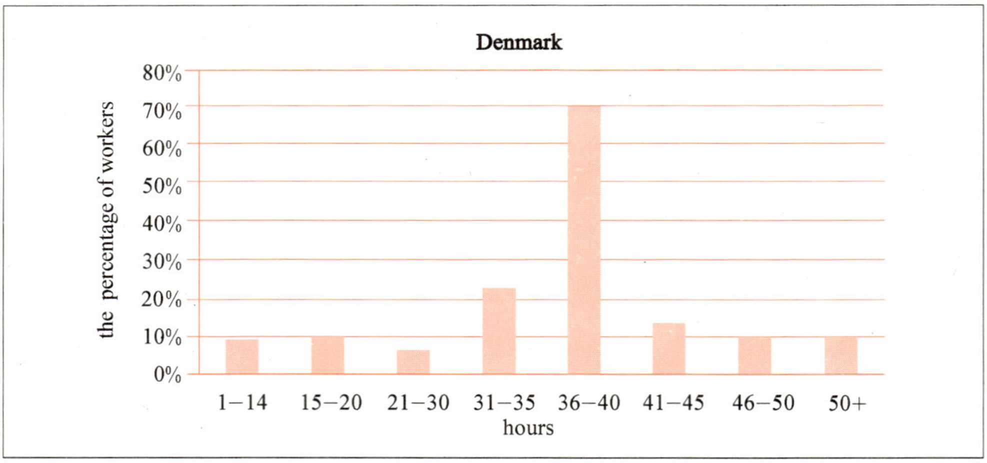
Denmark
80%
70%
60%
50%
40%
30%
20%
10%
0%
the percentage of workers
1–14
15–20
21–30
31–35
36–40
41–45
46–50
50+
hours

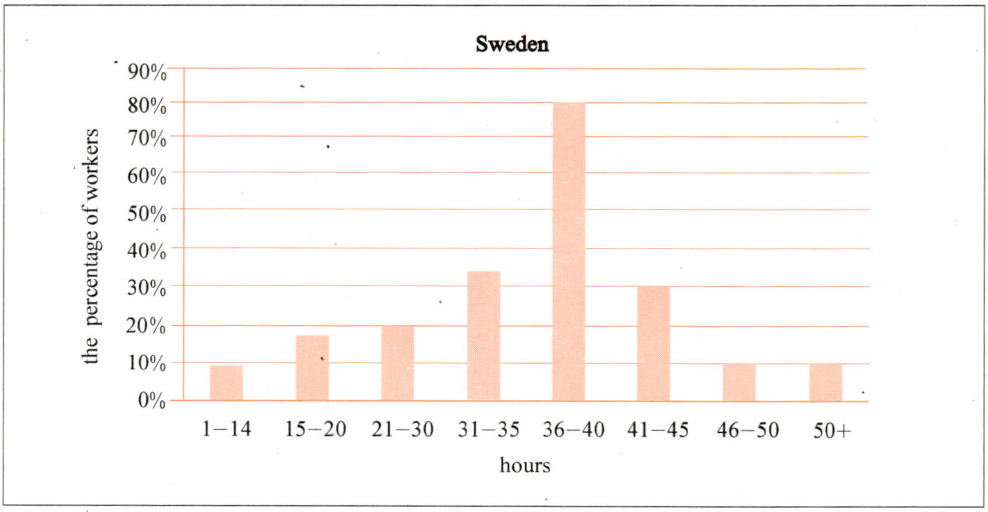
Sweden
90%
80%
70%
60%
50%
40%
30%
20%
10%
0%
the percentage of workers
1–14
15–20
21–30
31–35
36–40
41–45
46–50
50+
hours

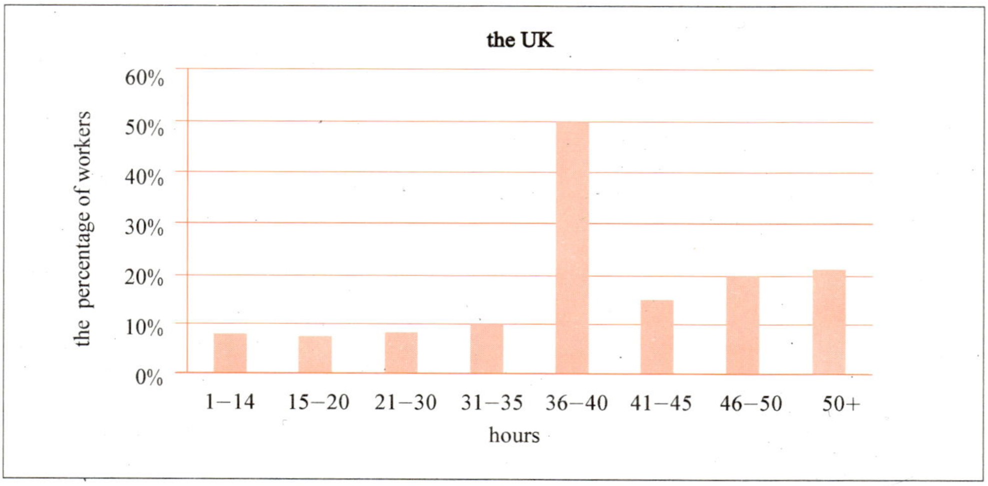
the UK
60%
50%
40%
30%
20%
10%
0%
the percentage of workers
1–14
15–20
21–30
31–35
36–40
41–45
46–50
50+
hours

(5) The chart below shows the average class size in six countries in 2006, and compares them with world average class size.

Summarize the information by selecting and reporting the main features, and make comparisons where relevant. (2015.05.30)

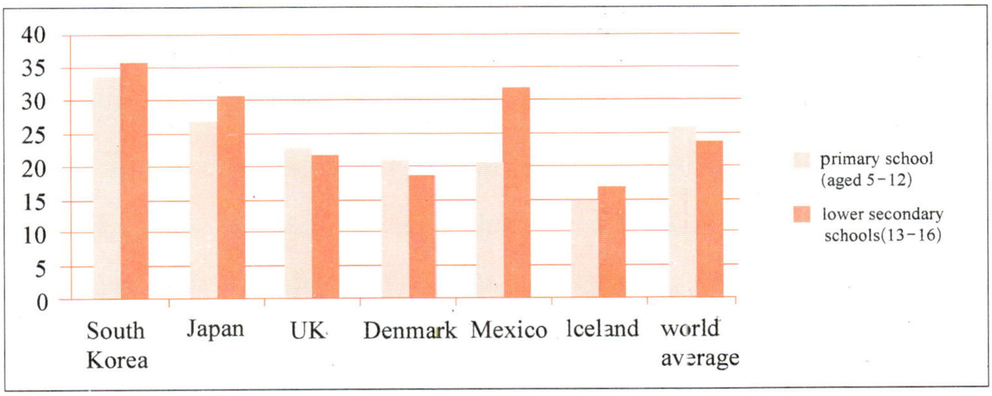

(6) The chart below gives information about the unemployment rate of people aged between 15 and 24 and the overall unemployment rate of five European countries in 2005.

Summarize the information by selecting and reporting the main features, and make comparisons where relevant. (2015.07.23)

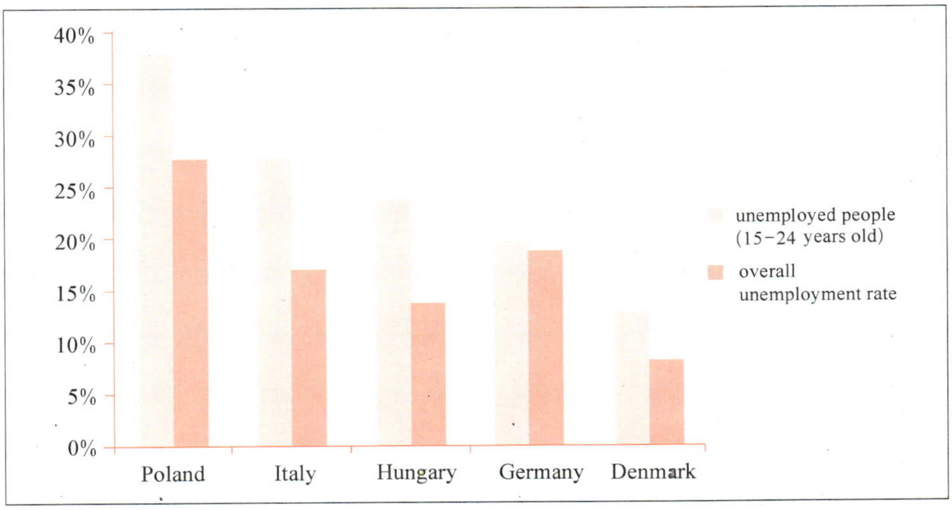

(7) The bar charts below show the amount of fruit exported to different countries in 2012.

Summarize the information by selecting and reporting the main features, and make comparisons where relevant. (2015.11.07A 卷)

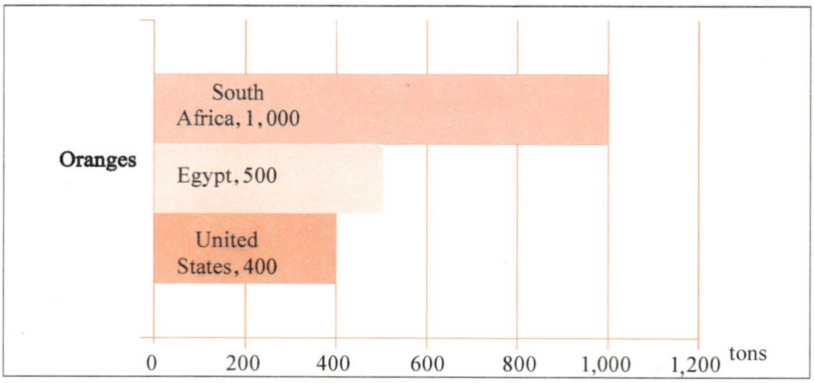
Oranges
South Africa, 1,000
Egypt, 500
United States, 400
0
200
400
600
800
1,000
1,200
tons

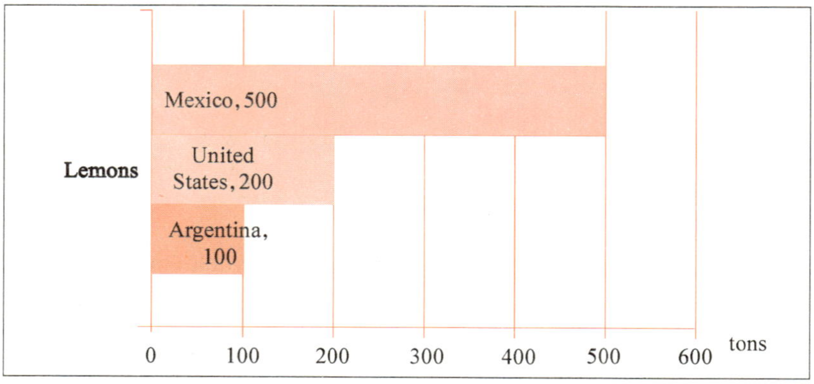
Lemons
Mexico, 500
United States, 200
Argentina, 100
0
100
200
300
400
500
600
tons

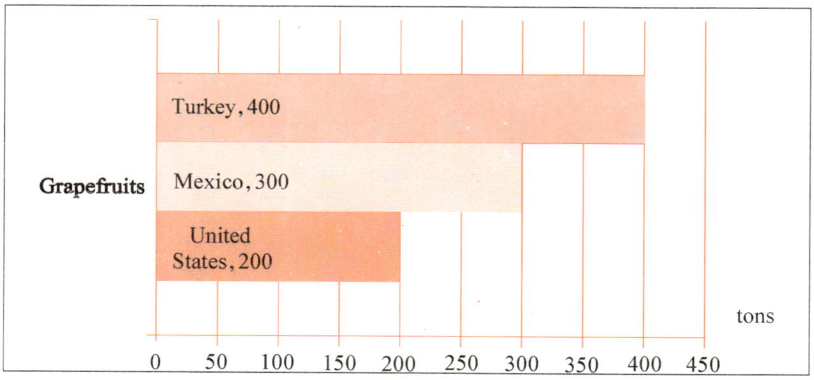
Grapefruits
Turkey, 400
Mexico, 300
United States, 200
0
50
100
150
200
250
300
350
400
450
tons

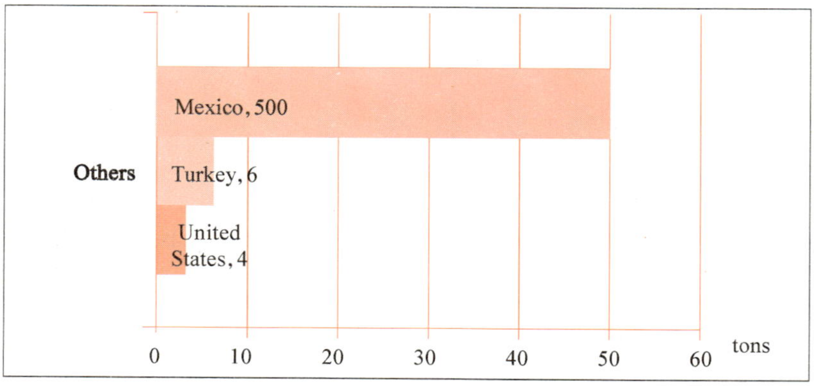
Others
Mexico, 500
Turkey, 6
United States, 4
0
10
20
30
40
50
60
tons

(8) The table below shows the percentage of "very good" rated by the first year students.

Summarize the information by selecting and reporting the main features, and make comparisons where relevant. (2015.02.12)

	Pre-course information	Teaching	Tutor	Printed Resources	Other Resources
Economics	59%	95%	90%	81%	60%
Law	72%	62%	76%	70%	80%
Commerce	95%	95%	93%	86%	81%

(9) The table below shows the salaries of secondary/high school teachers in 2009.

Summarize the information by selecting and reporting the main features, and make comparisons where relevant. (2015.05.09)

Country	Starting	After 15 years	Maximum	Years taken to reach the top salary
Australia	36,000	54,000	54,000	9
Denmark	58,000	48,000	48,000	8
Luxemburg	80,000	85,000	130,000	30
Korea	36,000	48,000	48,000	35
Japan	28,000	36,000	83,000	37

(10) The table below gives information about annual salaries of five employment sectors in Australia in 2006.

Summarize the information by selecting and reporting the main features, and make comparisons where relevant. (2015.06.18)

Employment sectors	Maximum	Minimum	Average
Sales	216,100	27,000	70,000
Engineering	145,080	38,500	80,000
IT and Telecommunications	100,080	38,000	79,000
Education	69,000	33,000	50,000
Traveling	67,000	32,000	45,000

Chapter 3 Dynamic Graphs
动态图

Section 1　A Quick Scan

什么是动态图？

动态图是体现一定时间段内变化趋势的图表。它描述的都是过去时间段内的变化，有时也会延伸到将来给出预测数据。动态图包括线图(line)，柱状图(bar)，表格(table)，饼状图(pie)。以下就是一些常见的动态图。

Line

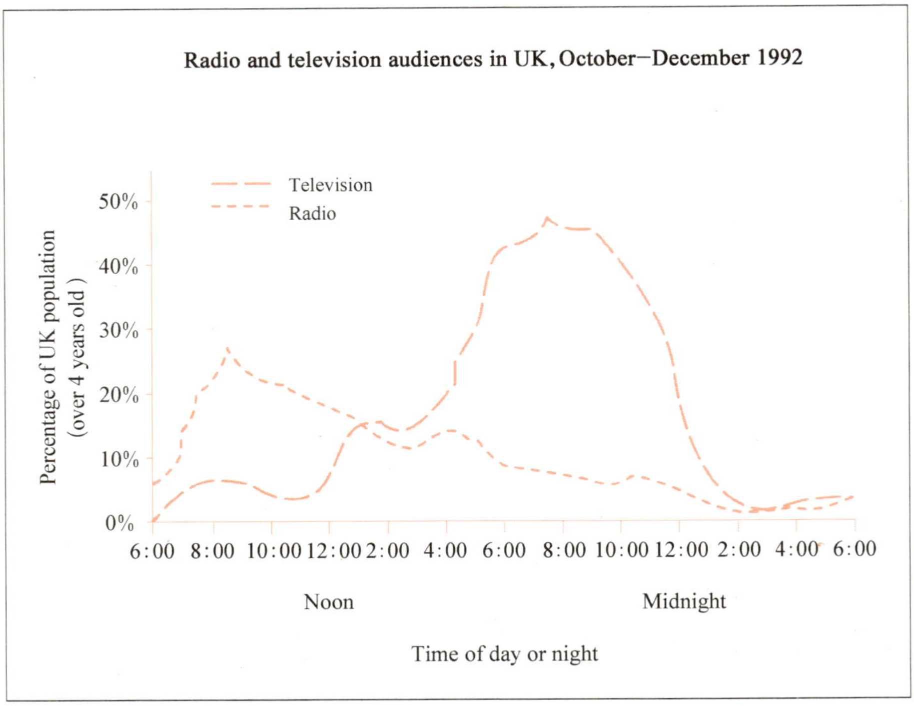

Bar

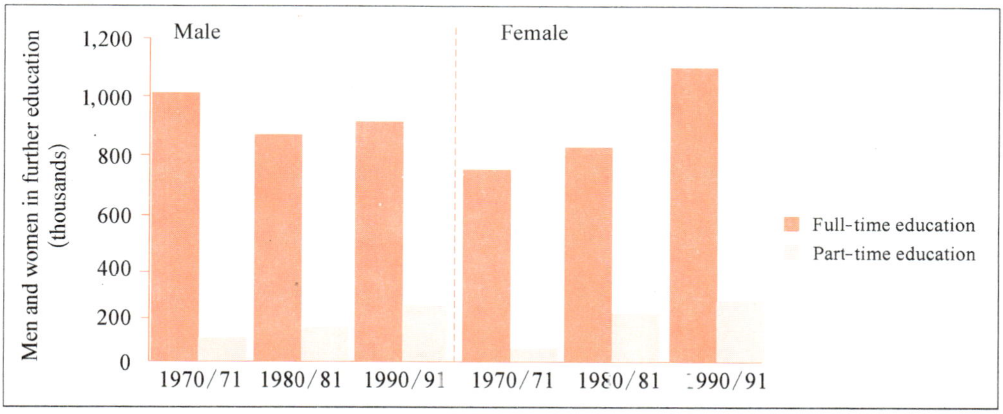

Table

the number of people taking part in a wildlife survey

Year	Adult	Children	Total
2001	36,000	12,000	48,000
2003	212,000	36,000	248,000
2005	332,000	32,000	364,000
2007	331,000	31,000	362,000
2009	270,000	270,000	540,000

Pie

Populations of Yemen and Italy

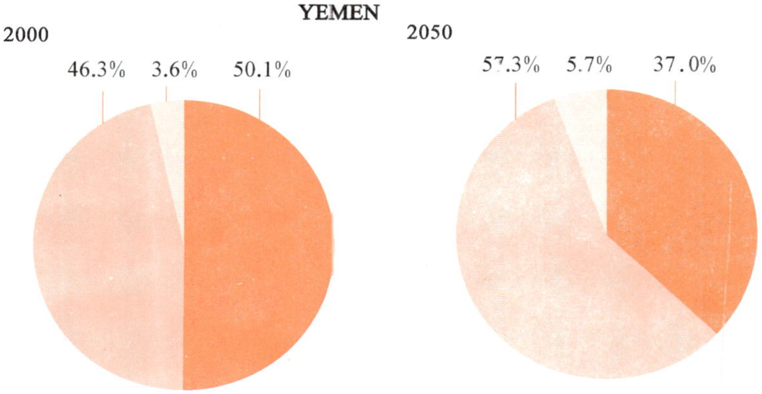

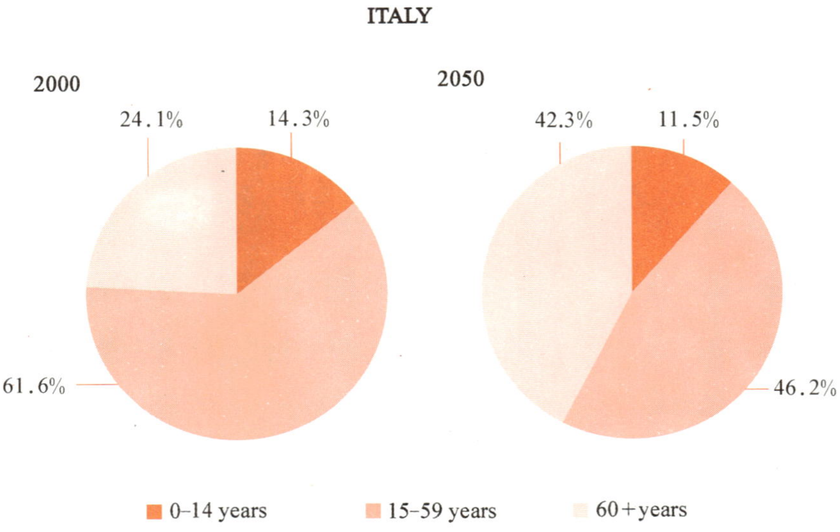

Section 2　Language Input

动态图最直观的形式是线图，同时还可以以柱状、表格还是饼的形式呈现，它们所用到的基本语言是非常接近的。描述动态图时要突出趋势的变化，同时也不要忽略某个时间点不同对象之间的静态描写及数据比较。

Part 1　表示趋势变化的基本表达

1. verb + adverb

最常见的表示变化的意思就是“上升/增加”和“下降/减少”，常见的动词和词组如下：

decline　drop　fall　rise　rocket　shoot up　go down　go up　grow　halve　improve　increase　jump　plummet　plunge　soar　surge　decrease　double

练习 1：请使用以上动词和词组的过去式形式将合适的词填入下表。

表示“上升/增加”	表示“下降/减少”	表示“大幅度上升/增加”	表示“大幅度下降/减少”

注意：后两列的单词无须跟副词搭配。而前两列的单词必须跟不同的副词搭配才能表达变化的幅度。

你能识别以下副词吗？

considerably drastically dramatically gradually marginally modestly negligibly rapidly remarkably sharply significantly moderately slightly steadily strikingly

练习 2：请将以上副词填入下面的横线上。

(1) a big change ____________________

(2) a small change ____________________

(3) a medium-size change ____________________

(4) a fast change ____________________

(5) a slow change ____________________

(6) a consistent increase or decrease ____________________

2. adjective + noun

动词加副词基本上都可以转化成形容词加名词，需要掌握不同词性之间的变化。

练习 3：请完成以下表格

	动词过去时	名　词
(1)	rose	
(2)	fell	
(3)	levelled off	
(4)	declined	
(5)	soared	
(6)	plummeted	
(7)	increased	
(8)	dropped	
(9)	fluctuated	
(10)	plunged	
(11)	decreased	
(12)	dipped	
(13)	recovered	
(14)	jumped	
(15)	surged	
(16)	grew	

练习 4：请写出相应的形容词。

（1）dramatically ________________

（2）considerably ________________

（3）steadily ________________

（4）negligibly ________________

（5）remarkably ________________

3. 介词的使用

在导入数据时难免会用到介词，常见的介词有 at，to，by。at 一般表示某个值，to 一般跟在表"上升"或"下降"的动词后表示"达到某个值"，by 后面一般跟的是净增量或净减量。有时也会用到 from ... to 和 between ... and 来表示数据的动态变化。

另外在表达时间时也要用到介词，如从 2010 年到 2015 年，可以说 from 2010 to 2015，也可以说 between 2010 and 2015，还可以说 during the period from 2010 to 2015。如表示在具体的某一年，就用介词 in 即可。此外，until，by，since 也会用来引导时间。

练习 5：阅读以下段落并选出合适的介词。

As regards Robbie's Bakery, income started (1) to/at £55,000 in 2000 and remained stable (2) at/to this figure (3) during/until 2005. At this point, there was a sharp rise (4) to/at £70,000. Between 2007 and 2008, the figure went up (5) to/by around £30,000 (6) to/from £70,000 (7) at/to nearly £100,000. Finally, income grew gradually, and peaked (8) at/to £105,000 in 2010. If we look at Lovely Loaves, earnings fluctuated (9) between/at £80,000 and £90,000 in the first five years, and then there was a sharp fall (10) to/at £40,000 in 2008. Finally, the figure levelled off (11) to/at £40,000, and finished (12) to/at the same figure.

练习 6：请补出下列段落中缺省的介词。

If we look at Bernie's Buns, income started £20,000 in 2000, and then there was a slight rise £25,000 in 2001. At this point, the figure fell back just over £20,000, followed by a slight increase just under £40,000. Earnings then levelled off £39,000, and then fell marginally £38,000. Income then rose £23,000, £38,000 £61,000. In the next two years, there was a gradual rise around £62,000, and then the figure peaked around £65,000.

4. 对数据的进一步说明

如果说能用正确的语言罗列数据，你只是做到了第一步。为了使句型更多样化，特点更突出，有必要学会对数据加以评价。以下就是常用的一些手段。

1）加入静态比较

The income of Lovely Loaves fell significantly to around £40,000 in 2008, **which meant that it earned far less than the other bakeries.**

2）表明极值

There was a considerable rise in the takings of Robbie's Bakery in the last two years to £105,000, **this figure being the peak level of income during the whole period.**

3）添加额外的动词

The income of Robbie's Bakery rose sharply in 2008, **rocketing to just under £100,000.**

4）强调最高级

Lovely Loaves earned just over £80,000 in 2000. **This meant that it had the highest income of the three bakeries in that year.**

练习 7：针对所给的线图，来完成以下句子。

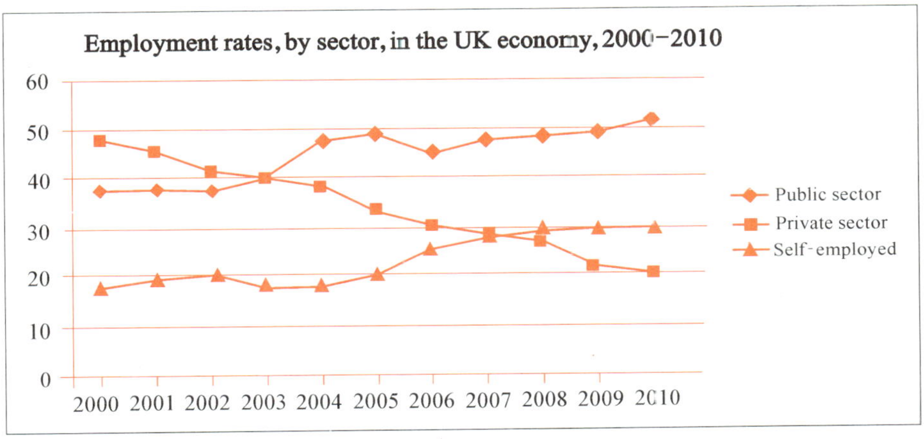

（1）Forty-eight per cent of people worked in the private sector in 2000, which meant ______________________________

（2）There was a slight rise in the percentage of people who worked in the public sector, to just over 50% in 2010, this figure being ______________________________

（3）The percentage of people employed in the public sector rose sharply between 2002 and 2004, soaring ______________________________

（4）The percentage of people who worked in the private sector went down steadily to 20% in 2010. This meant ______________________________

Part 2 其他语言要素

1. 题目的常见改写方式

由于图表作文经常涉及数据，在首段落的题目改写中不妨用上 how many/how much, the number of/the amount of 之类的词。

例子：

原题：**The chart shows information about visitors to Australia, 2000 – 2008.**

Summarize the information by selecting and reporting the main features, and make comparisons where relevant.

改写方式 1：The graph shows information about ***how many people visited*** Australia, over an eight-year period between 2000 and 2008.

改写方式 2：The graph illustrates data about ***the number of people who visited Australia***, over an eight-year period between 2000 and 2008.

练习 1：完成以下表格。

topic	how many/how much	the number of /amount of
(1) DVD sales, UK and USA (2005 – 2008)	The graph shows information about how many DVDs were sold in the UK and the USA from 2005 to 2008.	
(2) Chocolate production, Colombia (1997 – 2007)		

2. 如何写 overview(概述)

(1) Sth. went up/down generally/significantly + 时间状语

例：The output of cars in Toyota went up significantly during the period from 2000 to 2010.

(2) there be 句型

There was a general/significant upward/downward trend in ...

例：There was a significant upward trend in the number of cars produced in Toyota over the period from 2000 to 2010.

(3) Sth./时间段 saw/witnessed ... 句型

Sth. saw a general/significant upward/downward trend during/in/...

时间段 saw a general/significant upward/downward trend in sth.

例：The output of cars in Toyota saw a significant upward trend from 2000 to 2010.

The decade from 2000 to 2010 saw a significant upward trend in the output of cars in Toyota.

3. 衔接手段

1) 先后顺序

由于动态图的描述基本上可以按照时间线索进行，对先后顺序的表述就显得比较重要了。请看下面这一段文字，划出跟时间顺序有关的词。

Income of Bernie's Buns started at £20,000 in 2000, and after that there was a slight rise to £23,000 in 2001. Following this, the figure fell slightly to £21,000 in 2002, after which income rose sharply in 2003. At this point, the number levelled off until 2005. Next, there was a slight dip in 2006, but this was followed by a sharp increase to £60,000 in 2008. Subsequently, income went up gradually in the last two years.

练习 2：根据括号里的关键词来链接句子。

(1) Income began at just over £80,000. Income went up slightly to £95,000 in 2001. (and then)

____

____

(2) There was a steady fall to £80,000. Income recovered to £90,000 in 2004. (after which)

____

____

(3) Earnings dropped sharply to just over £60,000. There was a slight dip. (At this point)

____

____

(4) There was a slight rise to just under £60,000. The figure went down considerably. (Subsequently)

____

____

(5) Income fell significantly to £40,000. The number levelled off. (Next)

____

____

2）转换话题

动态图中往往是将多个对象的动态变化进行比较。在文章写作中，很可能遇到不同对象之间的切换，或不同比较维度之间的切换，就需要掌握一些话题转换的表达式。

The graph shows information about the amount of money which was earned by three bakeries in London, over a ten-year period between 2000 and 2010.

Overall, what stands out from the graph is that there were considerable upward trends in the income of both Bernie's Puns and Robbie's Bakery, while the earnings of Lovely Loaves saw a considerable fall over the period in question. Another interesting point is that Lovely Loaves was the most popular bakery in 2000, but in 2010, Robbie's Bakery earned more money than the others.

Looking at the details, as regards Bernie's Puns, income started at £20,000 in 2000, then there was a fluctuation over the next three years, at which point it levelled off at just under £40,000 until 2006. Then the figure went up significantly, finishing at around

£65,000 in 2010. If we look at Robbie's Bakery, the trend was similar. Having remained stable at approximately £55,000 in the first half of the decade, income then rose sharply, reaching nearly £100,000 in 2008. There was then a gradual rise to around £105,000 in 2010.

By contrast, the income of Lovely Loaves went in the opposite direction. Takings fluctuated around £90,000 until 2004. After that, despite falling sharply to just over £40,000 in 2008, the figure then levelled off in the last two years.

除了以上划横线部分的表达式,还可以用 regarding, as for, with respect to 来表达话题的转换。

注意:使用以上衔接手段时,一般需要添加代词作为主语。如:

Regarding the income of Bernie's Buns, ***it*** started at £20,000 in 2000, and then ...

练习 3:根据括号里的衔接词来改写句子。

(1) The income of Robbie's Bakery began at just under £60,000. (with respect to)

____

(2) The amount of money which was earned by Bernie's Buns in 2000 was £20,000. (if we look at)

____

(3) The earnings of Robbie's Bakery remained stable during the first five years of the graph. (as for)

____

(4) Income for Lovely Loaves fluctuated considerably between 2000 and 2005. (regarding)

____

Part 3 预测

在近几年的动态图中,经常会出现对未来一段的时间的预测。在图表上表现为数据从过去延展至将来某一点时间。不仅要注意时态的变化,也要了解如何表达对未来数据的预估。一般可以采纳以下两种句型。

(1) Sth. is estimated/predicted/forecast/projected/likely to reach/rise to/decrease to/remain at + 数据 + 时间

(2) It is estimated/predicted/forecast/projected/likely that sth. will reach/rise to/decrease to/remain at + 数据 + 时间

例:60 岁以上的老年人在 2050 年预计将达到 50 万。

The population aged 60 and above is predicted to reach 500,000 in 2050.

It is projected that the population aged 60 and above will reach 500,000 in 2050.

Section 3 Writing

实战演练：

The line graph below shows the land used for organic crops in two countries between 1985 and 2010.

Summarize the information by selecting and reporting the main features, and make comparisons where relevant.

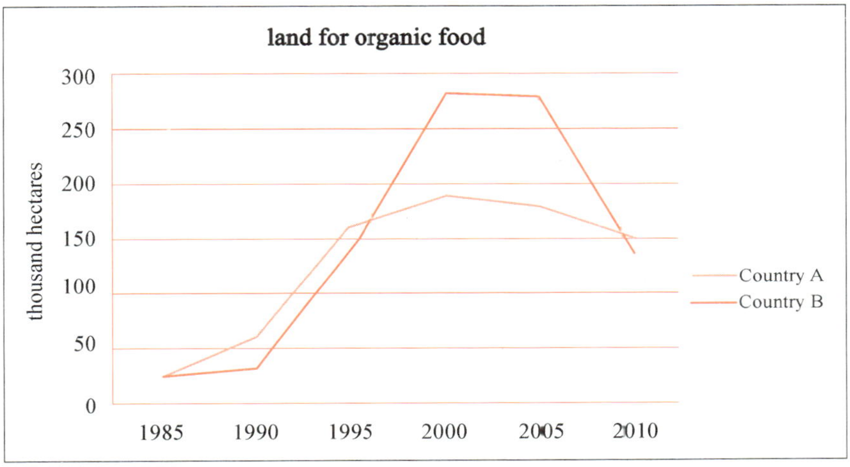

Part 1 图表分析

Key points:

(1) What does the horizontal axis represent?

(2) What does the vertical axis represent?

(3) What is the trend for Country A?

(4) What is the trend for Country B?

(5) Are there any similarities between the two countries?

(6) Which figures can you use? Why?

(7) In what order would you describe the information?

(8) What will be the most frequently used word in your writing? And how would you replace it with other words or expressions?

Part 2 预热-单句练习

写句子是写文章的基础，在写小作文前，考生需要具备的基本能力就是对随意抽取出来的一个数据可以自由用英文来表达。

例如：1990，Country B 对应的是 35，可以写成：

In 1990, around 35 thousand hectares was used to grow organic food in Country B.

The size of land for organic food in Country B in 1990 was around 35 thousand hectares.

练习 1：根据 Section 2 所给图表，请任意选取 5 个数据进行单句练习。

(1) ______

(2) ______

(3) ______

(4) ______

(5) ______

其次，还需要具备对任何一组数据进行比较的能力。

例如：2000：Country A vs Country B，可以写成：

In the peak year 2000, the size of land for organic food in Country B reached 280 thousand hectares, 100 thousand hectares larger than that for Country A.

练习 2：根据 Section 2 所给图表，请任意选取 5 组数据进行单句练习。

(1) ______

(2) ______

(3) ______

(4) ______

(5) ______

Part 3 思路梳理

一般来说，线图可以有两种思路：一是按时间来写；二是按线来写。看哪种讲得清楚就挑哪一种。在本题中，两种思路都可以。所以先按时间来写：

(1) 交代题目信息。

(2) 1985—1995：两个国家的土地使用趋势接近，都在增长。

(3) 1995—2010：两个国家的土地使用面积呈现完全不同的变化趋势，但最终趋于一致。

(4) 总结。

练习：你能按线的思路来写吗？请写在下面的横线上。

______

______

______

______

______

______

Part 4 首段落写作

原题：**The line graph below shows the land used for organic crops in two countries between 1985 and 2010.**

改写：The line chart illustrates the variation of the size of the land used for cultivating organic food in country A and country B from 1985 to 2010.

Part 5 主体段写作

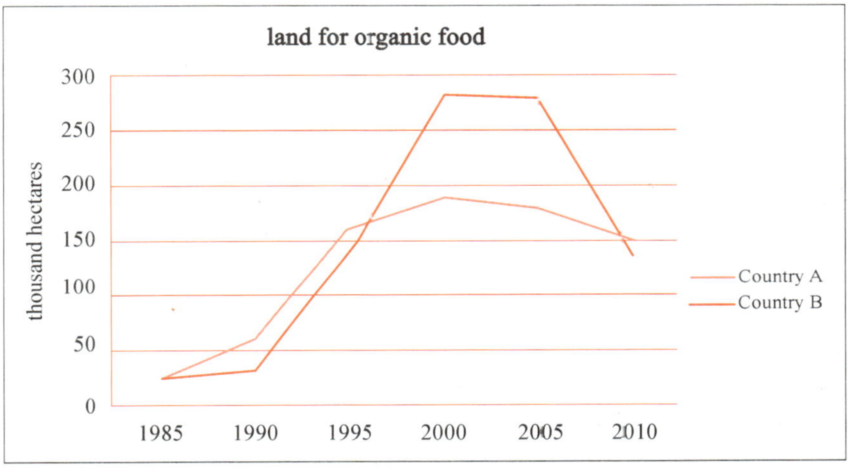

The trend in the two countries showed great similarity during the initial decade. In 1985, around 25 thousand hectares were used to grow organic food in both countries, which then saw an ongoing rise, though at a slightly different rate, in the land use until 1995, when the figures equaled again at approximately 170 thousand hectares.

After that, dramatic difference can be spotted. Land use in country A underwent less change, almost fluctuating between 150 – 180 thousand hectares. By contrast, for country B, the area continued to increase at the almost the same previous speed, peaking at 280 thousand hectares in 2000. The situation almost didn't change until 2005, after which there was an abrupt downward trend. Interestingly, during most of the last 15 years, far more land was used for organic crops in country B, while in 2010, the size was reduced to 140 thousand hectares, 10 thousand hectares smaller compared to that of country A.

练习：请根据第二种思路来写正文段落。

Part 6 结尾段写作

Sample

To sum up, despite the difference in the land use in these two countries during the 25 years, the area dedicated to organic crops was rather close both in the beginning and the end.

Part 7 真题练习

(1) The bar chart below shows the percentage of adults of different age groups in the UK who used the Internet everyday from 2003 to 2006.

Summarize the information by selecting and reporting the main features, and make comparisons where relevant. (2015.01.10)

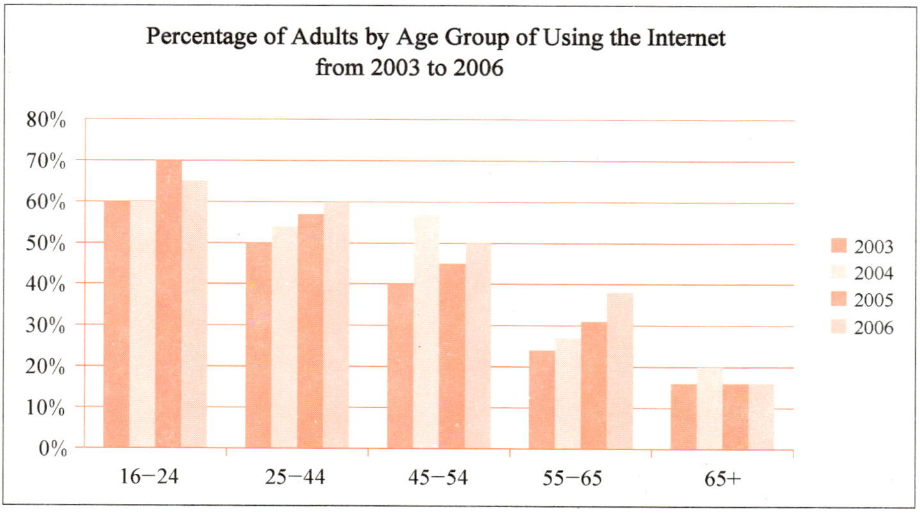

(2) The charts below show the proportions of water used for different purposes in Sydney in 1997 and 2007.

Summarize the information by selecting and reporting the main features, and make comparisons where relevant. (2015. 10. 10)

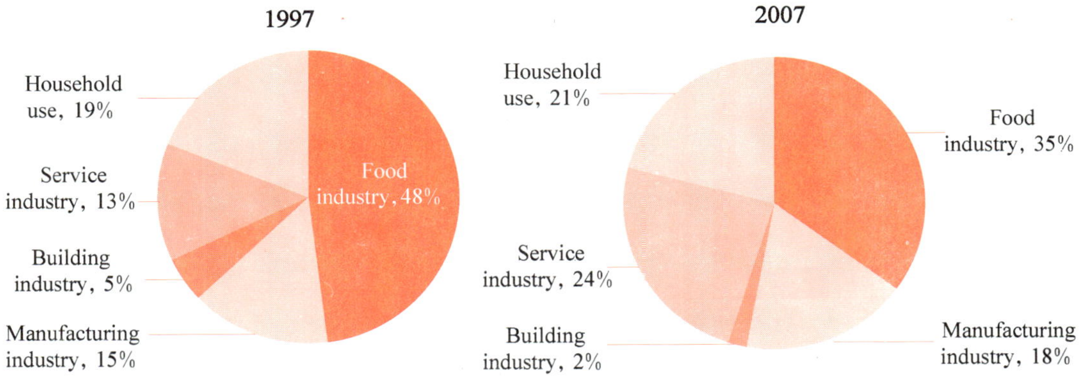

(3) The following charts show the distribution of the employment among agriculture, industry, and service in three countries in 1980 and a prediction for 2020.

Summarize the information by selecting and reporting the main features, and make comparisons where relevant. (2016. 03. 19)

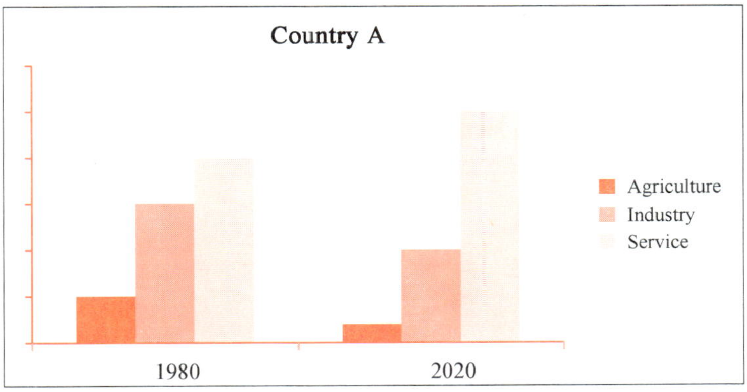

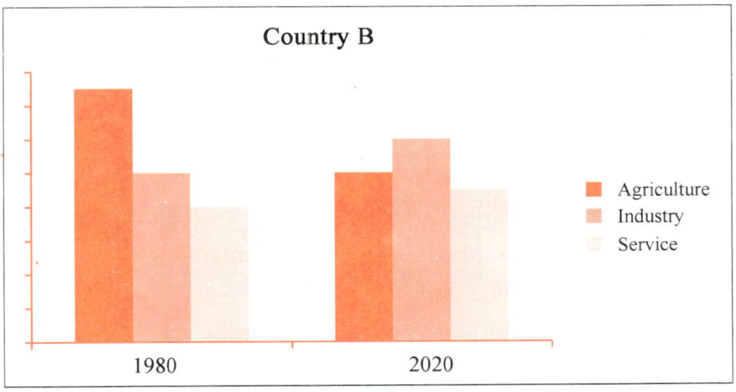

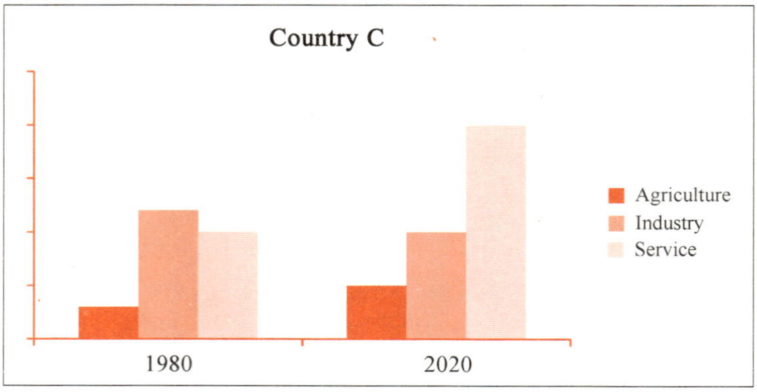

(4) The line graph shows the sales of children's books, adults' fictions and educational books between 2002 and 2006 in one country.

Summarize the information by selecting and reporting the main features, and make comparisons where relevant. (2015.01.17)

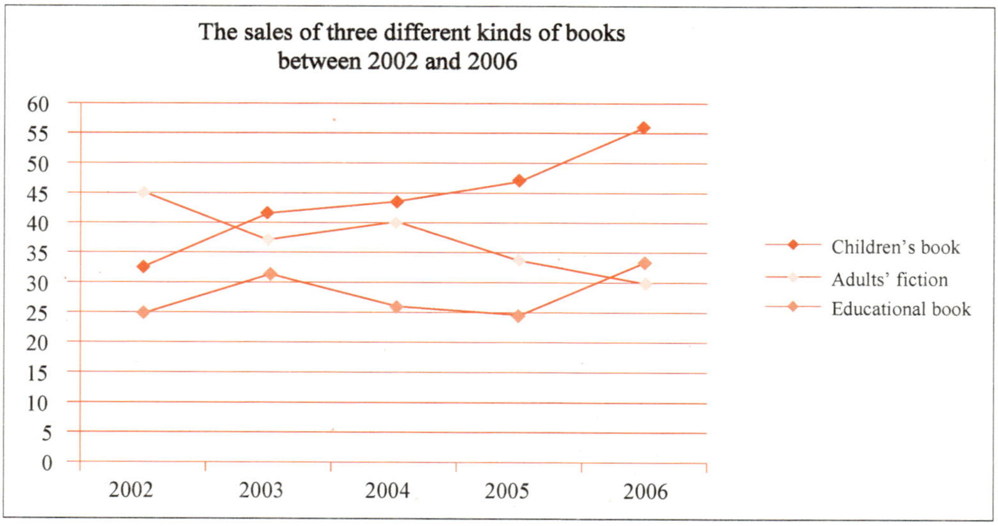

(5) The bar chart below shows the proportion of immigrants to Australia who came from five different countries in 1962, 1982 and 2002.

Summarize the information by selecting and reporting the main features, and make comparisons where relevant. (2015.11.21)

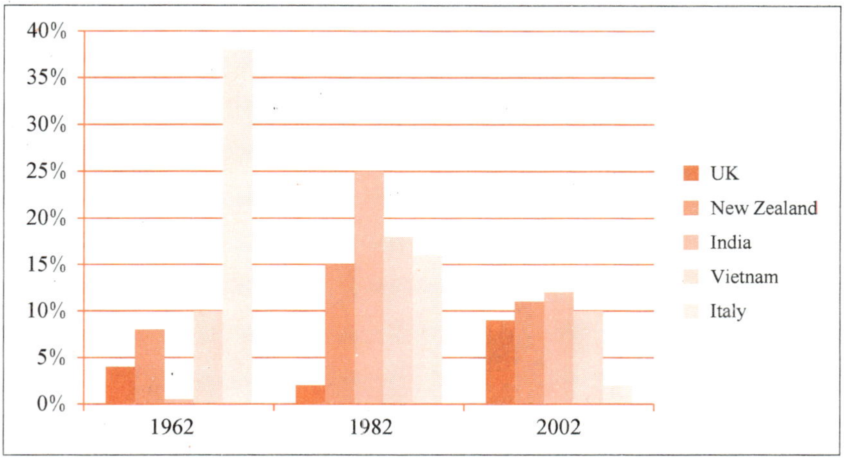

(6) The first graph shows the number of passengers travelling by train in Sydney. The second graph provides information about the percentage of trains running on time.

Summarize the information by selecting and reporting the main features, and make comparisons where relevant. (2015.06.27)

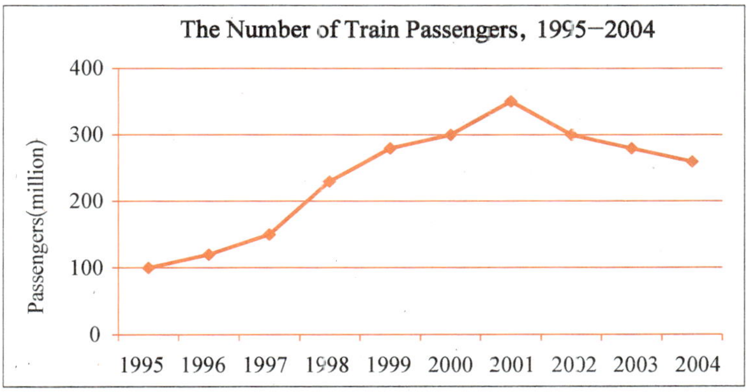

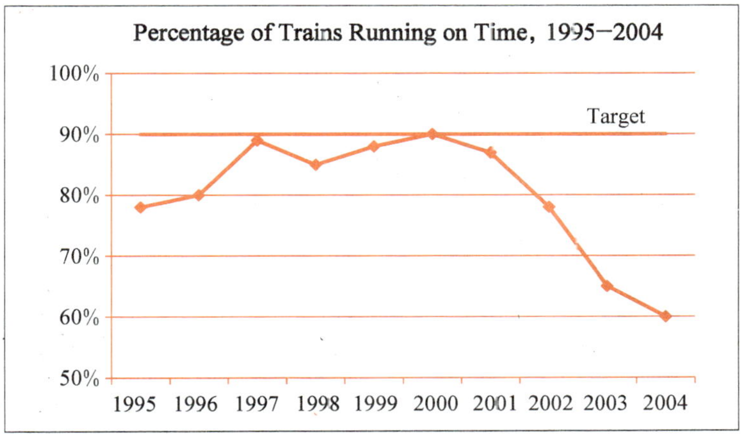

(7) The pie charts below show the percentage of five types of books sold by a bookseller between 1972 and 2012.

Summarize the information by selecting and reporting the main features, and make comparisons where relevant. (2015.08.13)

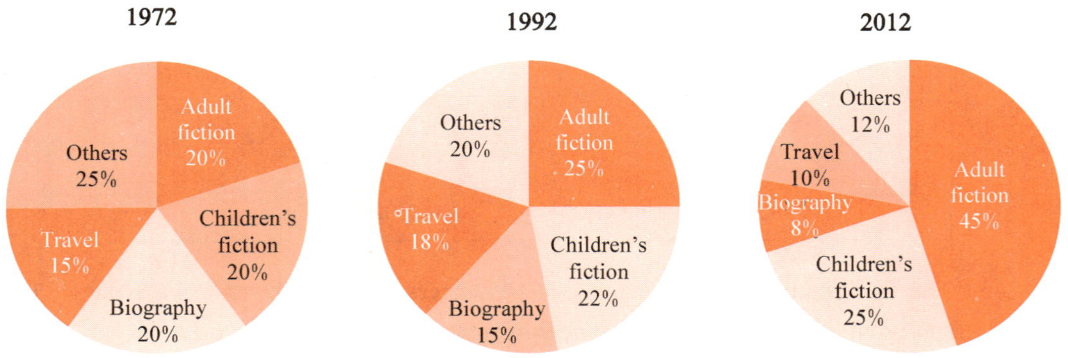

(8) The line graph shows the changes of average monthly salary and the prices of black and white TV and color TV in Japanese Yen from 1953 to 1973.

Summarize the information by selecting and reporting the main features, and make comparisons where relevant. (2016.02.18)

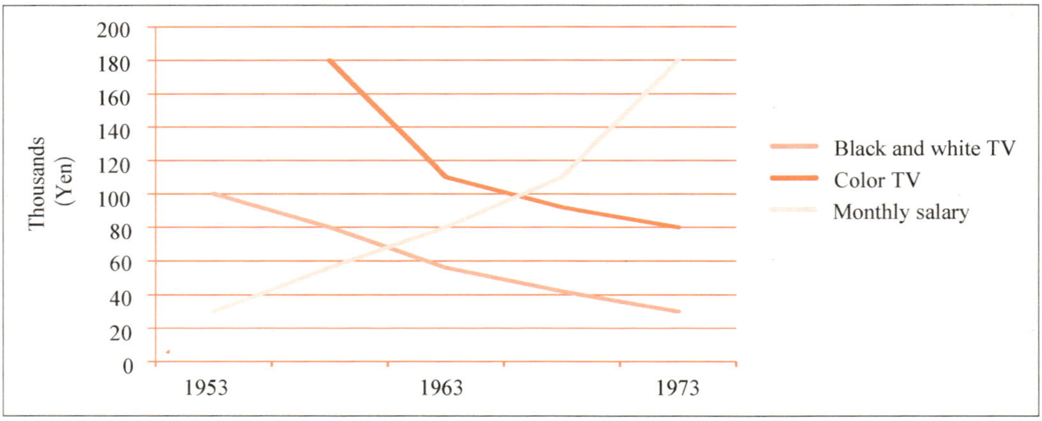

(9) The table below describes the changes of people (million) who went for international travel in 1990, 1995, 2000 and 2005.

Summarize the information by selecting and reporting the main features, and make comparisons where relevant. (2015.03.12)

1990	1995	2000	2005	Area
448.9	615.2	669.2	693.7	Total
18.2	20.8	26.9	28.7	Africa
80.5	112.5	118.2	113.2	America
60.2	80.3	117.4	135.8	Asia and the Pacific
280.2	390.3	393.2	400.2	Europe
9.8	11.3	13.5	15.8	Middle East

(10) The table shows population ratio of males per 100 females in six different areas in 1950 & 2005 (Africa, Asia, Europe, North and central America Oceania, North America).

Summarize the information by selecting and reporting the main features, and make comparisons where relevant. (2015.04.18)

1950	97.8	105.3	89.4	100.1	100	103.9
2005	99.2	104.9	92.8	96.9	97.5	99.8

Chapter 4 Maps and Flowcharts
地图和流程图

Section 1 Maps

什么是地图?

地图（Map）展现某一个地区的房屋、建筑物的分布状况，或者展现某一个区域的地貌特点。地图题包括“变迁类”地图题和“选址类”地图题两种。“变迁类”地图题展现同一地区在几个不同年份发生的变化，要求考生描述这些变化。“选址类”地图题一般是为商场、酒店等选址，会提供几个不同的区域作为备选方案，问考生哪个区域最适合建造商场、酒店或其他设施，并请考生给出理由。

Part 1 A Quick Scan

变迁类地图题

从过去到过去

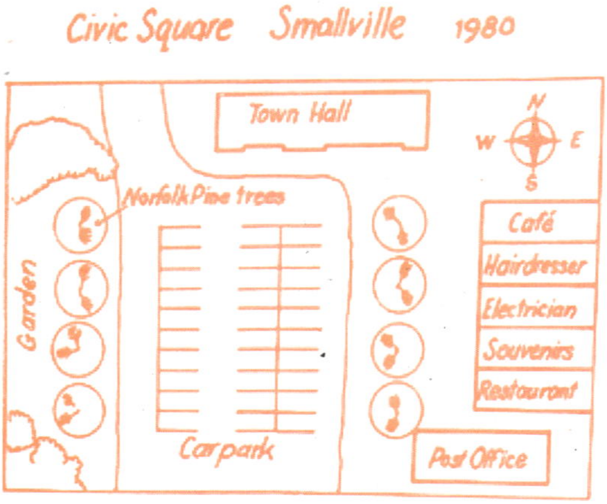

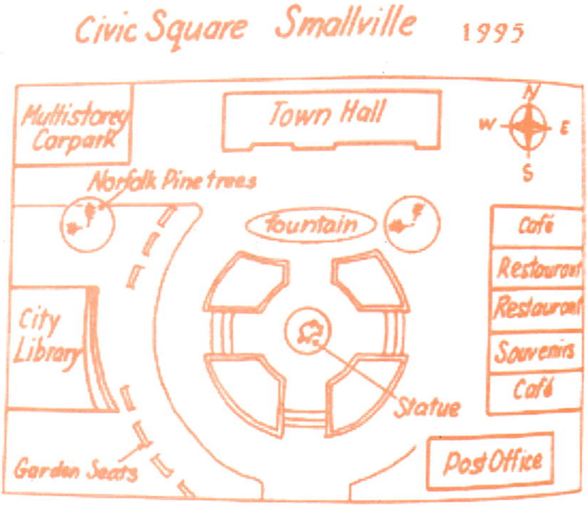

从过去到现在

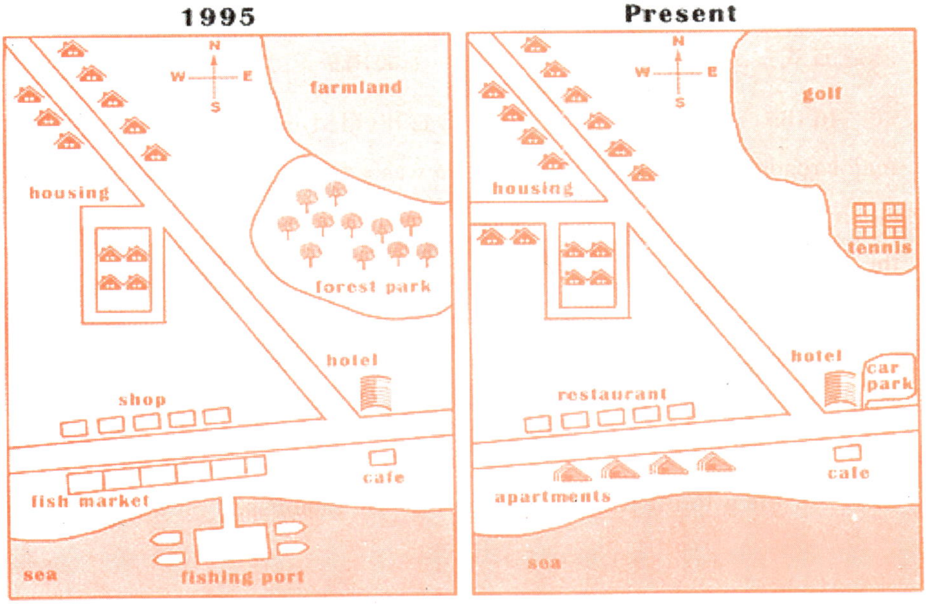

从现在到将来

School Site-present：600 students

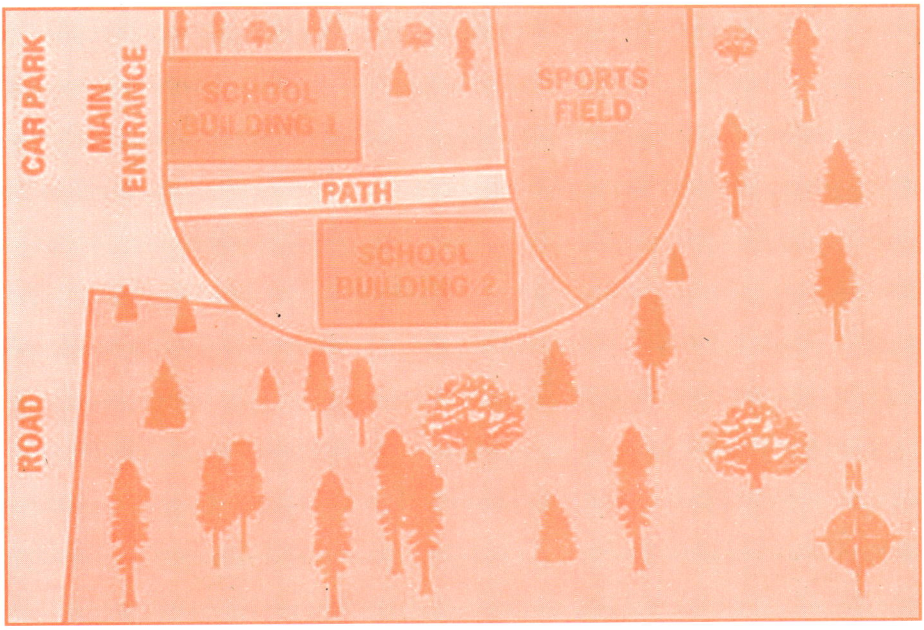

School Site – 2024: 1,000 students

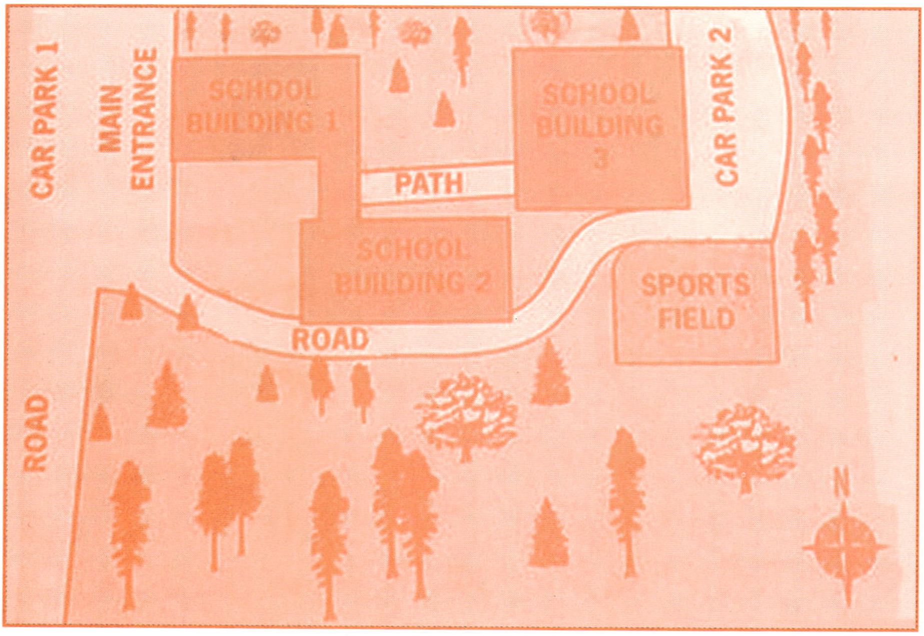

选址类地图题

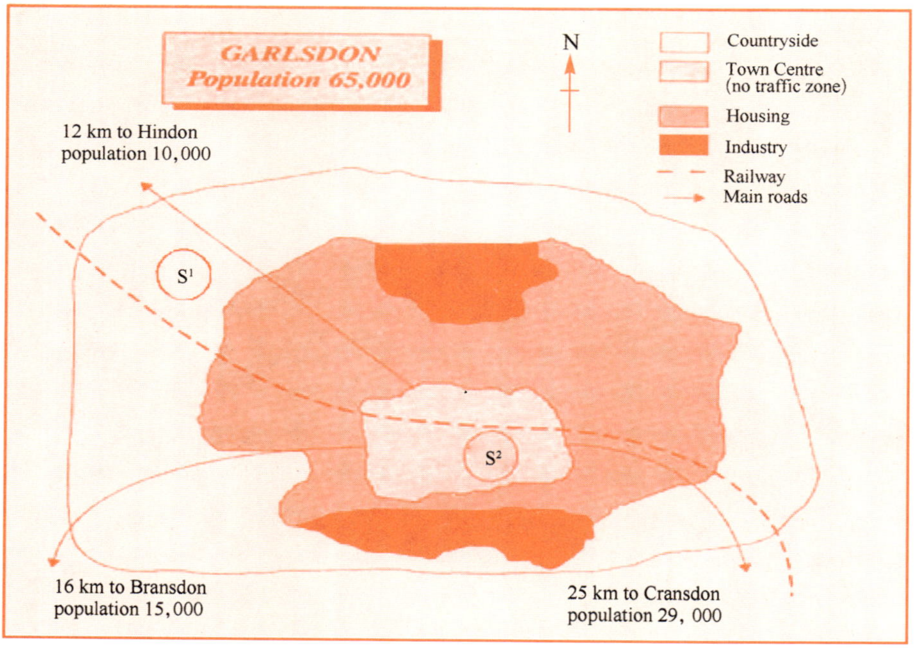

Part 2 Language Input

地图题分为静态地图题和动态地图题两种。在描写静态地图题的过程中，会用到描述方位、平行、交叉、相邻等的表达方式。在描写动态地图（变迁过程）的过程中，会用到描述数量增加/减少、规模扩大/缩小、从无到有/从有到无、方位移动的表达方式。

（一）静态地图

1. 方位介词

B is in the north of A. B 在 A 的北边（B 在 A 内部）

C is on the north of A. C 在 A 的北边（C 在 A 外部，C 和 A 接壤）

D is to the north of A. D 在 A 的北边（D 在 A 外部，D 和 A 可以接壤也可以不接壤）

注意：in/on/to 三个介词表示方位时的区别

例：

➢ Shanghai is in the east of China.（Shanghai 在 China 内部）

➢ Fujian Province is on the east of Jiangxi Province.（Fujian Province 在 Jiangxi Province 外部，两者接壤）

➢ Japan is to the east of China.（Japan 在 China 的外部，两者不接壤）

练习 1：用 in/on/to 三个介词表示方位。

例：Russia/China/north

Russia is on the north of China.

（1）Canada/North America/north

____

（2）Hainan Island/Guangdong Province/south

____

（3）Texas/the US/south

____

2. 方位动词

B **lies/is located/is situated** in the north of A.

注意："坐落于……"是 be located，不是 locate

例：The village locates in the east of the valley.　（×）

The village is located in the east of the valley.　（√）

练习 2：用 lies/is located/is situated ... 写出以下句子。

例：the UK/France/west/is situated

The UK is situated to the west of France.

（1）Ohio/Pennsylvania/west/lie

____

(2) Germany/France/east/is located

(3) Britain/the European Continent/west/lie

3. 中心/边缘

1）中心

A is in the centre/center of B. A 在 B 的中央。

A is in the middle of B. A 在 B 的中心。

2）边缘

C is on the border of D. C 在 D 的边缘。

C is on the edge of D. C 在 D 的边缘。

例：The scouts pitched their tents on the border of the lake.

The ranger lived in a cabin on the edge of the forest.

练习 3：用 in the centre/center of、in the middle of、on the border of 或 on the edge of 组词成句。

(1) shed/national park/on the border of

(2) expensive department store/London/in the center of/be located

(3) factory/town/on the border of/be situated

(4) library/campus/on the edge of/lie

(5) gym/neighborhood/in the middle of/be located

4. 相邻

A is **in the vicinity of** B. A 在 B 附近。

A is **in the proximity of** B. A 在 B 附近。

例：The plane crashed **in the vicinity of** the mountain area.

They bought a house **in the proximity of** the hospital.

C **is adjacent to** D. C 和 D 相邻。

例：The Johnson's property **is adjacent to** ours.

练习 4：用 in the vicinity of/in the proximity of/be adjacent to 写出以下句子。

(1) swimming pool/yard/in the vicinity/lie

(2) drug store/hospital/in the proximity of/is located

(3) my neighbor's yard/ours/be adjacent to

当主语内容信息量较大时，我们可以用倒装句，给主语带上定语部分，于是就有了以下的更加高级的表达方式：

In the vicinity of A lies B with . . . .

In the proximity of A is B, which is . . .

例如：

In the vicinity of the hotel lies a gym with all kinds of sports equipment.

In the proximity of Route 66 is a historic building, which was constructed in the 1860s.

练习 5：请翻译以下句子。

(1) 在博物馆附近有一家小商店，参观者可以在这里购买各种各样的纪念品。(in the vicinity of A lies B, where . . .)

(2) 在卖菜小贩的旁边有一家海鲜超市，供应新鲜的牡蛎和龙虾。(in the proximity of A is B with . . .)

5. 平行/交叉

1）平行

Road A **is parallel to** Road B. 路 A 和路 B 平行。

例：King's Street **is parallel to** Fourth Avenue.

2）交叉

Road C **intersects（with）** Road D. 路 C 和路 D 交叉。

例：Abby Road **intersects（with）** Crooked Road.（with 可以省略）

练习 6：请用 be parallel to 或 intersect（with）来翻译以下句子。

（1）人行道和 Lane Crawford 平行。

____

（2）两条路在喷泉附近相交。

____

（3）Marbury Road 和 Orchard Street 平行。

____

6. 容纳

（1）hold

例：The stadium can hold approximately 2000 spectators.

（2）have a capacity of

例：The city hall has a capacity of 300 people.

（3）accommodate

例：The school is not big enough to accommodate all the children from the local community.

练习 7：请用 hold/have a capacity of/accommodate 造句。

（1）这辆车最多可以容纳 20 名乘客。（hold）

____

（2）医院病房可以容纳 60 名病人。（have a capacity of）

____

（3）酒店有足够的房间来容纳 80 名游客。（accommodate）

____

（二）动态地图

1. 数量上升/下降

1）数量上升：increase/rise

例：The number of parking places increased from 10 to 25 during the twelve years.

注意：如果数量正好是成倍增长，还可以用 double，triple 等。

例如：There were 40 restaurants in the shopping mall in 2002. The number **doubled** in five years.

2）数量下降：decrease/decline/fall/reduce

注意：The number of gas stations decreased to 80. 是“加油站的数量减少到 80 个”。

The number of gas stations decreased by 80. 是“加油站的数量减少了 80 个”。

练习 1：请用括号里的词翻译所给句子

（1）在改建之后，客房的数量增长到 15 个。（rise）

____

（2）在三年内，车站的数量减少了 5%。（reduce）

____

（3）酒店房间的数量翻了一倍来容纳更多的游客。（double）

____

2. 规模变大

1）enlarge

例：They enlarged the barn in 2015.

The school was moved to the southeastern area of the town with an enlarged campus.

2）expand

例：They plan to expand the factory in two years.

The plan to expand the city will be implemented in 2020.

练习 2：请用括号里的词翻译所给句子

（1）小路被拓宽成了大路。（expand）

____

（2）我的邻居扩大了他的草坪。（enlarge）

____

（3）现在有了的更好的工作环境，带有被扩大了的办公室。（enlarge）

____

3. 规模缩小

1）shrink

例：The size of the swimming pool shrunk in 2013.

2）reduce

例：The farmland has been reduced to 14 acres.

注意：halve 可以表示“把……减半”

例：The risk of bankruptcy has been halved.

练习 3：请用括号里的词翻译所给句子

（1）在 2005 年市中心的规模大大缩减。（shrink）

____

(2) 在最近10年间,热带雨林已经减少了一半。(reduce)

____

(3) 为了给新的免税店让出空间,候机室被缩小了一半。(halve)

____

4. 从无到有

appear/emerge

例:A garage appeared in the northwestern area of the property.

练习4:请用括号里的词翻译所给句子

(1) 两年以后,那所小学旁边出现了一家书店。(appear/in the vicinity of)

____

(2) 楼梯旁边出现了一个衣帽间。(emerge)

____

5. 从有到无

disappear/vanish

例:The seafood market near the restaurants vanished in 2015.

练习5:请用括号里的词翻译所给句子

(1) 校园发生了很大的改变,食堂消失了。(disappear)

____

(2) 商场和它的停车场一同消失了。(vanish)

____

6. 方位移动

move/relocate

例:The library has been moved to the northeastern part of the campus.

练习6:请用括号里的词翻译所给句子

(1) 体育馆被搬迁到了市中心。(move)

____

(2) 他们决定将工厂搬到乡下去。(relocate).

____

Part 3 Writing

实战演练

The pictures below show the differences of the layout of a conference center between the present and its future plan.

Summarise the information by selecting and reporting the main features, and make comparisons where relevant. (2014.11.13)

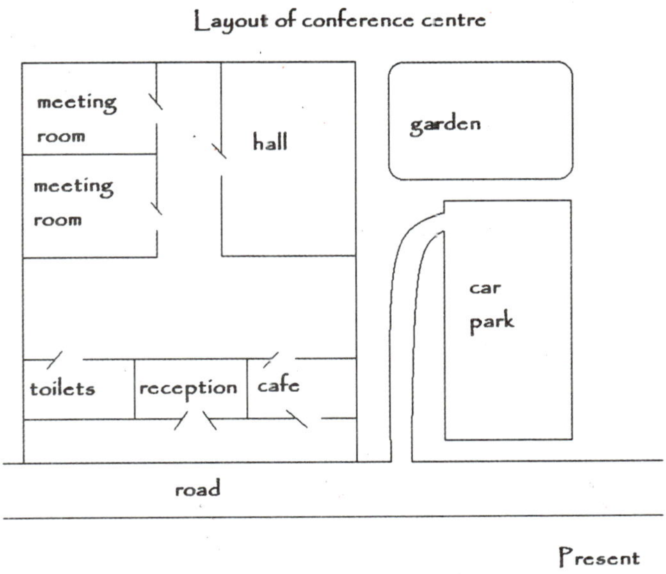

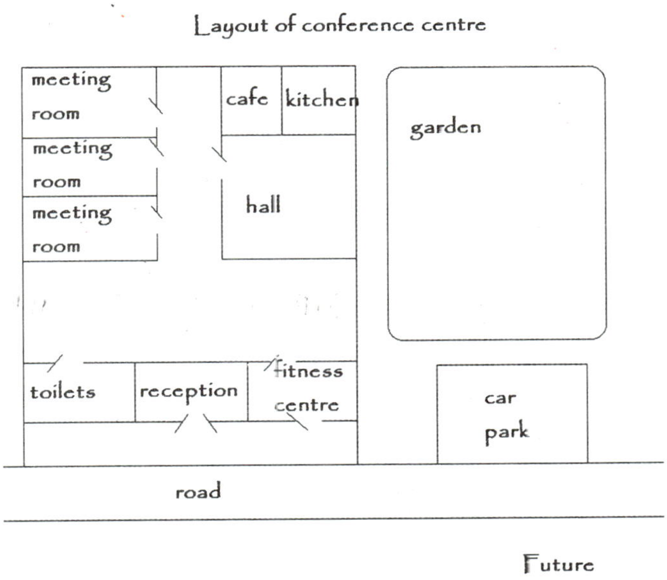

1. 图表分析

Key points:

(1) What tense should we choose to describe the two maps?

(2) Is there any change related to size?

(3) Is there any change related to numbers?

(4) Is there any change related to location?

(5) In what order would you describe the maps?

2. 预热-单句练习

变化 1：

停车场缩小而花园扩大了。

It is obvious that the car parking lot will be able to accommodate fewer cars, while the garden will be more spacious.

变化 2：

两个会议室将会被划分为三个。

After the reconstruction, the two meeting rooms will be divided into three meeting rooms

你还能看出哪些变化？请描写这些变化。

变化 3：

____

____

____

变化 4：

____

____

____

变化 5：

____

____

____

3. 思路梳理

(1) Overview：会议中心的室内室外都将发生变化

(2) 室内：(可按南北顺序来描述，从入口开始)

南面(从左到右)：左边 toilet 中间 reception 都不会改变，右边原来是 café 今后将会是 fitness centre

北面：西北角的会议室由 2 个变成 3 个

Hall 的面积将缩小到原来的 2/3，其中北面的 1/3 用来作 café 和 kitchen

(3) 室外：北面：garden 面积扩大了 3 倍

Car park 大面积缩小，原来位于东北角的入口和通向入口的道路将会消失，入口直接位于 road 上

(4) 总结：将来的会议中心设施配备更完善，也更环保

4. 参考范文

The maps given compares today's layout of the conference centre with the planned layout in the future. It is clearly seen that the change will happen both indoors and outdoors.

When you walk into the building, right in front of you is the reception area, to the west of which are toilets. These two facilities won't change in the future, but the current café to the east of the reception area will be replaced by a fitness centre. When you walk further, you will find two meeting rooms in the northwest, which will be converted into three. Opposite the meeting rooms is a hall of an equal size. However, its size will be reduced to two thirds of its original for the northern part will be dedicated for a café and a kitchen.

Outside the conference building, you can find a garden and a car park and they will remain in the future. Nevertheless, the garden is planned to be expanded southward to three times its current size. Correspondingly, the car park will shrink and its entrance will shift from the northeast to the south, just on the road.

Overall, the conference center in the future plan seems to offer more facilities, ensuring greater convenience and more leisure.

Part 4 真题演练

(1) The map below shows information about two plans of the layout of a training session.

Summarize the information by selecting and reporting the main features and make comparisons where relevant. (2015.8.1)

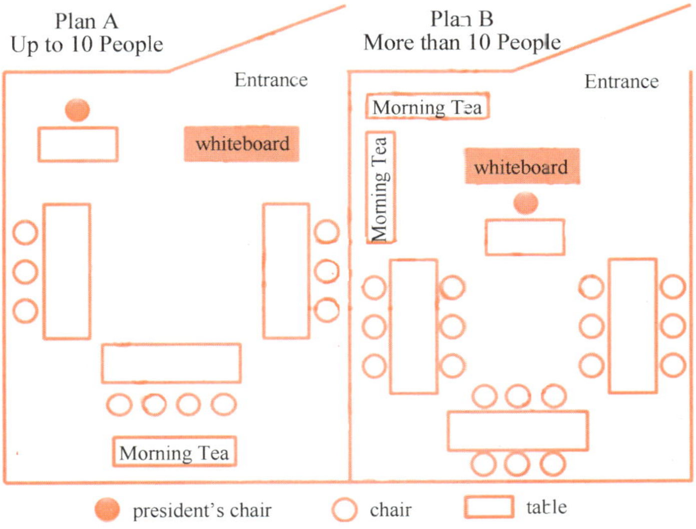

(2) The diagram below shows the development of the village of Kelsby between 1780 and 2000.

Summarise the information by selecting and reporting the main features, and make comparisons where relevant.

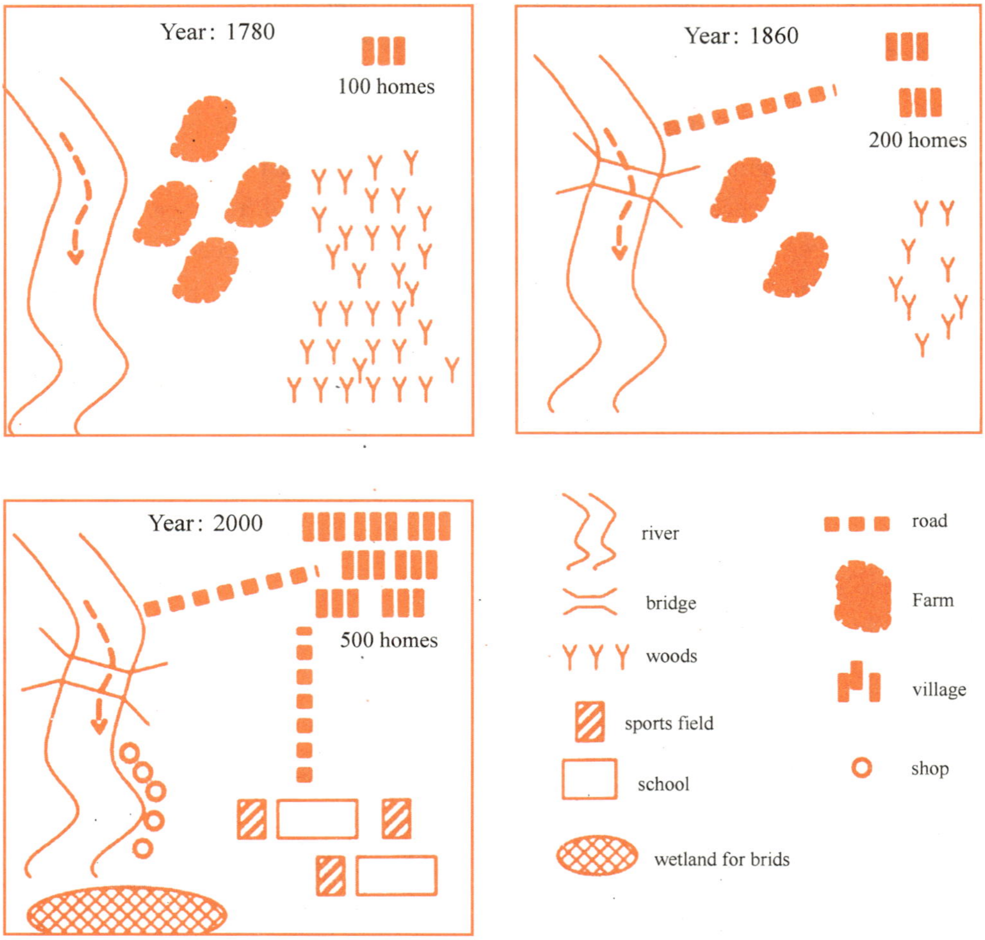

(3) The two maps below show an island, before and after the construction of some tourist facilities.

Summarise the information by selecting and reporting the main features, and make comparisons where relevant.

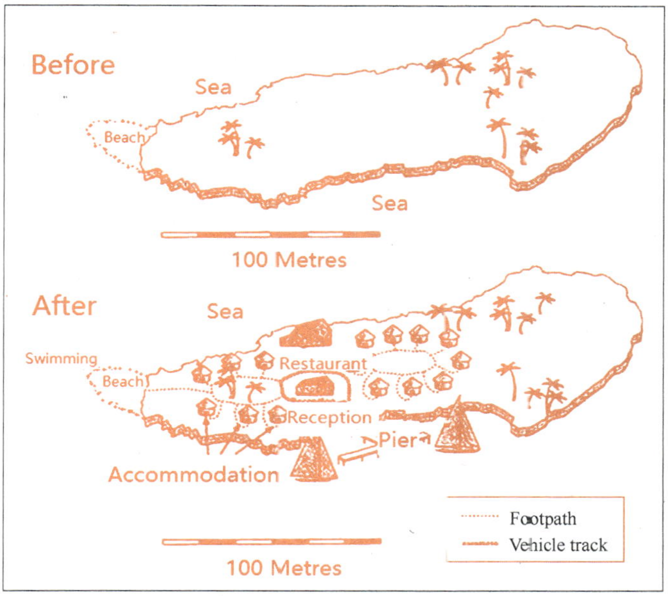

(4) Below is a map of the city of Brandfield. City planners have decided to build a new shopping mall for the area, and two sites, S1 and S2 have been proposed.

Summarize the information by selecting and reporting the main features and make comparisons where relevant.

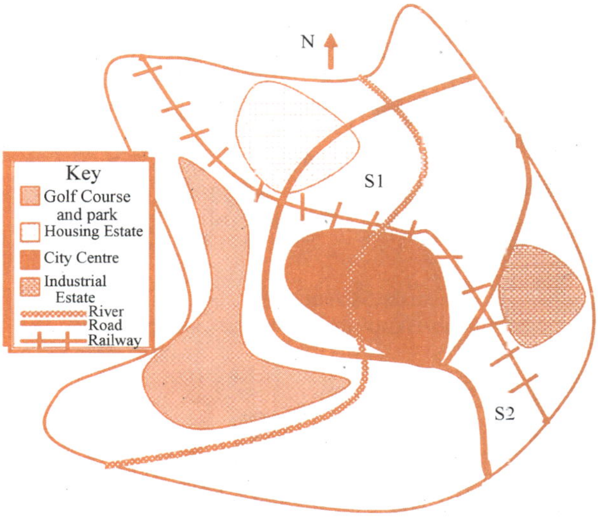

Section 2 Flowcharts

流程图一般分为工艺流程(industrial process)(如巧克力的制作)和自然进程(natural process)(如昆虫的生命周期),有时候也会出现一些生活类场景,如考驾照的流程。从所给流程图的要素来看，有时候出现的是名词，有时候出现的是动词。如果是前者，在写作过程中需要将动词补出，同样，如果是后者，需要将与动词相关的名词给补出来。

Part 1 A Quick Scan

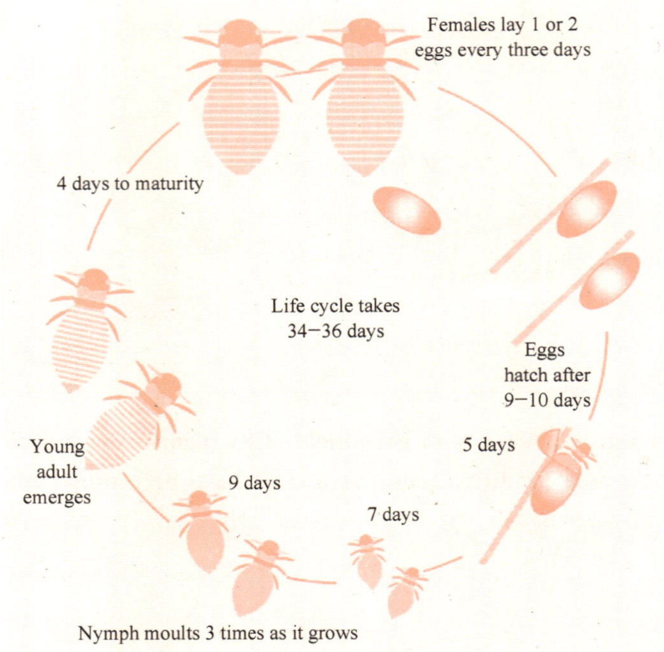

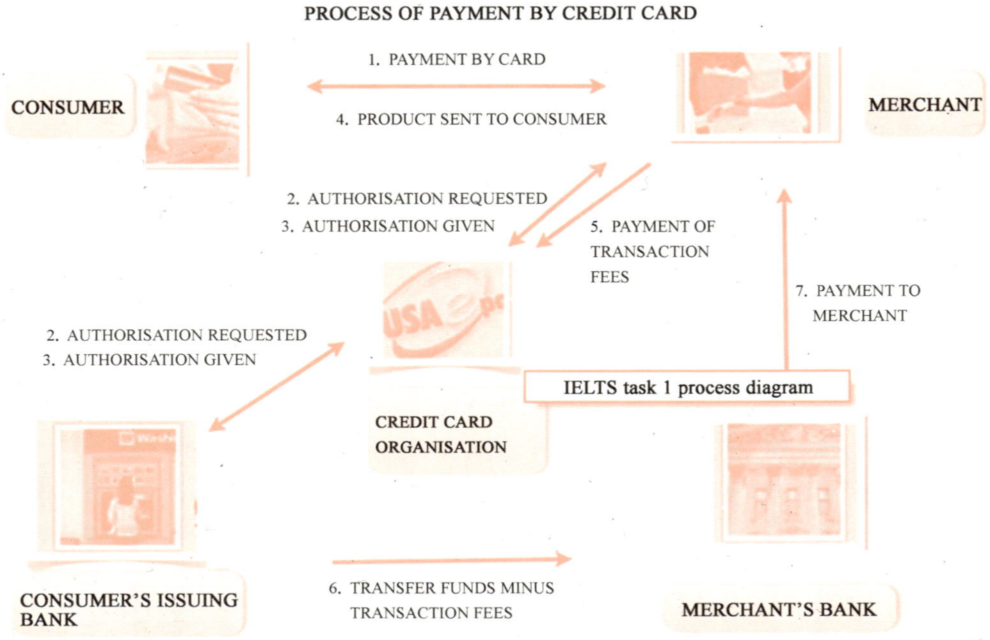

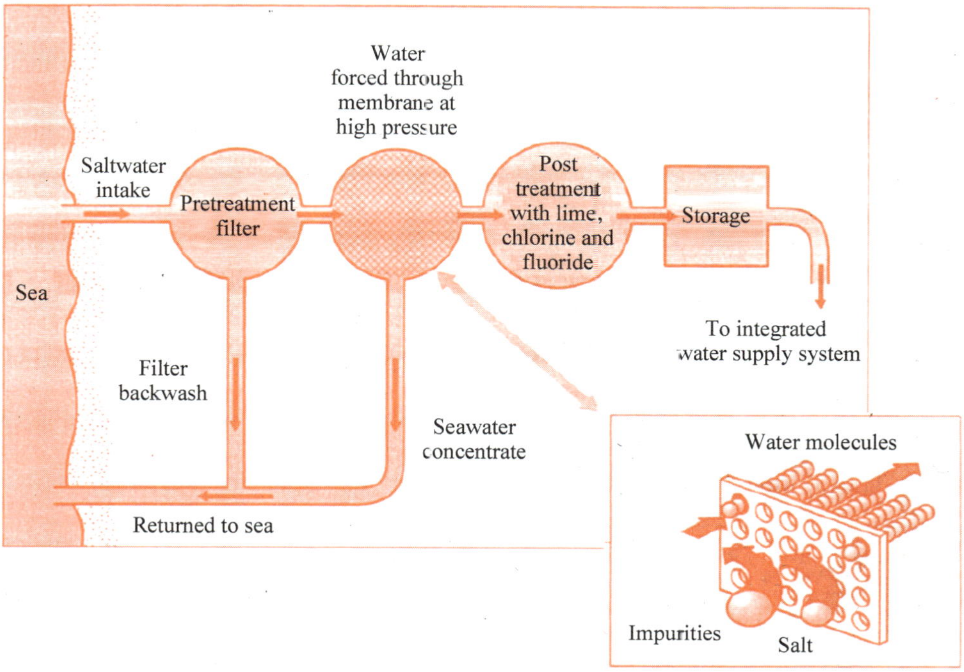

Part 2 Language Input

1. 被动语态

流程图中多用被动语态，动作由谁发出来并不重要。但是在自然进程中，可以用到主动语态的，如 The sun shines; The fruit ripes。

练习 1：完成以下表格。

动词	过去分词	动词	过去分词
grow		hold	
sow		grind	
sell		put	
take		cut	
wrap		weave	

练习 2：用被动语态翻译以下句子。

（1）橘子从西班牙出口到欧洲比较寒冷的国家。

____

（2）为了制作咖啡粉，咖啡豆需要先在机器里磨碎。

____

(3) 大米装袋后被运到超市。

____

(4) 巧克力棒被包在银色的纸中然后再装箱。

____

2. 衔接手段

在流程中,需要按步骤来描写。在这个步骤中,需要用到合适的衔接词才能使语句过渡自然。

练习 3:请将以下衔接表达式填入表格的合适位置。

Then　First of all　Subsequently　The first step is that　Finally　After that
At this point　The next step is that　Following this　To begin with
The following step is that　Initially　The last step is　and then　after which

Next	The first stage is	The last stage is

练习 4:用括号里的词来改写句子。

(1) The tea leaves are picked and then they are put in the sun to dry. (once)

____

(2) The tea leaves are picked from the tea plants and packed into boxes, (after)

____

(3) The boxes are loaded onto a lorry and then they are taken to supermarkets, (when)

____

(4) You put the tea bag in the cup and then you can pour hot water into it. (once)

____

3. 定语从句和目的状语

由于流程图多用被动语态,句型会稍显单调,为了使句型多样化,同时也是为了内容更具体化。需要对基本句型做一个补充,如在名词结尾的句子后,对该名词作进一步的说明,就可以用上 which 或 where 等引导的定语从句。在时间名词后可以接上 when 定语从句进行扩充。此外,对于某些特定步骤,可以解释一下该步骤的目的是什么,这是可以用上 in order to 或 so that 等衔接词。

练习 5：用括号中的词来连接两个句子。

(1) The fruit is sent to a factory. It is put into cans there. (where)

____

(2) The biscuits are put in the oven. They are cooked. (in order to be)

____

(3) The farmer waters the plants. This makes them grow more quickly. (which)

____

(4) The mushrooms are stored in a dark room. This helps them to stay fresh. (so that)

____

Part 3 Writing

实战演练：

The pictures below show how tomato ketchup is made.

Summarize the information by selecting and reporting the main features and make comparisons where relevant.

1. 图表分析

Key points:

(1) Do you know all the verbs necessary to describe each picture?

（2）Do you know all the purposes of each step?

2. 预热-单句练习

把每张图写清楚是写好整篇流程图的基础。

例：picture 3：The selected tomatoes are delivered to the factory by van.

练习 1：根据所给图表，请任意选取 5 张图片进行单句练习。

（1）______________________________

（2）______________________________

（3）______________________________

（4）______________________________

（5）______________________________

其次，还需要具备对任何两个图片进行链接的能力。

例如：对于 picture 5 &6，可以写成：

After being poured into a container, the tomatoes are crushed.

练习 2：根据所给图表，请任意选取 2 组相邻进行单句练习。

（1）______________________________

（2）______________________________

3. 参考范文

The given pictures demonstrate the way of making tomato ketchup step by step. Overall, there are 15 steps to be done to produce a bottle of ketchup.

First of all, a farmer picks up tomatoes from his farm and put them in baskets. Then, he selects only good tomatoes from the ones he picked. After being sent to factory, the tomatoes will have a removal process in order to get rid of stalks, seeds and skins. Having been collected into containers, the processed tomatoes are crushed and turned into liquid. Subsequently, with adding sugar, salt and vinegar, they are ready to be cooked. This process turns tomatoes into a liquid form which is called ketchup. After boiling, the ketchup is left to cool for two hours before being poured into bottles which are then labelled. In order to make quality the best, inspectors check all their products. At just before the final stage, only the selected bottles are packed and delivered to supermarkets. Finally, the customers enjoy the tomato ketchup with their food.

Part 4 真题练习

（1）The flowchart below shows the process of water cycle

Summarize the information by selecting and reporting the main features and make comparisons where relevant.

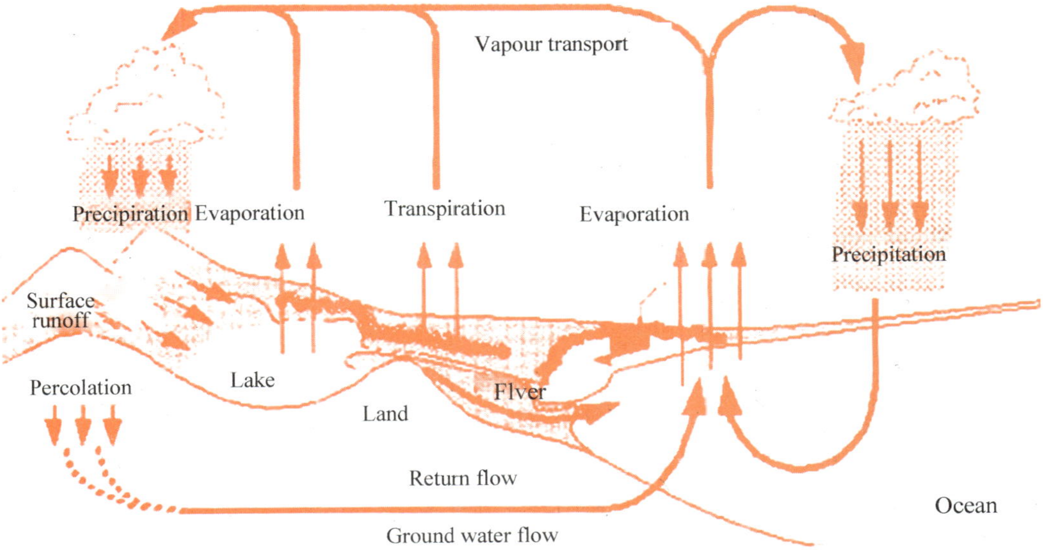

(2) The diagrams below give information of three methods to recruit new employees. Summarize the information by selecting and reporting the main features and make comparisons where relevant.

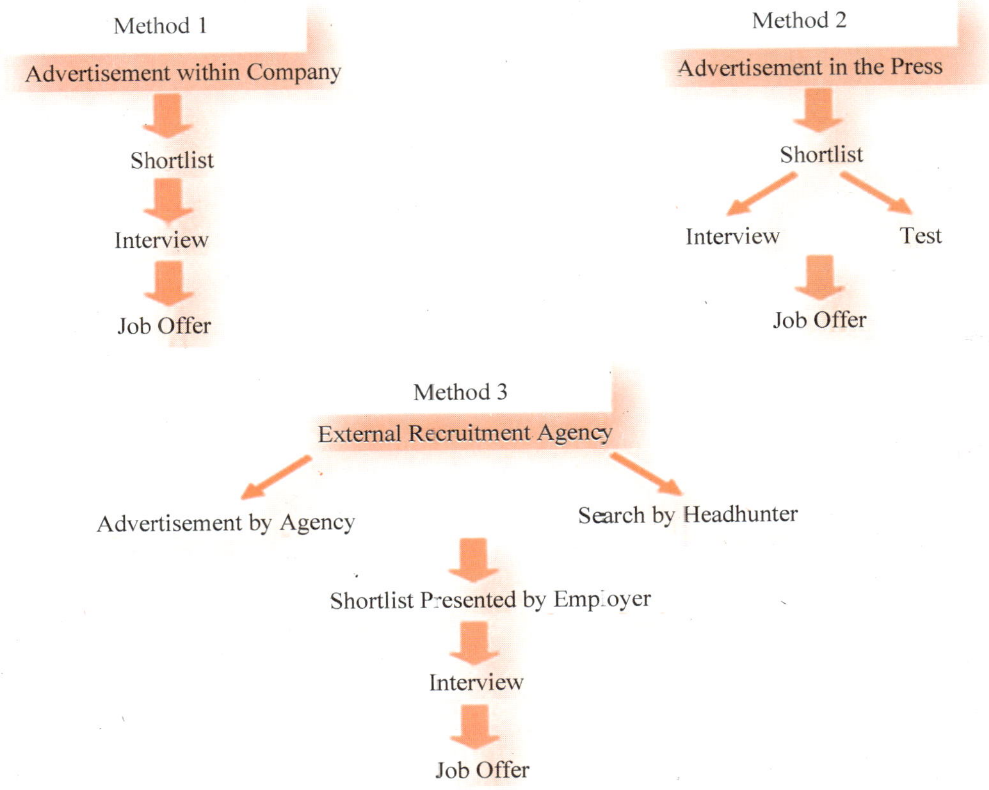

(3) The information in the diagram below describes the bread making process.

Summarise the information by selecting and reporting the main features, and make comparisons where relevant.

The Bread Making Process

Chapter 5 Topic: Education & Technology

教育类、科技类大作文

Section 1 Education

Part 1 考什么

重点范围

教育的本质

(1) What do you think a good education should cover?

> 考题例子：
>
> Some people think university education should prepare students for employment. Other people think the university has other functions. Discuss both views and what do you think the function of university education. (2009.10.24)

选科目

(2) What kind of subjects do you learn in high school or university?

(3) Are there any subjects that you are not good at or interested in?

(4) Do you think you should learn all subjects or just some? Why?

(5) Do you think students should learn international news?

(6) Why do most male students like science while most girls are better at arts or language learning?

> 考题例子：
>
> In some countries, secondary schools aim to provide a general education across a range of subjects. In others, children focus on a narrow range of subjects related to a particular career. Which do you think is appropriate in today's world? (2015.10.08)

大学教育

(7) Do you think university education is necessary for all?

(8) Who should pay for university tuition fees? Why?

考题例子:

Too much emphasis has been put on going to university for academic study. We should encourage more people to receive vocational training because of lack of trades people, such electricians and plumbers. To what extent do you agree? (2015. 11. 21B 卷)

次要范围

课余安排

(9) What is the best way to spend the after-class time?

(10) Do you think it important for students to volunteer in community service?

教育问题和校园问题

(11) Are you satisfied with the current education? Why or why not?

(12) What student problems do you find at school? What are the causes?

学习方式

(13) What is your preferred way of learning (e. g. studying alone vs. studying in a group; learning from teachers vs. learning from the Internet; leaning a skill independently vs learning a skill from a teacher)?

(14) What kind of role does rote-learning play in study?

学习地点

(15) What kind of school do you prefer to go to, a public school or a private one? Why?

(16) What are the advantages and disadvantages of overseas study?

教师话题

(17) Should teachers stay in one school all the time or change schools to teach?

(18) Should teachers be allowed to design what they are going to teach?

(19) Should teachers be evaluated by students?

间隔年

(20) Would you like to have a gap year after graduating from high school?

外语学习

(21) What is the best time to start learning a foreign language? Do all students have to learn a foreign language?

其他

(22) Should students live at school?

(23) What factors do you think a school should consider in recruiting new students?

(24) What kind of students should be rewarded?

(25) Do you support homeschooling?

Part 2 思考维度

Part 1 所列范围几乎囊括了近10年所有雅思教育类考题。作为主流话题同时也是考生最熟悉的话题领域，教育类内容比较繁杂，具体的题目呈现形式可能更为多样化，但基本上跳不出以上这些基本问题范围。

为了更好地拓展思维，可以从题目考查的**本质**或**论据**出发，以不变应万变。以下就常考话题给出一些思维切入角度，可灵活应用到不同考题。

(1) What do you expect from **a young person fresh from college**?

(2) Who develops better in the real world, a person with **a wide knowledge scope** or one with **a deep insight into** one or a few particular areas?

(3) Should education **keep pace with** the trend of **globalization**?

(4) How do boys and girls differ in terms of brain, interest, talent, etc.?

(5) Is what you learn at university **closely related to** your future job?

(6) Does **government subsidy motivate** or **demotivate** students? Is education the **top priority** for the government?

(7) Does **excellence in academic performance outweigh** anything else for students?

(8) Does **unpaid service** require any ability of the provider?

(9) Does **exam-oriented teaching approach prevail** in your country? Do students like it?

(10) Do families and **high-tech products** also **account for** students' **poor performance** at school?

(11) Should we **adopt the same method** in learning different subjects? Are there any differences in the learning style for students of different age?

(12) Which is better, spending more time with **peers** or family members?

(13) What kind of problem would a student meet in a different culture?

(14) Who knows about students better?

(15) How to **ensure education equality**?

(16) Are all teachers **qualified**?

(17) Do you think it necessary for students to learn a foreign language? Is there anything more **meaningful** or interesting than learning a foreign language?

(18) Can parents be better than school teachers? Will **customized study miss out on some opportunities** beneficial to children?

An Illustration 思考维度 1

人们希望大学生毕业后有扎实的专业知识(**equipped with solid professional knowledge**)以便适应工作岗位的要求(**job requirements**)。

同时,雇主希望大学生在工作中能够有较好的沟通能力(**communication ability**),乐意与人合作(**willing to cooperate**),具有创新精神(**innovative**)。

整个社会希望大学生举止良好(**well-mannered**),尊重他人(**respectful**),不去做任何违反法律的问题(**won't do anything against the law**),对社会做贡献(**make contributions**),如多参加一些志愿者活动(**volunteer work**)以帮助社会弱势群体(**people in a disadvantaged position**)。

因此,好的教育应该提供完善的理论教育(**provide theory classes**)和实践机会(**practice opportunity**),这样,学生才能学以致用(**apply what they learn to practice**)。

人文和艺术的学习也同样重要,这可以陶冶情操(**cultivate their mind**),培养创造力(**develop creativity**)。

此外,学校应该开展丰富的课外活动(**a variety of extracurriculum activities**)来锻炼学生的组织能力(**organizing ability**)、领导能力(**leadership**)和团队精神(**team spirit**)。

然而更重要的是,道德教育(**moral education**)千万不能让位于(**give way to**)学术课程的学习(**academic study**)。这能确保学生具有良好的价值观(**life values**)和责任心(**sense of responsibility**),以后不会误入歧途(**go astray**),不会用自己所学到的知识来做非法的事情(**do illegal things**)。

对比你的答案和给出的示例,看看这些答案是不是囊括了"考什么 1",并部分解决了"考什么 9、10、11、23、24"?

☺ 雅思考试的真题几乎都包含在上述的那些问题中了,通过刚才的训练,再看以下一些雅思考题,是否心中基本上有答案了?

(1) Some people think the purpose of education is to prepare individuals to be useful to society. Others believe that the purpose is to help young people achieve their personal ambitions. Discuss both views and give your own opinion. (2014.4.12)

(2) Many people believe that teachers should take the responsibility to teach students to judge what is right and wrong and behave well; others feel that teachers should only teach academic subjects. Discuss both views and give your own opinion. (2011.5.28)

(3) Some people think university education should prepare students for employment. Other people think university has other functions. Discuss both views and what do you think the function of university education. (2009.10.24)

Part 3 话题词汇补充

poor student behavior	学生的不良行为
spoilt children	被宠坏的孩子
show consideration for others	为他人考虑
self-control	自我控制
self-discipline	自我约束,自律
show/have respect for teachers	尊重老师
obey school rules	遵守学校规定
graduate from high school	从高中毕业
primary school	小学
vocational school	职业学校
nursery school	幼儿园,托儿所
compulsory course	必修课
optional course	选修课
undergraduate	大学生
academic atmosphere	学术氛围
have/obtain/get access to	有权使用
a degree in economics	经济学学位
enroll in a course	参加某课程
pursuit of knowledge	对知识的追求
academic qualifications	学历资格
careers fair	招聘会
certificate	证书
extracurriculum activities	课外活动
interact with a lot of different people	与不同的人交流
learn information and basic skills	学习知识和基本技能
learn to communicate	学习沟通
be used to a strange environment	习惯于一个陌生环境

续表

make friends	交朋友
get on with other children of a similar age	与同龄人相处
economically independent	经济独立
have a broader view of life	对生活有更宽广的视野
cope with challenges	应对挑战
readapt to an academic environment	重新适应学术环境
broaden one's horizons	开阔视野
pick up languages	自然习得语言
acquire one's mother tongue	学习母语
maintain learners' enthusiasm	保持学习者的热情
have a command of a language	精通某种语言
unpaid community service	义务社区服务
to be a valuable member of a community	成为对社区有价值的成员
top priority	重中之重
give priority to sth.	优先考虑某事
increase one's employability	增强就业能力
reward sb. for sth.	因为某事奖励某人
provide a good role model	提供一个好的榜样
obtain/secure a position	获得一个职位
self-sufficient	自给自足
bully	欺凌
suffer from cultural shock	受到文化冲击的困扰
sense of loss	失落感
bleak career prospect	惨淡的职业前景
breadwinner	养家糊口的人
be ignorant of	对……无知
financial burden	经济负担
next generation	下一代
graduate unemployment	毕业生失业
adjust to	调节适应

续表

elite	精英
fruitful	有成效的
further studies	深造
global awareness	全球意识
impart knowledge	传授知识
liberal society	自由开放的社会
foster one's creativity	培养创造才干
physical co-ordination	身体协调性

Part 4 句子翻译

使用给出的单词和词组，把下列中文句子翻译成英文，注意给定单词和词组的形式有可能在句中发生改变。

Example：

- 学生糟糕的表现可能会引起课堂上的混乱。（student behavior）

Poor student behavior may result in chaos in classroom.

- 现代社会里孩子们从物质上被宠坏很常见。（spoilt）

It is normal in modern society that children **are spoilt** in material ways.

（1）他是一个自私的人，一点也不为别人考虑。（selfish，consideration）

____

（2）孩子们可以在团体活动中学会自我控制和纪律。（self-control，discipline）

____

（3）尊重老师和遵守学校规定是对学生的基本要求。（have respect for，obey）

____

（4）学校提供了一个供同龄孩子交流，交朋友，和学习如何相处的空间。（interact，get on with）

____

（5）对于很多学生来说，高中毕业意味着经济独立和独自应对挑战。（independent，cope with）

____

（6）现在选才不仅要看学历，还要看他有没有能力。（academic qualification，practical ability）

____

(7) 儿童母语的习得是以已有的知识经验为基础的。(acquire)

(8) 语言学家研究孩子们学语言的方法,发现一些大人也可适用的东西。(pick up)

(9) 在海外学习的人对生活有更宽广的视野和更好的个人资源去利用。(have a boarder view of, draw on)

(10) 每个人都应该花些时间在社区服务上。(invest, community service)

(11) 没有热情你什么事也办不成。(enthusiasm)

(12) 她精通法语。(have a command of)

(13) 数学是很多大学生的必修课。(compulsory subject)

(14) 终生学习对于增加就业能力是必需的。(essential, employability)

(15) 我们唯一能做主的是做一个好榜样还是一个坏榜样。(role model)

(16) 教师应该教会学生不要去欺凌他人。(bully)

(17) 大学经常在毕业典礼上要求他们的毕业生终生追求知识。(pursue, graduation ceremony)

(18) 我希望攻读化学学位课程。(chemistry degree)

(19) 这门课只有 5 个学生选了/注册。(enroll in)

(20) 他在一家商店获得了一份每周四百美元的工作。(secure)

(21) 许多人到国外时,都感受到文化冲击。(cultural shock)

(22) 学生们必须有使用图书馆的权限。(access)

（23）毕业前，我们会接受一些职业训练。（vocational）

____

Part 5　真题写作

2015 年 10 月 8 日真题

In some countries, secondary schools aim to provide a general education across a range of subjects. In others, children focus on a narrow range of subjects related to a particular career. Which do you think is appropriate in today's world?

Give reasons for your answer and include any relevant examples from your own knowledge or experience.

Write at least 250 words.

Step 1　审题

审题的目的有两个：

一是找出**题眼**（即关键词）是什么，以便在接下来的构思中围绕关键词展开；二是掌握题目中句子的**逻辑关系**和**问题指向性**，这对整体布局文章有关键的作用。

在本题中，很明显的**关键词**是 a general education, a range of subjects, a narrow range of subjects, a particular career。

此外，**带有定语的名词**、**限定性状语**也是关键词。可以确定在一定范围内进行讨论，而不是泛泛而谈。本题的限定名词是 secondary schools，意味着不能去谈小学或大学的情况。还有一个是 today's world，提示我们重视现在社会的特点和要求。以上这些关键词对拓展思路起着极其关键的作用。

其次，题干的部分形成**对比关系**，提示了在写作过程中可采取对比论证的策略。问题形式虽然是 Which do you think is appropriate in today's world? 看上去比较另类，实质上跟 Discuss both views and give your own opinion 是一样的。所以在写作中一定要双方都涉及，并加以评价。

练习：写出以下题目的关键词并分析句子内部/之间的逻辑关系

（1）Some teachers think it is effective for students to study in group while others think it is better to study alone. What are the benefits of each way and which one do you think is more effective?（2008.8.30）

关键词：____

逻辑关系：____

（2）Some people believe that studying in a college or university is the best way for students to prepare for their future career. Others think they should leave school as soon as possible to develop their career through work experience. Discuss both views and give your own opinion.（2013.3.9）

关键词：______________________________

逻辑关系：______________________________

(3) Many schools encourage students to evaluate and criticize their teachers in order to improve the quality of education, while others say this will lead to loss of respect for teachers. Discuss both views and give your own opinion. (2015.5.16)

关键词：______________________________

逻辑关系：______________________________

(4) Children find it difficult to concentrate on or pay attention to study at school. What are the reasons? How can we solve this problem? (2014.1.18)

关键词：______________________________

逻辑关系：______________________________

(5) The subjects and lesson contents are decided by the authorities such as the government. Some people argue that teachers should make the choice. To what extent do you agree or disagree? (2009.8.13)

关键词：______________________________

逻辑关系：______________________________

Step 2　构思

构思即思路拓展，必须建立在审题的基础上进行，不能偏离关键词。在这里可以对每个关键词进行延展（你可以补充更多你能想到的论据）：

(1) a general education/a range of subjects

优点：学得多，知识面广。

缺点：可能要学一些自己不感兴趣的或不擅长的。

(2) a narrow range of subjects/a particular career

优点：学得精，实用性强。

缺点：知识面窄。

(3) secondary schools

特点：孩子年龄还小，离就业还远，有可能兴趣指向性还不强。

(4) today's world

特点：① 信息化的社会，出现很多跨界，对复合型人才的需求比较大。

② 新问题层出不穷，需要一个综合性的思维和多角度的考虑。

练习：试着对 step 1 练习里的 5 个题目进行构思

Step 3　组织

经过 step 2 的构思后，会发现我们的 idea 是有一些了，但是不成体系，这个步骤就是以有逻辑的方法将构思好的内容串起来。推荐的方法是做一个 **outline**，这里必须融入自己的观点。

假设我们的观点是支持 a general education，就可以列出如下提纲（注意：这只是其中一种方案）：

- Paragraph 1：题目改写 + 观点（支持 a general education）
- Paragraph 2：主题句：在中学阶段学习所有科目是适应当今这个社会的发展的
  - ✓ 支持细节 1：每个学科的知识都是有用的
  - ✓ 支持细节 2：当今社会对复合型人才的需求是巨大的
- Paragraph 3：主题句：学少量跟就业有关的科目对中学生的未来发展未必有好处
  - ✓ 支持细节 1：中学生年龄尚小，兴趣指向或就业目标尚未定型
  - ✓ 支持细节 2：知识面窄对未来发展不利
- Paragraph 4：总结：重申观点

☺ **练习 1**：写出反面观点（即支持学习少量科目）的提纲

Paragraph 1：____

____

Paragraph 2：____

____

____

Paragraph 3：____

____

____

Paragraph 4：____

____

☺ **练习 2**

针对 step 2 的练习列提纲

Step 4　首段落写作

首段落写作的要点就是**改写题目**并表达自己的观点，改写题目的关键就是对关键词进行**同义替换**。改写的幅度视自己的英文程度而定，至少要改掉一些关键词，**切不可原题抄下**。

例子：In some countries, secondary schools aim to provide <u>a general education across a range of subjects.</u> In others, children focus on <u>a narrow range of subjects related to a particular career</u>. Which do you think is appropriate in today's world?

改写：Some high school students are required to **learn a wide range of subjects**, while others only **learn a few subjects for the employment purpose**. I think **a wider knowledge scope** is essential for personal development in the modern times

☺ **练习**：针对 step 1 的练习写出首段落

Step 5 主体段写作

主体段写作的要点是每一段要有一个**分论点**(central topic),建议考生把分论点以**主题句**(topic sentence)的形式给写下来,一般位于句首。

接下来就要用各种**细节**来支持主题句(即如何去论证),如果拓展能力强,一个支持细节也可以,如经常看到的考官范文一样,一段里只有一个充分展开的细节。这个细节可以是例子,也可以是原因加例子,也可能是原因加结果等等。如果拓展能力不强,可能会用到两到三个细节,这两到三个细节可以呈并列、递进或转折的关系。考生在写作的时候要注意衔接词的使用,更要注意的是句意之间的衔接,而不是形式上的衔接。

接下来,根据 step 3 提纲中的 Paragraph 2 部分展开写作。

Paragraph 2:主题句:在中学阶段学习所有科目是适应当今这个社会的发展的

✓ 支持细节 1:每个学科的知识都是有用的

✓ 支持细节 2:当今社会对复合型人才的需求是巨大的

Learning a range of subjects is likely to turn children into well-rounded, knowledgeable youngsters, who are badly needed in today's competitive society. (主题句) Every subject they learn at school will benefit them in their later life. (支持细节 1) A child destined to be an engineer, if good at grammar, may find himself better at expressing himself in both speech and writing in future. And a little knowledge of history will help him have a deeper understanding about his country and its heritage. (用两个例子对细节 1 的内容进行延展) **On the other hand,** (前面从知识的角度出来,接下来从社会要求方面来论述), we cannot blind ourselves to the social needs for talents with integrated skills. (支持细节 2) The information age we are in necessitates the grasp of computer skills for people from almost all industries. Furthermore, cross-border businesses are emerging rapidly, which can be well illustrated by Alibaba, an e-commerce giant entering the finance market. (这两句是对细节 2 的进一步展开) Such phenomena show that a person with limited knowledge won't fare well in today's world. (总结,强化本段主题句)

练习

请根据 step 3 的提纲写出 Paragraph 3

Paragraph 3:主题句:学少量跟就业有关的科目对中学生的未来发展未必有好处

支持细节 1:中学生年龄尚小,兴趣指向或就业目标尚未定型

支持细节 2:知识面窄对未来发展不利

Your paragraph:

Step 6 结尾段写作

结尾段是对全篇内容的总结,也是对观点的重申,也可以对全篇内容做个升华。但是要注意,在语言措辞上不能重复首段落。

这里的例子依旧是承接上个步骤

In summary, for secondary education, students should receive a general education not only for their future decision which leads them to a particular field but also for satisfying the social needs for talents with diverse skills.

练习:真题写作

针对 step 1 里的真题进行文章写作

Section 2 Technology

Part 1 考什么

重点范围

科技的影响

(1) What were the early technological products? How did they affect people's life?

(2) Is automation good or bad?

(3) What high-tech products do we often use? In what ways do they affect us?

(4) How does the Internet change the way we study, work, shop, do business and interact with others?

(5) How does technology affect our environment?

(6) In what areas do you think technology improves our life and in what ways it makes our life worse?

> 考题例子:
>
> In some countries, with the widespread use of the Internet, people have more freedom to work or study at home instead of travelling to work or college. Do the advantages of this development outweigh the disadvantages? (2014.4.26)

取代话题

(7) With the computer and Internet, we can do many things without going out. Can you list some?

(8) Is it still necessary for us to write a letter, read a printed book, go to a library, visit a museum, travel or learn from a teacher face to face?

考题例子：

Some people believe that printed books are no longer necessary in this digital era as all writings can be stored electronically. Others think that printed books still play an important role. Discuss both views and give your own opinion. (2014.3.13)

对孩子的影响

(9) Do children watch too much TV (play too much computer games)/spend much time on mobile phones or other electronic products? What are the advantages and disadvantages?

(10) Is there anything bad included in TV or computer games?

(11) How do computers or mobile phones affect children's creativity, reading and writing ability and communication ability?

考题例子：

Some people say that playing computer games is bad for children in every aspect. Others say that playing computer games can have positive effects on the way children develop. Discuss both views and give your own opinion. (2015.10.24)

次要范围

科技与艺术

(12) Which is more important, technology or arts?

太空技术

(13) What kind of effect does space technology have on us?

现代游戏与传统游戏

(14) What kind of games did children in the past play?

(15) What do children usually do in their spare time?

(16) What are the differences?

老年人使用科技产品

(17) Do old people use mobile phones and the Internet as much as the young generation? Why?

(18) In what ways can we encourage them to use high-tech products?

(19) What are the benefits and drawbacks if old people use the Internet?

科技与贫富差距

(20) Do you think the Internet enlarges or narrows the gap between the rich and the poor? Why?

Part 2 思考维度

大部分科技类话题都在以上问题中得以体现,科技类题目考查的核心比教育类相对要集中。科技一般来说是**改善效率**,对**物质文明有推动作用**。可能**对传统的东西会有一些颠覆**。考生可以试着从以下一些角度去思考。

(1) What do we lose when machines become popular in our work and life?

(2) How did technology **revolutionize** transport? What effects does it cause on our environment?

(3) Can technology be used to improve environment?

(4) Does technology **make people closer** or more **distant**?

(5) What do we lose when we get things **effortlessly**?

(6) Can **personal experience** be **replaced** by the Internet?

(7) What are the features of teenagers? How will they react to the negative content shown on TV or the Internet?

(8) What kinds of art form do you know? How does each form benefit you?

(9) In addition to **economic development** (**improvement** of our **living conditions**), what else do we need?

(10) Has any experiment been done on another planet?

(11) What technology or applications we are now using are attributable to space technology?

(12) What **physical problems** may happen to an astronaut?

(13) Are we **actively thinking** or **passively receiving information** when using a high-tech product?

(14) Is there any danger in the **virtual world**?

(15) With the Internet, can farmers improve their financial situation?

An Illustration 思考维度 1

(思考维度1)我们在生活和工作中使用各类机器。如在工厂里,自动化的普及(**the popularization of automation**)极大地提高了生产效率(**greatly improve production efficiency**),但是也造成了很多工人失业(**become unempolyed**)。另一方面,在流水线(**assembly line**)上操作的工人必须高度专注(**stay focused all the time**)重复一样的动作(**do repetitive things**),在某种程度上也成了机器的一部分。由于缺乏交流(**lack of communication**),工人在工作中容易感到厌倦(**feel tedious**)。在家里,我们使用洗衣机等节省劳力(**labor-saving**)的设备,在一定程度上从繁重的家务中解放出来(**liberate ourselves from busy housework**),但同时也缺乏了必要的运动。像电视机等娱乐设施容易使人们久坐不动(**sedentary**),甚至会增加肥胖的风险(**increase the risk of becoming obese**)。电脑和网络的普及更是减少了人们面对面交流的机会(**reduce the opportunities of face-to-face communication**),甚至有些人患上了社交恐惧症(**social phobia**)。亲人之间的关系也疏远了(**become alienated/estranged**)。

这样,我们是否部分解决了"考什么 1、2、3、4、6、9、10"?

再看以下一些雅思考题,是否心中有部分答案了?

Human society has made great technological progress in the last hundred years. Some people think this has negative effects on our life. To what extent do you agree or disagree? (2013.3.23)

There is a lot of physical work which has been replaced by machines. Do advantages of this trend outweigh the disadvantages? (2015.11.19)

Part 3 话题词汇补充

advanced/cutting-edge technology	尖端科技
scientific invention	科学发明
computer illiterate	电脑盲
create an online community	创建网络社区
call logs	通信记录
security cameras	监控摄像头
keep sb. under surveillance	使某人受到监视
invade one's privacy	侵犯某人隐私
upload one's information/photographs onto social network sites	将某人的信息或照片上传社交网站
explore the outer space	探索外太空
facilitate communication	促进交流
get access to information	获得信息
sustainable	可持续的

续表

interact with	与……互动
launch a space mission	开展太空任务
make a significant breakthrough	取得重大突破
make one's life easier	使人们生活更方便
optimize	优化
make an online purchase	网上购物
make progress	进步
medical advances	医疗进步
modem refrigeration techniques	现代制冷(冷藏)技术
reach a remote place	到达遥远的地方
double-edged sword	双刃剑
shorten the distance	缩短距离
violent	暴力的
self-centred	自我为中心的
substitute	替代品
virtual world	虚拟世界
a number of concerns	很多担忧
stay up to date with technology	紧跟科技潮流
surf the internet	上网
be indulged in	沉迷于
be available to	可被获得
radiation	辐射
hacker	黑客
virus	病毒

Part 4　句子翻译

使用给出的单词和词组，把下列中文句子翻译成英文，注意给定单词和词组的形式有可能在句中发生改变。

Example:

- 探索外太空对人类的可持续发展有着至关重要的意义。(explore, vital)

Exploring the outer space is vital for human's **sustainable development**.

- 现在有许多人建立网络社区来交朋友。(online communication)

Nowadays, a number of people **create online communities** to make friends.

(1) 大部分老年人都是不懂电脑,因此我们应该鼓励他们学习电脑知识。(illiterate)

(2) 面对面授课最大的好处就是促进交流。(face-to-face, facilitate)

(3) 自工业革命以来,我们生活的方方面面都出现了重大突破。(breakthrough)

(4) 学生花了大量的业余时间在上网。(surf)

(5) 沉迷于网络世界会使学生失去对学习的兴趣。(indulge, deprive)

(6) 来自电子产品的辐射会对健康造成负面影响。(radiation)

(7) 监控摄像头的使用在很大程度上制止了偷窃。(security cameras, prevent)

(8) 先进的科学技术给农村妇女打开了致富大门。(advanced science, prosperity)

(9) 科学发明可以造福人类,但另一方面,它有时也可能给人类带来灾难。(benefit)

(10) 当人们在社交网站上上传他人的照片,他们没有意识到他们的行为已经侵犯了他人隐私。(upload, invade)

(11) 警察一直在严密监视他。(under surveillance)

(12) 科技上的新发展能使人们的生活更轻松。(make life easier)

(13) 发现治疗艾滋病的方法将是医学上的一大进展。(medical advance)

(14) 所有新的医学进步都有潜在的不安全性,如果只考虑安全性问题的话,那就不会有任何进步了。(progress)

Part 5 真题写作

2013 年 3 月 2 日真题

Universities and colleges are now offering qualifications through distance learning from the Internet rather than teachers in the classroom. Do you think the advantages of this development outweigh the disadvantages?

Give reasons for your answer and include any relevant examples from your own knowledge or experience.

Write at least 250 words.

Step 1 审题

本题的关键词是 universities and colleges, distance learning from the Internet, teachers in the classroom。句子内部出现对比逻辑关系。根据问题,advantages 和 disadvantages 均需提及。观点可以是利大于弊,也可以是弊大于利。

Step 2 构思

构思必须从关键词出发,更细致一些,可以从关键词的特点出发,进而得出相应的优缺点还有结果。当然,构思切入的角度不止这一种,只不过这一种是比较常用,暂且给它们做如下命名:

F (features) + Advantages/Disadvantages + Effects + (Examples)

在本题中,可以对 distance learning 在做个细化的分类,有实时课程(real time course),也有录播课程(recorded course),两者的性质略有不同。

	Features	Advantages/Disadvantages	Effects	Example
Distance learning	实时:① 基本上没有人数限制	① A:几乎所有学生(包括乡村地区的或身体残疾的)都可以参与	① 好的教育资源得到了传播	① 一个残疾的学生通过远程教育得到了大学文凭
	② 老师与学生没碰过面	② D:老师不了解听课的学生,讲的内容可能针对性不强	② 可能花同样的时间,效果不如面授课程有效	② 可描述个人的一次经历
	录播课程:① 可重复播放	① A:灵活性强,学生不受时间限制和次数限制进行学习	① 与自己的学校学习或工作不形成冲突,可以是有效的补充	
	② 价格比较低廉	② A:几乎所有学生都读得起	② 对渴求知识但经济条件不好的学生来说是个不错的选择	
	③ 只有老师的讲课,没有互动	③ D:学生的问题得不到解决	③ 学习效果差	

续表

	Features	Advantages/ Disadvantages	Effects	Example
Teachers in the classroom	① 面对面授课,互动性强 ② 老师会组织各种课堂活动 ③ 上一遍,很少重复	① A: 有问题可及时提问 ② A: 向同学学习,与同学互相帮助 ③ D: 基础差的学生可能跟不上	① 学习效果好 ② 锻炼了其他能力如组织、合作能力 ③ 个别学生会自暴自弃	

当我们列出这样一张表格时,其实把主体段落的大纲和逻辑基本都解决了。

练习

用上述方法对以下题目进行列表构思:

(1) In some countries, with the widespread use of the Internet, people have more freedom to work or study at home instead of travelling to work or college. Do the advantages of this development outweigh the disadvantages? (2014.4.26)

(2) Mobile phones have made life easier: anyone can use a mobile phone to answer/make work calls or home calls at any place 7 days a week. Do you think this development has more positive effects or negative effects on the individual and society? (2010.9.4)

(3) Some people say that playing computer games is bad for children in every aspect. Others say that playing computer games can have positive effects on the way children develop. Discuss both views and give your own opinion. (2015.10.24)

(4) Some people say modern children's games do not develop a wide range of skills, while traditional games can be much better for developing such skills. To what extent do you agree or disagree? (2008.11.29)

(5) It is not necessary to travel to other places to learn about other cultures. We can learn as much as from books, films and the internet. To what extent do you agree or disagree? (2014.10.18)

Step 3 组织

经过 step 2 的构思,思路已比较清晰,具体的写作思路还是要根据自己的观点而定,对上一步骤的内容可以做一定的筛选。

- Paragraph 1: 题目改写 + 观点(远程教育只能作为补充,如果替代真实课堂就会弊大于利)
- Paragraph 2: 主题句: 远程教育确是有好处,但仅仅依赖它来完成学业是不够的
  - ✓ 支持细节 1: 人数没有限制,使身体受限的人等得到教育机会
  - ✓ 支持细节 2: 存在弊端,上课效果不如线下课好(可描述 step2 里的负面影响)
- Paragraph 3: 主题句: 线下课的好处不能被替代

✓ 支持细节 1：老师了解学生，上课内容针对性强，互动性好
✓ 支持细节 2：课堂各类活动能锻炼学生各方面的能力
- Paragraph 4：总结：重申观点

Step 4 首段落写作

例子：Universities and colleges are now offering qualifications through distance learning from the Internet rather than teachers in the classroom. Do you think the advantages of this development outweigh the disadvantages?

改写：Nowadays, students can obtain a university degree by **taking online courses** instead of **learning from a teacher face to face**. I think such courses are complementary to **classroom teaching**, and if the former takes over the latter, it will bring more negative effects.

练习

针对 step 2 的练习写出首段落

Step 5 主体段写作

根据 step 2 的构思和 step 3 提纲中的 paragraph2 部分展开写作

Paragraph 2：**主题句：远程教育确是有好处，但仅仅依赖它来完成学业是不够的**

✓ 支持细节 1：人数没有限制，使身体受限的人等得到教育机会
✓ 支持细节 2：存在弊端，上课效果不如线下课好（可描述 step2 里的负面影响）

Long-distance learning, though bringing us great benefits, is far from the most effective means the majority can rely on to finish the university education.（主题句）It is remarkable that an online course can admit almost an unlimited number of students（支持细节 1 中的特点）, typically more than ten times the size of a normal classroom teaching（加入对比）. This form of teaching is particularly beneficial to those who crave for knowledge but are confined by their physical disability.（支持细节 1 中的结果）**However**, we cannot expect the same learning effect as we attend the face-to-face lecture.（支持细节 2，与细节 1 形成转折）This is mainly because online teachers have never met the students before, unware of the listeners' weaknesses and interests, so that their teaching may not fully meet the students' needs. Another factor is lack of interaction, leaving problems arising from the courses unsolved.（对细节 2 进行解释，即网课的特点和缺点）

练习

请根据 Step 3 的提纲写出 Paragraph 3

Step 6　结尾段写作

这里的例子依旧是承接上个步骤

To sum up, it is sensible for universities to deliver online courses for this move benefits a greater number of young people, while classroom teaching should still occupy a dominant position because it is the most effective way to achieve the best learning effect.

练习：真题写作

针对 Step 2 里的真题进行文章写作

Chapter 6 Topic: Media & Law
媒体类、法律类大作文

Section 1 Media

Part 1 考什么

重点范围

媒体的影响

(1) What is the effect of negative information shown on media?

(2) Is violence contained in films and computer games?

(3) Is watching TV good for children? Why or why not?

(4) Why is news media important in our country? Is its influence positive or negative?

(5) Are people's ideas influenced by newspapers?

> 考题例子:
>
> A tendency that the news reported in the media focuses on problems and emergencies rather than the positive developments is harmful to both the individual and our society. To what extent do you agree or disagree? (2012.04.14)

广告的影响

(6) Do advertisements make people look the same? Why or why not?

(7) What's the influence of advertising on people's life?

(8) Do the high sales of popular consumer goods reflect the power of advertising?

(9) Should all forms of advertising be banned?

(10) What are the effects of advertisements aimed at children?

> 考题例子:
>
> Advertising discourages us from being different individuals by making them want to be or to look the same. Do you agree or disagree? (2015.07.11)

次要范围

真实性

(11) Should we trust journalists? What qualities should they have?

(12) How do you think the information on the Internet?

媒体暴力

(13) Should the amount of violence on the TV program be reduced? Why?

(14) Should the media report details of crimes?

阅读与看电视

(15) Which one is better, reading or watching TV?

(16) Will radio be replaced by TV?

国际新闻

(17) Should secondary school students learn international news?

质量与数量

(18) Will people pay more attention to quantity rather than quality because of advertising?

Part 2 思考维度

Part 1 所列范围几乎囊括了近几年所有的媒体广告类考题。媒体与广告类话题与人们生活息息相关,并且无处不在。但是考题范围相对比较限定,具体的题目呈现形式可能更为多样化,但基本上跳不出以上这些基本问题范围。可以根据以下的思考维度进行切入,将这类话题进行总结并且灵活应用在各类考题中。

(1) Apart from **promoting products**, what other advantages can advertising bring us?

(2) Can you identify **various forms of** advertisements?

(3) Do advertisements focus on the **features and functions** or effects of products?

(4) Which **target group** is easily influenced by advertisements?

(5) Do ads tend to enhance or **eliminate individualism**?

(6) Why do ads become more **entertaining**?

(7) Do you get **fragmented information** or **a deep insight**?

(8) Do you learn **actively** or **passively**?

(9) Do you get old information or **updated information**?

(10) Do you tend to be **focused** or **distracted**?

(11) Do you **learn independently** or **interactively**?

(12) What types of news do you usually read or watch?

(13) To what extent do you **rely on** news in your daily life?

(14) Does international news offer **global vision**?
(15) Do journalists report news **objectively** or **exaggeratedly** or in a **biased** way?
(16) Is news **manipulated** by some **authorities**?
(17) Does **detailed coverage** of negative events **cause panic** or **sense of insecurity**?

An Illustration 思考维度 1

作为消费者和生产商之间的桥梁，广告可以提供消费者最新的产品信息(**the latest information**)，便于人们购买(**purchase**)和选择商品。

除此之外，广告还有利于刺激人们的购买冲动(**evoke impulse buying**)，增加产品的销量(**boost sales**)，以此带动经济的发展(**promote economic development**)。

同时，广告也成为了很多产业的支柱与收入来源(**a main source of income**)，尤其是媒体业。

但是广告会带来很多问题。对消费者最直接的影响就是会增加产品的成本导致价格上涨(**add to the cost of the products**)。

而且，很多广告只提及产品的优点(**claim products' advantages only**)，是一种不公正(**unfair**)，不全面的信息。很多广告甚至宣传虚假和夸张的信息(**false and exaggerative information**)，来误导(**mislead**)和欺骗(**cheat**)消费者。甚至一些广告上面还有许多不良信息(negative information)的传播，比如一些色情(**pornography**)与暴力(**violence**)信息，对于小孩来说是非常不利的(**adverse**)。

最后，广告会导致消费者冲动购买(**impulsive purchase**)，导致一些不必要的浪费。

当然，值得注意的是广告分为商业广告(**commercial advertising**)和公益广告(**public service advertising**)，商业广告有利有弊，但是公益广告还是有教育宣传(**publicity**)功能的。

对比你的答案和给出的示例，看看这些答案是不是囊括了"考什么 1"，并部分解决了"考什么 7、8、9、10"?

☺雅思考试的真题几乎都包含在上述的那些问题中了，通过刚才的训练，再看以下一些雅思考题，是否心中基本上有答案了?

(1) A high percentage of advertisements on TV are aimed at children. What are the effects of this situation on children? Should television advertisements be controlled? (2014.4.24)

(2) People are surrounded by many kinds of advertising which can influence their life. Does the positive effect of this trend outweigh the negative effect? (2015.12.5)

(3) Advertising encourages people to buy in quantity rather than promoting its quality. To what extent do you agree or disagree? (2012.7.7)

Part 3　话题词汇补充

prevalent	无处不在的
objective	客观的
biased	不客观的
celebrity	名人
journalists	记者
the press	新闻界
coverage	报道
misleading	有误导性的
dependable	可靠的
up-to-the-minute	非常及时的
sway	影响
informative	增长见闻的
entertaining	娱乐性强的
alienation	疏远
a ready means of relaxation	一种方便的休闲方式
inevitable	不可避免的
give rise to	引起
have negative influence on	对……产生不良影响
be aware of	意识到
be surrounded by	被包围
impose restrictions on	施加限制
extremely costly	花费高
run an advertisement	做广告
interfere	干扰
be interrupted by	打断

续表

in defense of	捍卫
play a crucial role in	起重要作用
boost the sales of	促进销量
impulsively	冲动地
allocate one's budget	分配预算
an overwhelming number of	大量的
take advantage of	利用
financial burden	经济负担
make a substantial contribution to	做出巨大贡献
vulnerable mentality	脆弱的心理
weighty responsibility	巨大的责任
dominate the headline	主宰头条
on behalf of	代表
sense of insecurity	不安全感
detailed crime coverage	报道犯罪细节
boost newspaper circulation	促进报纸销量
television rating	收视率
exaggerated	夸张的
go uncontrolled	不控制
give free publicity	免费宣传
an indispensable tool	必不可少的工具
simultaneously	同步地
flood the TV screens	充斥着电视屏幕
imitate the scenes	模仿画面
be exposed to	暴露在

续表

distinguish right from wrong	区分对错
aggravate the financial burden	增加经济负担
breakthrough	突破
cultivate one's creativity	培养创造力
tackle difficulty	解决困难

Part 4 句子翻译

使用给出的单词和词组，把下列中文句子翻译成英文，注意给定单词和词组的形式有可能在句中发生改变。

Example：

● 电视的存在使得家庭成员之间关系疏远了。（alienation）

The existence of TV has brought about **alienation** among family members.

● 对于每天从事常规的繁忙工作的人来说，看电视是一种比较方便的休闲方式。（a ready means of relaxation）

TV provides **a ready means of relaxation** for people who spend their days doing routine and busy jobs.

（1）我们会发现我们被各种各样的广告所包围。（find oneself surrounded by）

____

（2）政府应该对广告施加严格的限制。（impose restrictions on）

____

（3）做广告的成本是相当高的。（costly，put up）

____

（4）广告促进产品销量，并且促使人们买一些根本不需要的东西。（boost the sales of goods）

____

（5）他们不可能被那些广告左右。（sway）

____

（6）很多广告把孩子们作为他们的目标群。（overwhelming，target group）

____

（7）现代大众传媒对我们的日常生活和整个社会的影响巨大是不可否认的。（mass media，undeniable）

____

（8）似乎坏消息主宰了各种媒体的头条。（dominate the headlines）

____

（9）毫无疑问，那些看了这些杂志的青少年将会有一种错误的世界观。（it is no doubt that）

____

（10）很多细节报道都有失偏颇或者夸大其词。（biased，exaggerated）

____

（11）记者报道犯罪行为最主要的目的是促进报纸的销量或者提高电视的收视率。（boost ... circulation and television rating）

____

（12）如果这样的报道仍不禁止，这将会对人们造成更严重的影响。（go uncontrolled）

____

（13）通过看电视，人们可以同步知道世界正在发生的事情。（simultaneously）

____

（14）青少年会去模仿电视节目中的暴力与犯罪行为，从而沦为罪犯。（imitate the scene）

____

（15）电视节目可以培养孩子的创造力和解决困难的能力。（cultivate one's creativity）

____

Part 5 真题写作

2016 年 7 月 9 日真题

There are many advertisements directed at children, such as snacks, toys and other goods. Parents argue that children are under pressure. Advertisers claim that the advertisements provide useful information. Discuss both views and give your own opinion.

Give reasons for your answer and include any relevant examples from your own knowledge or experience.

Write at least 250 words.

Step 1 审题

本题第一句是背景句，其中的例子 snacks 和 toys 最好在文章中要提及，可以作为例证展开。第二句和第三句是观点句，相对立，分别对应广告的一个弊端和一个好处。这里的 under pressure 要结合上下文理解，指的是 Children are easily influenced by advertisements and likely to ask their parents to buy the advertised goods.

Step 2　构思

负面观点：under pressure

1）从广告出发：广告产品可能对孩子无益，导致对健康不利

2）从孩子出发：缠着父母要买，对父母造成困扰，增加经济负担

正面观点：useful information

通过广告和产品了解外部世界

我的观点：广告无所谓好坏，孩子无鉴别能力，重点看父母的引导

在讨论双方观点时可以客观地给出观点持有方的理由，也可以融入自己的观点。

Step 3　组织

Outline：

- Paragraph 1：背景句＋题目改写
- Paragraph 2：父母对广告持有负面观点

✓ 支持细节 1：广告产品可能对孩子无益，导致对健康不利（例子：糖果）

✓ 支持细节 2：孩子缠着父母要买，对父母造成困扰，增加经济负担

- Paragraph 3：广告商认为广告给孩子提供有用信息

✓ 支持细节 1：孩子通过产品和广告可以认知外部世界

✓ 支持细节 2：例证：车子玩具让孩子了解真实世界

- Paragraph 4：自己的观点：广告无所谓好坏，孩子无鉴别能力，重点看父母的引导

Step 4　首段落写作

例子：There are many advertisements directed at children, such as snacks, toys and other goods. Parents argue that children are under pressure. Advertisers claim that the advertisements provide useful information. Discuss both views and give your own opinion.

首段落写作中最重要的原则是对关键词进行**同义或近义替换**。

在所给例子中，可以将 directed at 改成 aimed at, targeting at，将 such as snacks, toys and other goods 改成 ranging from food to toys，将 provide 改成 offer，将 useful 改成 valuable，将 information 改成 messages 或 knowledge.

此外，可以**备一些常用词汇**（多与观点表达相关），如 hold the opinion that, assert, believe 等，来替代 argue，claim 等。对于双边讨论类，还可以用上 a controversial issue, a topic of discussion/debate 等表达式。

改写的另一个原则是**词性的转换**。如 advertisements 可以表达为 advertised goods, advertisers 可以转换成 people in the advertising industry。

对于题目中出现较抽象的词，可以**进行解释说明**。如本题的 under pressure，可以解释为 are greatly influenced and eager to buy the advertised goods.

综合以上方法，可以这样来改写：

There are many advertisements aimed at children ranging from food to toys. This has become a topic of debate between parents and people in the advertising industry.

我们也可以着眼于句型，**对原句型加以一定的改变**。这里，第一句是背景句。二三两句是观点句。我们可以将背景句作为原因，两种观点作为结果。可以写成：

Nowadays, an increasing number of advertisements targeting at children have caused a divide in the opinion between parents and advertisers.

也可以将背景用介词短语引入，重点强调双方观点的不同：

In view of the increasing advertisements aimed at children flooding the TV screen, parents worry that their children are negatively affected, while advertisers claim these ads provide valuable information.

原则：题目改写并不是尽可能多的替换掉原题的词汇，而是要在保证不牺牲句子流畅度和地道性的前提下做修改，尤其要替换掉一些关键词。

练习：改写以下题目

(1) The news media have become more influential in people's lives. Some people think it's a negative development. To what extent do you agree or disagree? (2016.1.23)

____

____

____

(2) We can get knowledge from news, but some people think we should not trust the journalists. What do you think? And what do you think are the important qualities that a journalist should have? (2016.3.5)

____

____

____

(3) Nowadays, a large amount of advertising aiming at children should be banned because of its negative effects. To what extent do you agree or disagree? (2016.2.20)

____

____

____

(4) Today we are surrounded by all kinds of advertising and this is having an increasing effect on our lives. Do the positive effects of advertising outweigh the negative effects? (2015.12.5)

____

____

____

(5) Advertising discourages people from being different individuals by making them look the same. Do you agree or disagree? (2015.7.11)

Step 5　主体段写作

接下来，根据 step 3 提纲中的 paragraph 2 部分展开写作

- Paragraph 2：父母对广告持有负面观点

✓ 支持细节 1：广告产品可能对孩子无益，导致对健康不利（例子：糖果）

✓ 支持细节 2：孩子缠着父母要买，对父母造成困扰，增加经济负担

Most parents hold a negative view about this phenomenon.（主题句） They assert that the advertised goods such as snacks and toys that have a strong appeal to children are mostly unnecessary or even do harm to children's health.（支持细节 1）Take snacks for example. To attract children visually, snack producers often use food coloring, a kind of additive. Taking too many additives is definitely detrimental to children's health.（举例说明支持细节 1）Another strong argument is that children, who are poor in self-control, are very likely to pester their parents to buy what they see on TV commercials. Such behavior sometimes is irritating, and some parents will reluctantly give in. Also it incurs unnecessary family spending.（支持细节 2）

练习：根据 Paragraph 3 的提纲来进行段落写作

- Paragraph 3：广告商认为广告给孩子提供有用信息

✓ 支持细节 1：孩子通过产品和广告可以认知外部世界

✓ 支持细节 2：例证：车子玩具让孩子了解真实世界

Step 6　结尾段写作

- Paragraph 4：自己的观点：广告无所谓好坏，孩子无鉴别能力，重点看父母的引导

In my opinion, there are both desirable and undesirable goods and advertisements. As children are too young to differentiate the good from the bad, it is parents' duty to control the time children spend watching TV commercials and to teach them what is within and what is beyond their need.

练习：真题写作

针对 Step 4 练习中的真题进行文章写作

____

____

____

____

____

____

____

____

____

Section 2 Law

Part 1 考什么

重点范围

青少年犯罪

(1) What are reasons for and solutions to juvenile delinquency?

(2) Should young adults who commit crimes be treated equally with adults?

考题例子：

In some countries, a high proportion of criminal acts are committed by teenagers. Why has this happened? What can be done to deal with this? (2015.6.18)

惩罚措施

(3) What is the most common solution to crime?

(4) Can better education prevent people from becoming criminals?

(5) Should young criminals be sent to jails?

考题例子：

Some people think all lawbreakers should be put into prison, while others believe that there are better alternatives. Discuss and give your opinion. (2013.2.16)

犯罪是否无法避免

(6) Can crimes be prevented?

考题例子：

Many people are afraid to leave their homes because of their fear of crime. Some people believe that more actions should be taken to prevent crime, but others feel that little can be done. Discuss both views and give your own opinion. (2015.09.03)

次要范围

武器的影响

(7) Can a police force with guns reduce the level of crime?

监狱功能

(8) Will criminals commit crimes again after they are set free from prison?

媒体报道的影响

(9) Why do people feel unsafe either at home or out?

先天与后天因素

(10) Are most crimes caused by people who are bad by nature?

Part 2 思考维度

犯罪类话题近几年有增多趋势，主要围绕青少年犯罪、坐牢，以及解决犯罪问题的方法来考。当然，犯罪类也出现了新题，会和教育、媒体类进行结合。重点还是要思考总结犯罪的原因、措施，以及影响来发散思维。

(1) What are the **internal and external factors** for **juvenile delinquency**?

(2) Will **juveniles imitate** what they see and hear on mass media?

(3) What is the result when teenagers **are addicted to** computer games?

(4) What is the influence of families on children?

(5) Should exam-oriented education be responsible for **juvenile delinquency**?

(6) What is the influence from **peers**?

(7) Is **censorship** useful to reduce the crime rate?

(8) Do criminals **realize their faults** after they are set free?

(9) Do education and job training serve to solve **criminal acts**?

(10) Do guns have **deterring effect on** potential criminals?

An Illustration 思考维度 1

青少年犯罪(**juvenile delinquency**)的原因是多方面的。首先由于青少年自身心智不成熟(**mentally immature**),有时不能做出正确判断(**distinguish right from wrong**)。有时候家长太忙于工作而无暇顾及孩子(**pay little attention to their children**),导致孩子交上了不良朋友(**be in bad company**)。有些家长对孩子过于严厉,给孩子施加太大压力(**impose too much pressure on children**)而使得孩子变得叛逆(**become rebellious**),甚至做出一些违法的事情(**do things against the law**)来主张自己(**assert themselves**)。从外部环境来看,大众媒体上经常出现暴力场景(**scenes of violence**),由于经常接触到这些场景(**frequent exposure to these scenes**),青少年容易将暴力看作是处理冲突的常见途径(**regard violence as a normal means to solve conflicts**)。随着高科技技术越来越容易被获得(**become accessible to common people**),网络犯罪(**cyber crime**)的比率也不断在上升,其中不少就是一些年轻的黑客(**young hackers**)做的。

这样,我们是否部分解决了"考什么 1、6、9、10"?

再看以下一些雅思考题,是否心中有部分答案了?

Children are committing more crimes. What are the causes? How to punish them? (2014.8.2)

People are afraid to leave their homes for fear of crimes. Some people believe that more actions should be taken to prevent crimes while others think that little could be done. Discuss both sides and give your own opinion. (2015.9.3)

Part 3 话题词汇补充

crimes = offences = criminal acts	罪行
commit a crime	犯罪(动词短语)
stringent	严厉的
punishment/penalty	惩罚
the crime rate = the incidence of crime	犯罪率
rampant	猖獗的

续表

violate the law	违法
restrict	限制(自由等)
impulsive	冲动的
consequence	后果
circumstance	处境,状况
reform/rehabilitate criminals	改造罪犯
lengthy jail terms	漫长的刑期
put sb. into the prison/jail	把某人关进监狱
sentence sb. to death	宣判某人死刑
capital punishment	死刑
juvenile delinquency	青少年犯罪
immature/immaturity	不成熟
be liable to do	有做某事的倾向
be addicted to doing	沉迷于
indulge in	放纵(做某事)
be engaged in	忙于
encounter	遇见
single-parent family	单亲家庭
domestic violence	家庭暴力
prevent sb from doing	防止某人做某事
have deterring effect on	有威慑性的影响
censorship	审查制度
for the sake of	为了……目的
realize one's mistakes	认识到自己的错误
rebellious	叛逆的

续表

abolish	废除
alternative	选择
learn a lesson	吸取教训
distinguish	区分
be attributed to	归因于

Part 4　句子翻译

使用给出的单词和词组，把下列中文句子翻译成英文，注意给定单词和词组的形式有可能在句中发生改变。

Example：

- 应该废除死刑。（abolish）

Capital punishment should be **abolished.**

（1）他从监狱释放了。（release）

______

（2）青少年不能判断对错因为他们不成熟。（immaturity）

______

（3）青少年容易模仿电视和电影中的暴力场景。（be liable to）

______

（4）当青少年沉迷于网络游戏，他们需要很多钱来支持。（be addicted to）

______

（5）沉迷于虚拟世界很容易让青少年与外界隔离。（isolate from）

______

（6）家长忙于工作没有时间陪伴孩子。（be engaged in）

______

（7）应该采取像严格的媒体检查制度这样的行为来预防青少年犯罪。（censorship，for the sake of）

______

（8）然而，青少年很叛逆，不愿意听从父母的意愿。（rebellious）

______

（9）越来越多的人开始挑战现存的死刑制度。（capital punishment）

______

(10) 犯罪记录不断被刷新。(renewed)

____

(11) 我们应该保留送犯人进监狱的举措。(put sb into prison)

____

(12) 青少年犯罪归因于不断增长的离婚率和家庭暴力。(be attributed to)

____

Part 5 真题写作

2015 年 4 月 25 日真题

Young people who commit serious crimes, such as a robbery or a violent attack should be punished in the same way as adults. To what extent do you agree or disagree?

Give reasons for your answer and include any relevant examples from your own knowledge or experience.

Write at least 250 words.

Step 1 审题

本题把 young people 和 adults 进行比较,可见 young people 在此指的是未满 18 岁的青少年。这样可以去比较两类人群的不同特点,从而倾向于对年轻人要从轻处理。另外一个关键词是 serious,该词凸显了罪行的严重性,可以基于这一点强调惩罚不应看年龄。所以该题的观点倾向于单边比较好。单边观点的好处是立场鲜明,容易让考官看懂,但缺点是观点数量的减少意味着论据必须要充分。虽然不是双边讨论类,但是依旧可以在主体段的第二段先讲一个反方观点,分析反方观点,再把它反驳掉。

Step 2 构思

Agree:从 serious crimes 出发,可以从例子 a robbery 和 a violent attack 出发,强调这些罪行给个人、家庭和社会造成巨大的财产损失和人身伤害。也可以从现实数据出发,强调青少年犯罪率在上升,如果不加重惩罚,起不到威慑作用。

Disagree:从 young people 本身的特点出发,强调他们的心智不成熟,他们的犯罪动机多是由于外部原因影响,或由于家庭的疏忽从而走上犯罪道路,应该给予他们更多的机会重新悔过。

注意:在实际写作中选其中一个观点即可。

Step 3 组织

在此,选择 agree 这个观点。

Outline:

- Paragraph 1:题目改写 + 观点(同意)
- Paragraph 2:量刑的依据应该看罪行本身

✓ 支持细节 1：抢劫这样的恶性事件给受害者带来了经济损失，如果是抢银行，则会对社会造成巨大损失

✓ 支持细节 2：暴力袭击会造成伤亡，对受害者及受害者家庭带来巨大的伤害，甚至会伤及无辜，造成恐慌

- Paragraph 3：对年轻人从轻处理是不当的(驳斥段)

✓ 支持细节 1：(反方理由)年轻人是由于不成熟才走上犯罪道路的

✓ 支持细节 2：(正方观点)法律面前人人平等

✓ 支持细节 3：(正方观点)近几年青少年犯罪率上升，如果从轻处理则不利于遏制这个趋势

- Paragraph 4：重申观点

Step 4　首段落写作

例子：Young people who commit serious crimes, such as a robbery or a violent attack should be punished in the same way as adults. To what extent do you agree or disagree?

题目改写：

In modern days, it is no longer rare to see teenagers commit serious crimes including robberies and violent attacks. Therefore, I think they should receive equal punishment as adults.

Step 5　主体段写作

在主体段写作中，因果论证是最常见的论证方法之一。通常需要掌握必要的衔接手段。

	conj.	prep.	adv.	verb phrase
cause	because since as	due to thanks to as a result of		result in lead to give rise to
effect	so so that		therefore as a consequence accordingly	result from be attributed to be credited to

词性不同代表着用法不同。

例：父母对他长期疏忽，他走上了犯罪的道路。

Because his parents paid little attention to him, he began to do things against the law.

As a result of long-term parental negligence, he began to do things against the law.

His parents neglected him for a long time. Therefore, he began to do things against the law.

Long-term parental negligence led him to do things against the law.

- Paragraph 2：量刑的依据应该看罪行本身

✓ 支持细节 1：抢劫这样的恶性事件给受害者带来了经济损失，如果是抢银行，则会对社会造成巨大损失

✓ 支持细节 2：暴力袭击会造成伤亡，对受害者及受害者家庭带来巨大的伤害，甚至会伤及无辜，造成恐慌

现在将 Paragraph 2 的支持细节 2 分解一下，就会发现这里是因果关系

Cause	Effect	Further effect
Violent attack	1) Injury or death 2) Hurt passers-by	1) Hurt victims and their family members 2) Cause panic

在表达这层关系时可以灵活使用上述衔接手段，也可以用上定语从句或分词结构。

Voilent attacks will lead to injuries or even death, making victims and their families suffer both physically and mentally. Or even worse, some passers-by will be injured, and this often gives rise to great panic.

练习：根据 Paragraph 2 的提纲将段落写完整。

____

____

____

____

____

____

____

____

- Paragraph 3：对年轻人从轻处理是不当的(驳斥段)

✓ 支持细节 1：(反方理由)年轻人是由于不成熟才走上犯罪道路的

✓ 支持细节 2：(正方观点)法律面前人人平等

✓ 支持细节 3：(正方观点)近几年青少年犯罪率上升，如果从轻处理则不利于遏制这个趋势

Paragraph 3 是驳斥段，含有让步成分。

Sample：

I think it is imporper to be lenient with the young people who committed serious crimes. Despite some voices that many youths do things against the law because they are mentally immature, it should not become an excuse for them to get away with their offences. Law should be respected by everyone. And punishment should be fair no matter the offender is above or under 18. My second argument is that the past years have seen an ongoing rise in the crime rate among teenagers. This trend would not be easily curbed if we treat them in a different way as we do to adults. That is to say, a sentence to imprisonment has a better deterring effect than making a young offender do some compulsory community service.

Step 6 结尾段写作

- Paragraph 4：重申观点

In summary, anyone who commits a severe crime, no matter how old he is, should receive corresponding punishment. This serves as a useful warning for all and guarantees social justice.

练习：真题写作（尽可能使用因果论证）

(1) In some countries, a high proportion of criminal acts are committed by teenagers. Why has this happened? What can be done to deal with this? (2015.6.18)

(2) A recent newspaper article reports that a 14-year-old boy who seriously destroyed the school got a punishment to clean streets instead of being sent to prison. Do you think young criminals should be sent to jail? (2016.1.14)

(3) Research suggests that the majority of criminals who are sent to prison would commit crimes when set free. Why do you think is the case? What can be done to solve this problem? (2009.6.13)

(4) Many people nowadays do not feel safe when they either are at home or go out. What are the reasons and what to do to solve this problem? (2015.6.27)

(5) Some people think most crime is the result of circumstances such as poverty and other social problems. Others believe that most crime is caused by people who are bad by nature. Discuss both views and give your own opinion. (2014.11.8)

Chapter 7 Topic: Environment & Government
环境类、政府类大作文

Section 1 Environment

Part 1 考什么

重点范围

环境保护的责任

(1) Who should be responsible for environmental protection?

考题例子:

The environment problems facing today's world are so great that there is little ordinary people can do to improve the situation. Governments and large companies should be responsible for reducing the amount of damage being done to the environment. To what extent do you agree or disagree with this statement? (2009.10.03)

环境保护的原因和措施

(2) What are environmental problems?

(3) What are the causes of environmental problems?

(4) How to solve environmental problems?

(5) Do human activities make the Earth a better place to live in?

(6) What benefits does international cooperation bring to world environmental protection?

考题例子:

People generally know that the environment is important. However, most individuals still don't take responsibility to protect the environment. Why is this? What should be done to encourage people to protect the environment? (2006.3)

自然资源

(7) What are the causes of water shortage?

(8) Why is more and more rubbish produced nowadays?

(9) Is nuclear energy the best source of power in meeting ever-increasing energy needs?

(10) Is there not enough recycling of waste materials in some countries?

(11) Compared with fossil fuels, such as coal, oil and natural gas, what are the advantages and disadvantages of the use of alternative sources of energy, including wind, and solar power?

(12) Should people look for sources of oil and gas in remote and untouched natural places?

> 考题例子：
>
> The natural resources such as oil, forests and fresh water are being consumed at an alarming rate. What problems does it cause? How can we solve these problems? (2015.08.01)

动物保护

(13) Should animals be used in medical experiments?

(14) Is it necessary for people to protect wild animals?

(15) What is the function of a zoo?

(16) What is the function of animals in people's daily diet?

> 考题例子：
>
> In modern life, it is no longer necessary to use animals as food and in other products like clothing and medicines. To what extent do you agree or disagree? (2016.03.12)

次要范围

环境与科技

(17) Does the development of modern technology lead to environmental pollution?

(18) Can technology solve environmental problems?

交通拥挤

(19) Does traffic jam happen in most cities? What are the causes?

(20) How to address traffic congestion effectively?

环境与汽车

(21) Should the unlimited use of cars be discouraged?

(22) What are the problems that car use will bring?

(23) Should cheap air travel be encouraged?

Part 2 思考维度

Part 1 所列范围几乎涉猎了所有雅思环境类相关的考题,包括资源、交通、动物。环境是当今社会的一个热门话题,针对目前环境的现状,具体的题目呈现形式可能更为多样化,但基本上跳不出以上这些基本问题范围。

为了更好地拓展思维,可以从题目考查的本质或论据出发,以不变应万变。以下就常考话题给出一些思维切入角度,可灵活应用到不同考题。

(1) Is human being the **culprit** of environmental **pollution**?

(2) Do people know how to **preserve** environment effectively?

(3) Can environmental problems be **addressed** by individuals or companies?

(4) Why is the **consumption** of energy increasing **at an alarming rate**?

(5) Is **alternative energy** more expensive and less productive than **fossil fuels**?

(6) What does the development of technology bring to environment and people?

(7) Will people face **energy crisis** in the future? Are there any **remedies**?

(8) Is road **construction** able to **satisfy the need** of an **ever-increasing** number of cars?

An Illustration 思考维度 1

环境问题是当今世界面临的巨大挑战之一(**one of the biggest challenges**),这些环境问题产生的原因主要是由人口增长(**population growth**)、工业发展(**industrial development**)与长期的人类活动(**long-term human activities**)造成的。

但是大部分人都没有保护环境的意识(**environmental awareness**),他们把精力放在了生活中更急迫的事情(**more urgent things**)上,如住房、求职、养育孩子。即使有些人采取了一些环保的措施(**take measures**),但因受不到支持和鼓励(**lack support and encouragement**),没有激情和动力(**passion and motivation**)继续下去。很多人觉得自己的努力是微弱的和徒劳的(**negligible and futile**),不可能明显地改善环境(**unlikely to improve the situation significantly**),也有很多人以环境为代价牟取利益(**make profits at the expense of environmental damage**)。

所以环境问题的解决需要从多方面入手。首先从全球层面(**at the global level**),需要国际合作(**international cooperation**),为环境保护制定国际化标准(**set international standards**)。其次,政府应该颁布法律(**enact laws**),倡导低碳(**low carbon**)生活方式。从科技层面来说,应该开发新能源(**exploit alternative energy**),投资节能(**energy-saving**)经济。此外,公司应该生产环保(**environmentally friendly**)

产品，倡导绿色消费习惯（**green consuming habit**）。最后，人们应该提高环保意识（**raise public's green awareness**），从身边的小事做起。

对比你的答案和给出的示例，看看这些答案是不是囊括了“考什么3和4”，并部分解决了“考什么1、5、11、17、19”？

雅思考试的真题几乎都包含在上述的那些问题中了，通过刚才的训练，再看以下一些雅思考题，是否心中基本上有答案了？

（1）Fossil fuels, such as coal, oil and natural gas, are used in many countries. The use of alternatives sources of energy, including wind, and solar power, is encouraged. Is this trend a positive or negative development?（2009.5.30）

（2）Nowadays, technology developments are causing environmental problems. Many people think that we should live a simpler life while others believe that technology can solve environmental problems. Discuss both views and give your own opinion.（2009.2.12）

（3）Environmental problems are too big for individual countries and individual people to address. We have reached the stage where the only way to protect the environment is to address it at an international level. To what extent do you agree or disagree?（2011.5.7）

Part 3 话题词汇补充

Heatwaves and droughts	热浪和干旱
devastate the natural world	毁坏自然世界
dump waste	倾倒废物
food shortages	食物短缺
greenhouse gas emissions	温室气体排放
power stations	发电站
(burning) fossil fuels	（燃烧）化石燃料
emit all sorts of dangerous gases (such as carbon monoxide)	排放各种危险气体（比如一氧化碳）
solar panels	太阳能板
renewable energy	可再生能源
deforestation	森林退化（森林砍伐）
natural habitats	自然栖息地

续表

biodiversity	生物多样性
endangered species	濒危物种
extreme weather conditions	极端天气情况
the extinction of . . .	……的灭绝
illegal logging	非法采伐
employ wind and solar energy	利用风能和太阳能
energy efficiency	能源利用率
avert the impact of	避免某些影响
conserve energy	节约能源
contaminate	污染(缓慢的无法察觉的,例如化学物质的污染)
have an impact on	对……有影响
a threat to . . . /be under threat	对……是一个威胁/处在威胁之下
vicious cycle	恶性循环
be permanently damaged	遭到永久破坏
soil erosion	土壤侵蚀
discharge	排放
at the cost of	以……为代价
biosphere	生物圈
non-biodegradable material	不能进行生物降解的材料(白色污染)

Part 4　句子翻译

使用给出的单词和词组,把下列中文句子翻译成英文,注意给定单词和词组的形式有可能在句中发生改变。

Example:

大多数专家同意热浪和其他极端天气有增长的趋势。(heatwaves, extreme weather conditions)

Most experts agree that there is an increasing trend of **heatwaves** *and other* **extreme weather conditions**.

(1) 气候变化不仅会对人类有严重影响,而且会毁坏自然界和造成濒危物种的灭绝。

(devastate the natural world, the extinction of ...)

____

(2) 我们已经在世界上很多地方看到,土壤侵蚀导致了食物短缺。(soil erosion, food shortages)

____

(3) 不能被忘记的是亚马逊盆地的非法采伐仍然是森林退化的一个主要因素。(the Amazon Basin, illegal logging, deforestation)

____

(4) 个人可以通过减少使用化石燃料来为环境保护做出小贡献。(make a contribution to, fossil fuels)

____

(5) 现在已经不可能说人类活动不会影响天气状况。(It is no longer possible to ...)

____

(6) 一个显而易见的解决方法是使用更多的风能和太阳能。(employ)

____

(7) 风能和其他可再生能源有助于将二氧化碳排放量降低到一个可接受的水平。(wind energy, renewable energy, carbon dioxide)

____

(8) 提高你家里的能源利用率并非难事。(energy efficiency)

____

(9) 投资可再生资源有助于避免二氧化碳排放带来的影响。(avert the impact of ...)

____

(10) 不能进行生物降解的材料不会自然地腐烂或溶解。(non-biodegradable material, decay, dissolve away)

____

(11) 环境保护在有些地方已经陷入恶性循环。(a vicious circle)

____

(12) 科学家们好奇全球变暖会给生物圈带来怎样的影响。(global warming, biosphere)

____

(13) (人们)正在做出许多努力来保护濒危物种。(endangered species)

____

(14) 环境可能会因为空气污染而被永久破坏。(be permanently damaged)

____

(15) 土壤侵蚀的加速可能会影响到农业地区的环境。(accelerate, soil erosion)

___

(16) 他们以牺牲环境为代价追求盈利。(at the cost of)

___

Part 5 真题写作

2014年7月26日真题

Some people think that environmental problems are too big for individuals to solve. Others, however, believe that the problems cannot be solved if individuals do not take actions. Discuss both views and give your own opinion.

Give reasons for your answer and include any relevant examples from your own knowledge or experience.

Write at least 250 words.

Step 1 审题

在本题中,很明显的**关键词**是 environmental problems, individuals, too big to solve, take actions。所以我们讨论的对象是环境与人的关系。

本题是环境类的老话题,考的是环境问题是否个人能力所及,审题时先注意两边的观点讨论的范畴,一方认为对环境问题人们感到无能为力,too ... to 这个词组要理解清楚,另一方认为必须靠人们解决环境问题,主体讨论对象都是围绕人和环境来进行。

其次,题干的部分形成**对比关系**,问题形式是 Discuss both views and give your own opinion。所以在写作中一定要双方都涉及,并加以评价。

练习:划出以下题目的关键词。

(1) With the increasing demand for energy sources of oil and gas, people should look for sources of oil and gas in remote and untouched natural places. Do the advantages outweigh disadvantages of damaging such areas? (2014.6.28)

(2) In modern life, it is no longer necessary to use animals as food and in other products like clothing and medicines. To what extent do you agree or disagree? (2012.4.28)

(3) Some people argue that too much attention and too many resources are given to the protection of wild animals and birds. To what extent do you agree or disagree? (2015.1.31)

(4) Nowadays, technology developments are causing environmental problems. Many people think that we should live a simpler life while others believe that technology can solve environmental problems. Discuss both views and give your own opinion. (2009.2.21)

(5) Nuclear energy is the best source of power in meeting ever-increasing energy needs. To what extent do you agree or disagree? (2013.9.7)

Step 2 构思

构思即思路拓展，必须建立在审题的基础上进行，不能偏离关键词。在这里可以对每个关键词进行延展（你可以补充更多你能想到的论据）：

切入角度	无能为力（观点 1）	靠人解决（观点 2）
Environmental problems	自然灾害造成环境污染（acid rain, sand storm）	环境问题是由人类活动造成的
	人类活动造成环境污染跨越了国境（global warming, oil spoil）	集体的力量比较强大
Individuals	人的资金有限	公司的任何政策受到个体的影响
	个人的能力有限	政府的措施需要人的实施才有效

通过以上分析，可以对两边观点进行充分分析，既从人和环境的角度解析了环境问题人们无能为力的原因，也从相应的角度回答了个人努力可以改善环境的措施。讨论全面，思维切入多样性。

☺ **练习 1**：试着对 step 1 练习里的 5 个题目进行构思。

Step 3 组织

经过 step 2 的构思后，下一个步骤就是选择自己有想法的论点，用巧妙的逻辑将构思的内容链接起来，以下的 outline 是选择了第二个观点。那么对于第一个观点，可以承认它合理之处，但是整体上要加以否定，因为这两个观点是对立的。

Outline:

- Paragraph 1：背景句 + 题目改写 + 观点（支持观点 2）
- Paragraph 2：讨论一方的观点：确实，有些环境问题的严重了已经超出了人类的想象
  - ✓ 支持细节 1：人类很难抵御自然灾害
  - ✓ 支持细节 2：人类活动造成的危害已超越了国境
- Paragraph 3：讨论另一方观点：环境问题只能靠人类采取措施才能解决
  - ✓ 支持细节 1：人类是环境问题的罪魁祸首
  - ✓ 支持细节 2：集体的力量可以影响政府的决策
- Paragraph 4：总结：重申观点

☺ **练习 2**：针对 Step 2 的练习列提纲。

Paragraph 1：______________________________

____

Paragraph 2: ______________________________

____

____

Paragraph 3: ______________________________

____

____

Paragraph 4: ______________________________

____

Step 4　首段落写作

首段落写作的要点就是**改写题目**并表达自己的观点，改写题目有很多种方式，可以**同义词**转换，**词性**转变，也可以进行句型转变，改写的幅度视自己的英文程度而定，至少要改掉一些关键词，**切不可原题抄下**。

例子：Some people think that environmental problems are too big for individuals to solve. Others, however, believe that the problems cannot be solved if individuals do not take actions. Discuss both views and give your own opinion.

改写：The environmental problem is **one of the biggest challenges** facing **human beings**. However hard it would be for **individual persons** to solve it, they need to **do their utmost** to alleviate the pollution whether for the sake of their current living conditions or the future generation.

练习：针对 step 1 的练习写出首段落。

Step 5　主体段写作

每一个主体段落的写作都是围绕一个中心（即分论点）展开，该分论点应该通过不同的论证方式加以充分地展开，其中举例论证（exemplification）是最常见的论证方法之一。例子可以与原因放在一起，作为原因的补充来论证主题句，也可以单独成一段来论证总论点。前者的用法更常见。此外，在任何一个句子里都可以加上例子来丰富句子的内容。

举例逻辑词：

介词（词组）：

Like/such as（不放开头，后面加名词）

接在名词后面，后续接名词或动名词

副词词组

For example/for instance

用法灵活，接句子。一般位于句首，有时也置于句中或句末。不管哪种位置，都必须用逗号将它与句子其余部分分开。

动词词组

Take . . . for example/take . . . as an example

在省略号处填入名词或动名词,单独成句。

常用句式:

A case in point is that . . . 一个典型的例子是……

示范:

(1) Teamwork brings students many benefits, such as making them learn how to compromise and helping others.

(2) Teamwork benefits students in many ways. For example, they will learn how to compromise and help others.

(3) Technological advance sometimes produce negative effects on our environment. Take the increasing car use for example. A lot car exhaust pollutes the air we breathe.

(4) Technological advance sometimes produce negative effects on our environment. A case in point is that a lot of waste gas emitted from increasing cars pollutes the air we breathe.

接下来,根据 step 3 提纲中的 paragraph3 部分展开写作

- Paragraph 3:讨论另一方观点:环境问题只能靠人们采取措施才能解决

✓ 支持细节 1:人类是环境问题的罪魁祸首

✓ 支持细节 2:人类影响了政府的决策

Despite the fact that some environmental problems are too challenging for individuals to address, we cannot take it as an excuse to shrug off the responsibility of protecting environment(承上启下)(主题句) **In the first place,** human beings are the culprit of environmental pollution.(支持细节 1)For example, deforestation and reclamation were common in the past, which not only deteriorated our national environment but also endangered some rare animals.(举例过去的人类行为对环境的危害)Nowadays, pursuing economic acceleration necessitates heavier exploitation of natural resources and modern transportation vehicles like cars releases enormous waste gas.(再通过现在的事实,其中带有 cars 这个例子,来证明人类行为对环境的危害)**Moreover**, even if one person's strength is weak, people's unanimous voice will push the government to take effective measures.(支持细节 2)Take London in the early 20th century for example. Large amounts of waste gas emission due to industrial development severely polluted the air, leading many people to suffer from respiratory disease or even die. Then the public urged the government with righteous indignation to deal with the situation. Ultimately, clean air reappeared in London.(用伦敦历史上的雾霾治理来支持细节 2)

请运用举例来进一步解释以下句子

(1) New energy is more environmentally friendly.

(2) The development of technology makes us rely less on animals for food and medicine.

____

____

(3) Many animals are on the edge of extinction.

____

____

(4) It is dangerous of utilizing nuclear power.

____

____

Step 6 结尾段写作

结尾段是对全篇内容的总结,也是对观点的重申,所以结尾不能出现新的论点。可以适当提到建议呼吁的部分。

这里的例子依旧是承接上个步骤

In short, whatever environmental problem we face, we need to do our best to make contributions, which will lead to greater efforts at the governmental level. And meanwhile, we have to reduce the activities which do good to economic development at the expense of environment and resources.

练习:真题写作

针对 step 1 里的真题进行文章写作

Section 2 Government

Part 1 考什么

重点范围

政府投资

(1) What is the priority of the government?

(2) Should the government fund artists?

(3) Which area should the government invest in? Arts or public facilities?

(4) Are sports and art in school more important than professional sports and art events in communities?

(5) Should the government spend a lot of money on the restoration of old buildings in major cities?

(6) Do local films need support from the government?

考题例子:

Many people think arts like painting and music can not directly improve people's quality of life. Therefore the government should spend money on other things. Do you agree or disagree? (2012.7.28)

政府的责任

(7) Is it individuals' responsibility to care for their diet and health?

(8) Whether the amount of noise should be strictly controlled?

(9) Should the use of fresh water be controlled?

(10) Should the government control the content of media?

(11) Who should decide people's lifestyle?

(12) Should free libraries and education be provided by the government?

(13) Should the government pay for road system and health care?

(14) Who should be responsible for tuition fees?

(15) Who should be responsible for providing financial support to old people after they retire?

(16) Should health care be free for everyone?

(17) Should the authority decide what students should learn?

(18) Should scientific research be carried out by government?

考题例子:

The government should control the amount of violence in films and on television in order to decrease the violent crimes in society. To what extent do you agree or disagree with this issue? (2011.05.19)

次要范围

国际援助

(19) Is international aid necessary?

(20) What kind of international aid should be given?

(21) Is aid money always able to get to the poor of this world?

Part 2 思考维度

政府类的话题相对比较集中,基本围绕政府的**社会责任**、**政府投资**,以及**国际援助**这三部分考点。其中前两部分考点最高频,需要了解政府的职能(民主、民治、民生)以及政府需要负责的范畴才能进行顺利写作。

(1) Where does the government's **revenue** come from?
(2) What is the **power** of government?
(3) What should the government **be responsible for**?
(4) Can art **enrich** people's **spiritual world**?
(5) Should people have the right to enjoy **social welfare**?
(6) Is there any **supervision** over private health care?
(7) What is the **importance** of education and health care for people and the country?
(8) Can all people **have access to** education and health care in your country?
(9) Is the world like **a big warm family**?
(10) Does **corruption** happen in some poor countries?
(11) Should government offer **scholarship** to college students?
(12) Does strict media control **have deterring effect on** potential criminals?
(13) Is a private company **profit-oriented**?
(14) How can people's **basic living quality** be ensured?
(15) What are the **undesirable consequences** if the government takes all responsibilities?
(16) Is medical treatment **costly**?
(17) Are teachers more **professional** than the government when choosing subjects?

An Illustration 思考维度 1

(思考维度 1)政府的每一分钱都来自于纳税人(**tax payer**);而且政府能立法(**enact laws**),能控制和支配(**dominate**)各种资源。所以政府对民生中各个领域负有最大责任(**take the major responsibility**)。原因是:

(1) 每个政府的基本责任(**basic obligation**)是保证国家安全(**ensure national security**),维护社会稳定(**maintain social stability**),加强社会福利保障体系(**social welfare system**),完善公共设施建设(**public facilities**)。

(2) 政府有能力,有相关资源(**dominate various resources**)。

(3) 政府要优先重视(**give top priority to**)教育,科技和基本人类需求(**basic needs**)的投资(**investment**),后投资文化娱乐设施(**entertainment facilities**)。

这样,我们是否部分解决了"考什么 1、2、3、7、8、9、10"?

☺ 再看以下一些雅思考题,是否心中有部分答案了?

Some people say the government should give priority to health care, while others believe that taxpayers' money should be spent on other important priorities. Discuss both views and give your opinion. (2015.7.23)

Some people think that the government should establish free libraries in each town. While others believe that it is a waste of money since people can obtain information from the internet at home. Discuss both sides and give your own opinion.（2012.1.12）

Part 3　话题词汇补充

give priority to ...	给……优先权
fund	赞助
restore	恢复
be responsible for	为……负责
invest in ...	在……上投资
make a decision	做决定
make progress	进步
carry out	执行
give international aid	给予国际援助
spend money on	在……上花钱
developed countries	发达国家
do volunteer work	做志愿者工作
basics	基本需求
public money	公款
go on strike	罢工
municipal	市政的
diplomatic	外交上的
authority	权威
domestic	国内的
empower	授权给……；使……能够
authorize	批准
dominate	控制，支配
administer	管理
dogma	教条
economic crisis	经济危机

续表

fiscal	财政的
industrialization	工业化
give financial support	给予财政支持
affect	影响
advocate	提倡
solve the poverty problem	解决贫困问题
give help to	给予帮助
pay the least cost	付出最少的代价
sponsor	资助
out of poverty	摆脱贫困
impoverished countries	贫穷国家
take actions	采取行动
raise the living standard	提高生活水平

Part 4 句子翻译

使用给出的单词和词组，把下列中文句子翻译成英文，注意给定单词和词组的形式有可能在句中发生改变。

Example:

政府应当优先考虑人民的基本需求。(give priority to ...)

Governments should give priority to the basic needs of their people.

(1) 在许多发达国家，教育和医疗都由政府来资助。(fund)

____

(2) 人们普遍认为当局应当为贫富差距负责。(be responsible for ...)

____

(3) 许多人怀疑投资艺术是否值得。(invest in ...)

____

(4) 他们认为保护历史建筑完全是浪费公款。(public money)

____

(5) 我曾花了两个月的时间在非洲西部的一个小村庄做志愿者工作。(do volunteer work)

____

（6）应该鼓励非政府组织在人道主义项目上投资。（NGOs；spend money on）

____

（7）和发达国家相比，发展中国家更加依赖农业。（developed countries）

____

（8）人们曾花了许多年从经济危机中恢复过来。（economic crisis）

____

（9）工业化可能有负面影响，例如环境污染。（industrialization）

____

（10）对于他们来说，脱离贫困是头等大事。（out of poverty）

____

（11）一个贫穷国家在当大多数人们还生活在贫困线之下时还要资助艺术家，这显然是不可能的。（an impoverished country；sponsor）

____

（12）因为贫困问题已经被解决，所以是时候提高人们的生活水平了。（solve the poverty problem；raise the living standard）

____

（13）政府应当采取实际行动来满足来自各行各业的人们的基本需求。（take actions）

____

（14）许多工业国家定期向贫穷国家提供帮助。（industrialized countries；give help to）

____

（15）面临严重的财政问题，他们不得不向其他国家寻求帮助。（fiscal）

____

Part 5　真题写作

2013 年 6 月 6 日真题

Some people think the government should be responsible for providing financial support to old people after they retire, but others believe individuals should save money for themselves. What is your opinion?

Give reasons for your answer and include any relevant examples from your own knowledge or experience.

Write at least 250 words.

Step 1　审题

本题的关键词是 government，financial support，old people，themselves 句子内部出现

对比逻辑关系。根据问题,观点可以是政府承担,也可以是人们自己承担。

Step 2　构思

构思必须从关键词出发,学会多角度切入,来分析自己支持的观点。切入的方法有很多,这里推荐一种主客体的切入方式,即把题干的主语和宾语作为切入点,再把两个角度细化进行分析。

在本题中,可以对主体 government 分析为什么应该政府负责任,在做个细化的分类,也可以从客体 old people 的角度分析政府承担的好处。

主客体	观点一	观点二
Government	① 政府的基本责任 ② 纳税角度 ③ 社会稳定性	① 政府的预算有限 ② 政府需要投资很多更重要的领域,比如医疗,教育。
Old people	① 缓解老人财政负担 ② 老人没有收入来源 ③ 养老金花费高	① 人们自己的责任 ② 老人的下一代应该承担部分责任 ③ 公司承担一部分

当列出这样一张表格时,其实把主体段落的大纲和逻辑基本都解决了。

练习

对以下题目进行列表构思:

(1) There are much more people who watch foreign films than people who watch local films. What are the causes? Should the government provide financial support to the local film industry? (2011.8.27)

(2) Many people think arts like painting and music can not directly improve people's quality of life. Therefore, the government should spend money on other things. Do you agree or disagree? (2012.7.28)

(3) The restoration of old buildings in major cities in the world costs the government a lot of money. This money should be used in new housing and road development. To what extent do you agree or disagree? (2013.7.27)

(4) Governments are encouraging industries and businesses to move from large cities to regional areas. Do the advantages outweigh the disadvantages? (2014.8.16)

(5) Some people think people working in creative arts should be financially supported by the government. Others think they should find financial support from other resources. Discuss both sides and give your opinion. (2015.10.31)

Step 3　组织

经过 Step 2 的构思,思路已比较清晰,具体的写作思路还是要根据自己的观点而定,对上一步骤的内容可以做一定的筛选。

- Paragraph 1：题目改写 + 观点（政府承担人们的养老）
- Paragraph 2：主题句：政府承担人们退休后的养老是政府的责任

✓ 支持细节1：政府的税收来自人们的税收

✓ 支持细节2：有利于社会的稳定性

- Paragraph 3：主题句：政府承担人们退休后的养老可以减少人们的财政负担

✓ 支持细节1：老人没有收入

✓ 支持细节2：养老金花费高

- Paragraph 4：总结：重申观点

Step 4 首段落写作

例子：Some people think the government should be responsible for providing financial support to old people after they retire, but others believe individuals should save money for themselves. What is your opinion?

改写：It is quite common these days for many people to **do a lot of savings** for **their retirement**. However, in my opinion, **paying the pension for the retired** is the government's responsibility.

练习

针对 Step 2 的练习写出首段落

Step 5 主体段写作

本节我们将用对比论证来解题：

对比论证分为两种，一种是具体情况的正反对比，拿两件事物或者两种观点进行正反比较。另一种是过去与现在的对比，常用于科技文比较多。对比论证应用比较灵活。

1）正反对比常用连接词：

A . . . , **while/whereas** B . . .

While/whereas A . . . , B . . .

A . . . . **By/In contrast**, B . . .

Unlike A who/which . . . , B . . .

常用句式：

. . . , which is in stark/sharp/striking contrast with the fact that . . .

……，这和以下事实形成鲜明对比。

e. g. (1) Students who go to university immediately after gradation can better adjust themselves to the academic life, **whereas/while** those who take a gap year off are very unlikely to refocus their attention on study.

那些毕业后直接上大学的学生能更好地适应大学生活，而那些参加间隔年的学生却很可能无法再专注于学习。

(2) Students who go to university immediately after gradation can better adjust

themselves to the academic life. **In contrast,** those who take a gap year off are very unlikely to refocus their attention on study.

(3) Unlike the students who go to university immediately after gradation, those who take a gap year off are very unlikely to refocus their attention on study.

2）今昔对比常用用法：

In the past, ... However, nowadays, ...

Eg. In the past, people used to communicate with others by writing letters or sending pigeons, which was time-consuming and unsafe. Nowadays, however, people can connect with others via the Internet and mobile phone anywhere. It is convenient and efficient.

根据 Step 2 的构思和 Step 3 提纲中的 Paragraph 2 部分展开写作

Paragraph 2：主题句：政府承担人们退休后的养老是政府的责任

✓ 支持细节 1：政府的税收来自人们的税收

✓ 支持细节 2：有利于社会的稳定性

Funding people's retirement is the government's obligation. The income of government mainly comes from the public in the form of taxes.（支持细节 1）In the past, the government did not levy tax on people under collective economy, and people had few private rights and lived in hardship. Nowadays, however, people can start business and work by themselves. They pay tax legally for national construction.（用过去与现在对比支持细节 1）When they get old, they are entitled to enjoy the corresponding social welfare.（支持细节 1 中的结果）Also, if this basic right cannot be ensured, social stability is bound to be damaged.（支持细节 2，对细节 1 结果假设递进）As everyone knows, many people in China are just struggling to make ends meet. They don't have enough money for their future retirement. When it is compulsory for them to pay for pension, they might try some illegal means to get more money. Instead, if the government pays for pension, ordinary people would not worry very much about their future and can concentrate on their current life.（用正反对比来支持细节 2）

练习

请根据练习中的第 1 题用对比论证方法来写一段主体段

Step 6 结尾段写作

这里的例子依旧是承接上个步骤

To sum up, it is the government's inescapable duty to cover people's pension after their retirement. Helping old people is also helping millions of families, which the foundation of social stability.

练习：真题写作

针对 Step 2 里的真题进行文章写作

Chapter 8 Topic: Social Issues and Others
社会类大作文及其他

Section 1 Social Issues

Part 1 考什么

重点范围

家庭

(1) Why do women have babies at a later time?

(2) Do you think maternity leave is necessary?

(3) Why do some people live away from their families?

(4) Why do some people continue to live with their parents after they have found a job?

(5) Some people work in a foreign country and therefore their family move to the country too. Is it a good thing?

> 考题例子：
>
> In some countries, many people have chosen to live by themselves in recent years. What has caused this to happen? Does it have a positive or negative effect on the development of society? (2014.9.27)

消费

(6) Do you follow the trend when you buy clothes?

(7) Some people like to follow others in choosing what to buy (e.g. clothes). Why? Is it a good thing?

(8) More and more people like to buy all kinds of household electrical appliances. Why? Is it a good or bad thing?

考题例子：

More and more people want to buy famous brands with clothes, cars and other items. What are the reasons? Do you think it is a positive or negative development? (2013.11.30)

城乡

(9) Do you prefer to live in a city or in the countryside? Why?

(10) Some industries and businesses have been relocated to the suburbs. Why? Is it a good thing?

(11) In the city you live in, is the population increasing or decreasing? Why? What problems has it caused? Any solutions?

(12) In the city you live in, are the schools, shops and businesses mixed or separated in different regions? Which layout do you prefer?

(13) Do you think there should be more trees or open space in your city?

考题例子：

There are more new towns nowadays. It is more important to include public parks and sports facilities than shopping centres for individuals to spend their free time. To what extent do you agree or disagree? (2016.4.16)

食品

(14) Are there any differences between the food you eat today and the food in the past?

(15) Is today's food better or more harmful to us?

(16) Some fruit and vegetables can be eaten all year around. Is it a good thing?

(17) Do you buy imported fruit and vegetables?

(18) Do you prefer traditional food or fast food? Why?

(19) Do you watch food advertising? Do you think it should be banned?

(20) Should shops be allowed to sell unhealthy food?

考题例子：

Today food travels thousands of miles from the farm to the consumers. Why is this? Is it a positive or negative trend? (2011.12.03)

工作

(21) Why do people work?

(22) Which do you value more in work, money, security or satisfaction?

(23) What do you think of people who change jobs constantly in his life?

(24) What are the advantages and disadvantages to working in the government?

(25) What kind of people are qualified to work in the government?

(26) Should workers work overtime?

(27) What aspects of a job applicant should an employer consider during an interview?

(28) Is an interview reliable to judge a person?

考题例子：

Some people believe that job satisfaction is more important than job security. Others believe that people cannot always enjoy their jobs and that a permanent job is more important. Discuss both views and give your own opinion. (2014.10.25)

次要范围

贫富差距

(29) What causes the wide gap between the rich and the poor? What effects does it cause? Are there any effective solutions?

(30) Do you believe the narrower the gap is, the happier the society is?

慈善

(31) In which way would you help the poor people, giving money directly to them or donating to a charity organization?

(32) Is there any difference between helping people in your own country and helping those in foreign countries?

(33) Should young people spend a period of time helping the community without being paid?

税收与贡献

(34) Do you think paying taxes means making contributions to society?

(35) As members of society, what other things can we do to contribute to society?

体育

(36) Which factor is more important to success in sports, physical fitness or the mental attitude?

(37) What dangerous sports do you know? Should individuals be allowed to choose dangerous sports?

(38) What are the effects of hosting an international game, for example the Olympic Games?

(39) Should the government spend more money developing professional sportsmen or building sports facilities for all people?

企业社会责任

(40) Apart from making money, what social responsibilities should a company take?

Part 2 思考维度

社会类话题包罗万象，以上几个领域是考得比较集中的。每个小标题又自成体系，所以在备考是我们更该关注这些小标题，而不是“社会类”这个抽象的概念。接下来的思考角度是针对每个重点小话题而给出的。

家庭

(1) Is women's **social status** improved?

(2) What are the **internal and external factors** that influence a woman's decision in having a baby?

(3) Can young people today **afford a house** or an apartment in a city?

(4) What are the differences between today's young people and those in the past?

(5) To what extent do you think **cultural shock** will affect one's life?

消费

(6) What kind of people like to **follow the crowd**?

(7) What kind of role does advertising play in people's decision to buy?

(8) Do you know the difference between needs and wants?

城乡

(9) To what extent do you **value convenience** in life?

(10) Is pollution a factor to be considered in **city planning**?

(11) Are some **job opportunities** only found in cities?

(12) Which does the government pay more attention to, **public health** or **economic development**?

食品

(13) What **harmful substances** are contained in today's food?

(14) How is technology **applied to the quantity and quality of food**?

(15) Do you eat **genetically-modified food**?

(16) Why is it possible for food to **travel a long distance**?

(17) What is the bad effect of **food advertising aiming at children**?

(18) Should shops **bear moral obligations** or just **care about profits**?

工作

(19) Apart from money, what else do you want to obtain from your work?

(20) What kind of job requires people to have **accumulated experience** in one specific field?

(21) What are the differences between people **fresh from college** and those **with many years' work experience**?

(22) What makes you feel successful? **Achievement in work** or **a balance between**

work and family?

(23) What skills are needed by today's employers?

(24) Is there anything **exaggerated** or **fake** in an interview?

(25) Can all qualities in a person be shown in an interview?

An Illustration 思考维度 1

现代女性受到更好的教育(**better educated**),跟她们父母相比,她们对婚姻持有不同的见解(**have a different attitude toward marriage**),尤其是反对包办婚姻(**object to arranged marriages**)。这种对婚姻的谨慎态度(**prudent attitude**)导致女性结婚时间推迟(**delay getting married**),自然而然,她们要小孩的时间也推迟了。另一方面,随着男女之间的教育公平(**education equality**)的实现,女性的社会地位(**social status/position**)也极大地提高了,这意味着她们在职场(**the working world**)中经常担任要职(**occupy key positions**),而打拼到那个位置(**struggle to reach that position**)时女性往往已经到了要孩子的年龄。她们往往陷入了两难境地(**in a dilemma**),如果贸然选择生孩子,她们很可能会失去当前的职位(**likely to be replaced**)或失去晋升的机会(**lose the opportunity to get promoted**)。因此,有一部分女性会选择晚要孩子甚至不要孩子。

对比你的答案和给出的示例,看看这些答案是不是囊括了"考什么 1"?

再看以下雅思考题,是否心中基本上有答案了?

In some countries around the world men and women are having children late in life. What are the reasons for this development? What are the effects on society and family life? (2015.5.21)

Part 3 话题词汇补充

domestic	国内的
bring up	养育
parenting	教养
sibling	兄弟姐妹
nuclear family	核心家庭
be independent from ...	从……中独立出来
white-collar worker	白领
better	提高,改善

续表

down-and-out	穷困潦倒
encounter	遭遇
job-hopper	跳槽的人
career life-span	职业寿命
stable	稳定的
competitive	有竞争力的
reliable	可靠的
win-win	对各方都有益的,双赢的
prevalent	普遍存在的,普遍发生的
account for ...	导致;解释
bring benefits to	给……带来好处
experienced	有经验的
ease the burden	减轻负担
learn a lesson from ...	从……中吸取教训
outweigh	比……重要
maximize	最大限度地利用(某事物)
adverse	不利的,有害的
take measures	采取措施
optimize	优化
for the sake of ...	为了
be short of ...	缺少
feasible	可行的
address a problem	处理问题
settle down	定居
mutual	相互的
trigger	引起
collaborate	合作,协作
influential	有影响力的

续表

facilitate	促进
giant	大公司，大企业，大国
enhance one's reputation	增加某人的声誉
economic growth	经济增长
take advantage of . . .	利用
inevitable	不可避免的
make contributions to . . .	为……做出贡献
be worth doing . . .	做……是值得的
drawback	缺点
a symbol of social status	社会身份的象征
in pursuit of individual happiness	为了追求个人幸福
consumption	消耗
offer more job opportunities	提供更多的就业机会
rapid pace of life	快节奏生活
stress-related illnesses	与压力有关的疾病
high cost of living	高额生活费用
give special care to . . .	给予……特殊关照
better medical services	更好的医疗服务
put the blame on . . .	归咎于……
unprecedented	前所未有的

Part 4　句子翻译

使用给出的单词和词组，把下列中文句子翻译成英文，注意给定单词和词组的形式有可能在句中发生改变。

Example：

这项政策应该可以促进国内市场的销售。（domestic）

This policy is supposed to promote the sales in the domestic market.

（1）在这样的情况下，女性可能没有太多的时间来工作，因为她要独自抚养孩子。（bring up）

____

(2) 对于单身父母亲来说,养育子女可能会更加压力重亘。(parenting)

____

(3) 手足之争常常会使父母焦虑。(sibling)

____

(4) 核心家庭的重要性正在取代大家庭的重要性,这是一个很大的社会变革。(nuclear families)

____

(5) 工会应当从政府中独立出来。(be independent from ...)

____

(6) 无论他们的专业是什么,大多数毕业生都希望在办公室工作,换句话说,他们都想成为白领。(white-collar worker)

____

(7) 人们上夜校以求上进。(better)

____

(8) 在找工作时,缺乏相关经验的人可能会遭遇困难。(encounter)

____

(9) 调查显示大多数跳槽的人认同金钱是首要考虑的因素。(job-hopper)

____

(10) 体育明星的高收入是合乎情理的,因为他们的职业寿命相对比较短。(career life-span)

____

(11) 一些人坚持认为日常生活必需品的价格应当保持稳定。(stable)

____

(12) 人们涌进大城市为了更好的工作机会。(for the sake of ...)

____

(13) 在过去的几年中,城市在以前所未有的速度扩张。(unprecedented)

____

(14) 个人应当支付更高比例的医疗费用来减轻政府的财政负担。(ease the financial burden)

____

(15) 应该采取可行的措施来防止人口过剩。(feasible)

____

(16) 研究表明工作过度会引起与压力有关的疾病,例如失眠。(stress-related illness)

____

Part 5 真题写作(利弊讨论类)

2014年4月15日真题

An increasing number of people change their career and places of residence several times during their life. Is this a positive or negative development?

Give reasons for your answer and include any relevant examples from your own knowledge or experience.

Write at least 250 words.

Step 1 审题

本题题目比较简单,关键词有 career 和 places of residence,切不可只涉及其中一方。Career 跟 job 其实不尽相同,前者可能从 reporter 变成了 teacher,而后者可能在同一行业也可能夸行业。而转变住所既可能是换工作导致的也有可能是其他原因。另外 an increasing number of 体现了一个动态趋势的变化,暗示着我们可以进行今昔对比。问题是利弊讨论,最好利弊双方都涉及。Positive 和 negative 之间用 or 来连接表示我们可以选择单边来写。但由于很多事物都是有利有弊,建议考生双边都涉及,这样构思的压力也会少一些。对于利弊讨论的另一种问题形式是 Do the advantages outweigh the disadvantages? 或 Do the benefits outweigh the drawbacks? 对于这种利弊权衡的问题,一定要双边都涉及。哪一方比重更重,就决定了我们的观点。

Step 2 构思

在此题中,可以将 career 和 places of residence 进行联系,如很多年轻人由于追求职业的发展,会放弃小城市稳定的公务员工作,去大城市的外企工作,或创业,这种 career 的转换可能都会影响住所的转变。还有一种常见的情况就是人们出国从事不同于以往的工作,可能会把家人都带到国外。讨论这些并不是本题的重点,因为本题并不是让我们写原因,但了解原因有助于我们去写利弊。我们都知道 cause 和 effect 是紧密联系在一起的,这一题表面是利弊讨论,其实倾向于 positive effects 和 negative effects。既然是 effects,我们的着力点可以广一点,可以是针对个人,也可以是家庭和社会。其实很多涉及影响或利弊的都可以从这几个角度切入。现在简单罗列如下:

Positive development:

(1) 对个人:可以通过尝试不同的职业来找到自己真正的兴趣所在,发挥个人的潜力,从而取得更大的成就。

(2) 对家庭:职业的改变往往会带来收入的提高,可以改善家庭的生活质量。

(3) 对社会:住所的改变会繁荣房地产市场和租房市场。

Negative development:

(1) 对个人:有些年轻人出于追求新鲜感去尝试不同的职业,但由于一个人的整体的工作时间相对有限,可能很难在某个领域有很深的造诣。如果工作居所从一地迁到另一地,或从国内到国外,还会面临文化适应的问题。

(2) 对家庭：由于工作的改变可能导致个人住所也发生改变，与原来的家庭人员分开住，反而成本支出增加了，同时家庭成员关系可能会疏远，尤其对有孩子的家庭来说。

(3) 对社会：人口流动性的增加会带来一些不稳定因素，对交通压力也比较大（如中国的春运）。

以上的分析比较详尽，在实际写作中，考生可以不必面面俱到，挑一部分容易写的作为重点。除了按 idea 的数量来确定观点的倾向性，还可以根据程度。

练习：试着对以下利弊讨论的 5 个题目进行构思。

(1) It is suggested that all the young adults should undertake a period of unpaid work helping people in the community. Does it bring more benefits or drawbacks to the community and the young people? (2015.7.4)

(2) In many countries today, people in cities either live alone or in small family units, rather than in large, extended family groups. Is this a positive or negative trend? (2013.8.3)

(3) In some countries, more and more adults continue to live with their parents even after they have completed education and found jobs. Do the advantages outweigh the disadvantages? (2015.4.30)

(4) More and more people buy a wide range of household goods like televisions, microwave ovens, and rice cookers. Do you think this is a positive or negative development? (2013.12.12)

(5) In many countries women are allowed to take maternity leave from their jobs during the first months after the birth of their baby. Do the advantages outweigh the disadvantages? (2016.2.27)

Step 3 组织

经过 Step 2 的详细构思后，只需筛选出一些放入作文中即可。假设对这一篇的观点是利大于弊，可以列出这样一个提纲。

- Paragraph 1：题目改写
- Paragraph 2：主题句：有很多好处

✓ 支持细节 1：对个人：可以通过尝试不同的职业来找到自己真正的兴趣所在，发挥个人的潜力，从而取得更大的成就。

✓ 支持细节 2：对家庭：职业的改变往往会带来收入的提高，可以改善家庭的生活质量。

✓ 支持细节 3：对社会：住所的改变会繁荣房地产市场和租房市场。

- Paragraph 3：主题句：但是坏处也不容忽视

✓ 支持细节 1：有些年轻人出于追求新鲜感去尝试不同的职业，但由于一个人的整体的工作时间相对有限，可能很难在某个领域有很深的造诣。

✓ 支持细节 2：如果工作居所从一地迁到另一地，或从国内到国外，还会面临文化适应的问题。

- Paragraph 4：总结：利大于弊

Step 4 首段落写作

例子：An increasing number of people change their career and places of residence several times during their life. Is this a positive or negative development?

改写：Unlike people in the past who mostly stayed in one job and in one place all their life, today's people, especially young men, pursue different work experience and change their living places accordingly.

注意：为了拉长句子，可以引入对比。尤其是很多雅思写作题目讲的是与过去不太一样的现象，可引入今昔对比。

Step 5 主体段写作

接下来，根据 Step 3 提纲中的 Paragraph 2 部分展开写作

- Paragraph 2：主题句：有很多好处

✓ 支持细节 1：对个人：可以通过尝试不同的职业来找到自己真正的兴趣所在，发挥个人的潜力，从而取得更大的成就。

✓ 支持细节 2：对家庭：职业的改变往往会带来收入的提高，可以改善家庭的生活质量。

✓ 支持细节 3：对社会：住所的改变会繁荣房地产市场和租房市场。

There are many advantages to moving between different jobs and places.（主题句）For most young people who have just finished college education, they are not very confident about what job is most suitable for them. Only by trying different work can they make adjustment and finally find the job they like best. By then, they will be able to bring their potential into full play, which is likely to result in success in career.（以上三句体现了对个人的好处，把这三句看成 ABC，我们可以发现 A 与 B 是因果关系，而 B 又导致了 C，C 句里面又含有因果关系）Furthermore, every job hopping in real life brings more financial returns and thereby improves life quality of the whole family.（这句还是针对跳槽带来的好处，扩展到家庭，所以用了表递进关系的 furthermore）Another contribution is that change of residence directly prompts the boom of the house leasing industry, creating many job opportunities for society.（最后一条是侧重住所改变对社会带来的经济效益，与前面两点形成并列关系，所以用 another contribution 来引导）

除了要注意段落内部句与句之间的衔接，也要注意段落之间的衔接。对利弊讨论类文章来说，两个主体段之间往往形成转折关系，最好用衔接词加以体现。

针对以下 Paragraph 3 的提纲，可以这样来写主题句。

- Paragraph 3：主题句：但是坏处也不容忽视

✓ 支持细节 1：有些年轻人出于追求新鲜感去尝试不同的职业，但由于一个人的整体的工作时间相对有限，可能很难在某个领域有很深的造诣。

✓ 支持细节 2：如果工作居所从一地迁到另一地，或从国内到国外，还会面临文化适应的问题。

Topic Sentence：However, we cannot overlook the negative sides of such trend.

练习：请将本段的细节内容补充完整。

However, we cannot overlook the negative sides of such trend.

Step 6 结尾段写作

由于首段落没有申明观点，末端一定要申明利大于弊。

In summary, being able to make a choice about what career to engage in and where to live is great progress, the benefits resulting from it far outweigh the drawbacks. However, change is not the purpose, but a necessary process to find what you are really interested in.

练习：真题写作

针对 Step 2 里的真题进行文章写作

Section 2 People-related Topics

Part 1 考什么

重点范围

孩子话题

(1) What is the effect of using modern technology (such as watching TV, playing computer games and using mobile phones) on children?

(2) Who has the greater influence on children, the school or the family?

(3) Which factor has the greater influence on children, family education or media?

(4) What is the effect of advertising on children?

(5) Should parents treat their children strictly or allow them to do what they like?

(6) Should new parents attend a parenting class in order to bring up their children well?

(7) Should children go to school earlier or try to stay in the home for as long as possible?

(8) Are children from poor families better at solving problems than those from rich families?

(9) Should all children learn a foreign language?

(10) What is the best time for children to start learning a foreign language?

(11) What are the differences between modern games and traditional games?

(12) What is the better way for children to learn, telling stories or watching TV?

(13) Do children today suffer greater pressure?

(14) Why are some children hard to concentrate on study?

考题例子:

Children can learn effectively from watching television. Therefore children should be encouraged to watch television regularly both at home and at school. To what extent do you agree or disagree? (2014.5.17)

老年人和年轻人

(15) What is the effect of an increasing number of old people in a society?

(16) What is the effect of an increasing number of young people in a society?

(17) How should a person make preparations for his future retirement?

(18) Do employers like to recruit young or older people? Why?

考题例子:

It is expected that there will be a higher proportion of old people than young people in the future in some countries. Do you think it is a positive or negative development? (2012.3.10)

性别话题

(19) Can women do the same job as men?

(20) Should a company employ the same number of men and women?

(21) Why are most students who study arts girls and most who study science boys?

(22) What are the differences between the role of a father and a mother?

(23) Should men and women share housework equally?

考题例子:

In many countries, women are able to join the armed forces now on the equal basis to men. However, some people think only men should be members of the army, navy and Air Force. To what extent do you agree or disagree? (2016.5.19)

次要范围

影响力

(24) Who are more important in our society, politicians or scientists?

(25) What do you think of celebrities engaging in charity?

收入

(26) Do you think it reasonable for people in the entertainment or sports industry to earn much more money than some professional people like doctors and lawyers?

Part 2 思考维度

讨论跟人有关的话题时，一般从人群的**特性**入手，也可以从社会大众对特定的人群的**看法**入手。再把这些特性、看法和事情联系起来，题目就容易拓展了。以下思考角度是针对重点话题给出。

孩子话题

(1) Are there any advantages that modern media and technology have but books don't have?

(2) Do children have **strong self-control**?

(3) How much time do children spend with teachers, their **peers** and their parents at different stages? Is it possible that one stage **is particularly important for a child's development**?

(4) In today's world, how long is a child **exposed to electronic products** or media?

(5) Are children **credulous**?

(6) Can children **distinguish between** what is right **and** what is wrong?

(7) What is the purpose of advertisements?

(8) Are all children similar in **personality** and hobbies?

(9) Which is more important, **following the social norms** or **promoting individualism**?

(10) What are the **features** of today's new parents?

(11) What is the purpose of a parenting course?

(12) What is best way for a child to become independent or **learn give-and-take**?

(13) In China, who takes care of children for most of the time?

(14) Is **unfavorable environment** always good for children's development?

(15) If children do not learn a foreign language, what might they spend time on?

(16) What kind of games did your parents play when they were very young?

(17) How can a person's **creativity** and **team spirit** be developed during a play?

(18) Should children **stay close to nature**?

(19) Are children required to learn more today?

(20) What things **are likely to distract children from study**?

老年人和年轻人

(21) What kind of problems do old people often face?

(22) Are **government revenues** limited?

(23) What will **be highly demanded** when the young population is **exploding**?

(24) What are the differences between the characteristics of older people and young people at work?

性别话题

(25) How are women different from men?

(26) What factors should a company **take into consideration** in **recruitment**?

(27) Are there any born differences between boys and girls?

(28) Is women's **literacy** and **social position** the same as before?

An Illustration 思考维度 21 和 22

(思考维度 21 和 22) 在很多发达国家和中国的发达城市,老年人的数量逐步在增加。在有些地方,甚至占了总人口的很大比例(**occupy a large proportion of the totoal population**)。这样的趋势(**trend**)给政府和社会都带来了很多重大影响(**make a great impact on the government and society**)。例如,由于老人容易生病,尤其很多老人有慢性病(**suffer chronic diseases**),这使得医疗资源(**medical resources**)供不应求。同时,政府需要从公共开支中拨出很大一部分来支付养老金(**allocate a lot from the public purse for pension payment**),这样有可能影响其他方面的投资(**investment**)。在另一方面,老龄化的社会(**an aging society**)相对比较稳定(**stable**),犯罪率(**crime rate**)也比较低。老年人口的增加还可以催生养老产业的兴荣(**boost the pension service industry**)。

这样,我们是否部分解决了"考什么 15"?

再看以下一些雅思考题,是否心中有部分答案了?

In many countries, the proportion of older people is steadily increasing. Does this trend have more positive or negative effects on the society? (2011.10.8)

Part 3 话题词汇补充

illiterate	文盲的,目不识丁的
live on	靠……生活
be indulged in ...	沉溺于……

续表

be addicted to ...	对……上瘾
family attachment	家庭归属感
mutual understanding	相互了解
alienation of feelings	感情疏远
be sick of ...	对……感到厌倦
generation gap	代沟
exchange of feelings	感情交流
strengthen family ties	加强家庭纽带关系
distinguish right from wrong	明辨是非
edifying	有教育意义的
couch potato	电视迷
be harmful to ...	对……有害
imitate	模仿
physical and mental health	身心健康
stimulate one's imagination and creativity	激发某人的想象力和创造力
unwholesome lifestyle	不健康的生活方式
jeopardize	损害
adapt oneself to ...	使自己适应……
the effect of using mobile phones on children	使用手机对儿童的影响
peer pressure	来自同伴的压力
strict	严厉的
a better way to ...	做……更好的方法
distract sb. from sth.	将某人的注意力从某事上转移开
age	变老
pensioner	退休人员
equal opportunity for ...	给……的平等的机会
influential	有影响力的
engage in	参与

续表

reasonable	合情合理的
learn to cooperate and compromise	学习合作和妥协
be reliant on ...	依赖……
broaden one's horizons	开阔某人的眼界
keep skills fresh and up-to date	使技能可以不断更新
balance A and B	平衡 A 和 B
eliminate age discrimination	消除年龄歧视
explode	激增，骤增
supervision	监管

Part 4 句子翻译

使用给出的单词和词组，把下列中文句子翻译成英文，注意给定单词和词组的形式有可能在句中发生改变。

Example:

- 探索外太空对人类的可持续发展有着至关重要的意义。(explore, vital)

Exploring the outer space is vital for human's **sustainable development.**

- 现在有许多人建立网络社区来交朋友。(online communication)

Nowadays, a number of people **create online communities** to make friends.

(1) 一定要有对于男生和女生来说都平等的大学教育机会。(equal opportunity for ...)

____

(2) 参加学校活动使学生们学会合作和妥协。(engage in; learn to cooperate and compromise)

____

(3) 一些教育学家认为小孩子应该早一点儿被送去上学，这样他们就不会过于依赖他们的父母。(be reliant on)

____

(4) 有一个增长的趋势是家长送他们的孩子们去国外读书来开阔孩子们的眼界。(broaden one's horizon)

____

(5) 即使是已经在这个行业里很久了的员工也要参加在职培训来使他们的技能不断

更新。(keep skills fresh and up-to date)

____

(6) 为了平衡学习和娱乐并不意味着学生应当完全放弃看电视。(balance A and B)

____

(7) 随着老龄化人口的增多,政府正面临着付退休金的困难。(aging)

____

(8) 年龄歧视应当在劳动市场中被消除。(eliminate age discrimination)

____

(9) 智能手机、笔记本电脑和其他电子产品的使用会使学生的注意力从学习上转移开。(distract sb. from sth.)

____

(10) 随着年轻人人口的激增,政府需要创造更多的工作机会。(explode)

____

(11) 年幼的孩子们需要他们父母的监管,因为他们没有很强的自制力。(supervision)

____

(12) 不是所有的电视节目都对孩子们有负面影响,因为有些电视节目是有教育意义的。(edifying)

____

(13) 现在在我们的社会里娱乐明星和体育明星变得越来越有影响力了。(influential)

____

(14) 来自同伴的压力可能是孩子们在学校的不良行为的因素之一。(peer pressure)

____

(15) 夫妻双方都应该承担起做家务和照看小孩的责任。(take the responsibility)

____

(16) 有越来越多的担忧是关于对电子游戏上瘾的孩子们的。(be addicted to ...)

____

(17) 大部分老年人都是不懂电脑,因此我们应该鼓励他们学习电脑知识。(illiterate)

____

Part 5 真题写作(report 文体)

Report 文体涉及的方面不是观点,而是直接让我们讨论原因、结果、解决方案等。一般会涉及两个方面。来看一下以下真题:

2010 年 9 月 25 日真题

A report indicated that many children between 7 and 11 spend too much time watching television and/or play video games. How does the problem affect the children, their families and society? What measures can be taken to control it?（影响 + 解决方案）

2014 年 1 月 18 日真题

Children find it difficult to concentrate on or pay attention to school. What are the reasons? How can we solve this problem?（原因 + 解决方案）

2010 年 3 月 6 日真题

Surveys show that in many countries, people are living longer but increased life expectancy has many implications for the aging individuals and for society as a whole. What are the possible effects of longer living on individuals and society?（两方面的影响）

2015 年 4 月 11 日真题

Nowadays, older people who need employment have to compete with younger people. What problems do this cause? And what are the solutions?（问题/负面影响 + 解决方案）

2015 年 11 月 21 日真题 A 卷

In some societies, the role of a mother differs in some ways from the role of a father. Why do you think these differences exist? How might the parental role develop in the future?（原因 + 预测）

通过以上各题，我们了解 report 文体的形式还是比较多样化的。审题时一定要注意答题要点，如 2010 年 3 月 6 日这一题考的是对个人和社会的影响，切不可只注重对一方面的影响。另外，对应的两个问题的回应比重最好也要相当。

从难度上来讲，report 文体低于观点类作文，因为它无须我们提出自己的观点并对观点进行有力的展开。Report 的两个问题基本上圈定了每个主体段落的主题句，方便了我们构思。支持句只需围绕小问题展开即可。支持句之间的逻辑关系多呈并列或递进结构。但每个细节依旧需要理由或例子的支持。

本小节选取 2015 年 4 月 11 日的考题进行写作分步骤讲解

Step 1 审题

本题题干比较简短，但是几乎每个词都值得去深思。如 nowadays 提醒我们这个现象是现今社会特有的，过去可能不常见。可以联想一下过去的社会，人们多是在国企或机关事业单位从事着稳定的工作，年龄大的人基本上会在一个单位里服务到老。Compete 这个词提示了人才市场可能是供过于求或者职场对人才的要求越来越高了。其次，对于两个主体 older people 和 younger people 的特点，也要进行分析。问题是关于 problems，也是负面影响，既然是影响，肯定有个作用点，可以从个人、家庭、企业、社会等方面进行联想。只有明确了问题所在，才能给出相应的 solutions。

Step 2 构思

其实年纪大的人和年纪轻的人各有自己的优缺点，在职场中竞争必有一方会失败，失败的一方并不是固定的，但很可能是他们这个年龄层次所具有的弱点导致他们竞争不过另一方。那就不妨从他们的弱点入手：

Older people: less energetic, less creative, know less about modern technology

Younger people: little experience, less prudent, less skillful in dealing with people

再观察一下我们的现实世界，刚毕业的年轻人由于以上弱点，可能在求职时屡次碰壁，即使他们的学术背景比较强或培养潜力很大，可能会因为雇主的一些偏见而失去机会，对自己以后的发展造成不利甚至对大学教育产生怀疑。另一方面，年级大的人在就业方面也未必如意，由于社会技术发展迅速，他们的技能上往往跟不上发展，很容易被淘汰，而他们又往往是家庭的顶梁柱，一旦失业，影响的面就更广了。

对于以上这些问题，重要的解决方案还是要从政府层面做出，或呼吁企业提高社会责任心。

练习

对出现在 Part 5 开头的其他题目进行构思

Step 3 组织

经过 Step 2 的构思，思路已比较清晰，现罗列如下。

- Paragraph 1: 题目改写
- Paragraph 2: 主题句：对 younger people 和 older people 均产生影响甚至对家庭也有影响

✓ 支持细节 1: younger people 找不到理想中的工作可能使他们失去发挥能力的机会，甚至会怀疑以前所受的教育

✓ 支持细节 2: older people 一旦在竞争中失败，可能会倍感压力，家庭生计也有可能受到影响

- Paragraph 3: 主题句：解决方案必须在政府和企业层面做出

✓ 支持细节 1: 政府应该提供再培训项目或提供小型创业项目等

✓ 支持细节 2: 企业需要在招聘中消除年龄歧视，并发挥一定的社会责任感，加强创新以提供新的就业机会

- Paragraph 4: 总结：可强调只有从企业、社会双方面加强努力才会将目前的负面影响降到最低

Step 4 首段落写作

例子：

Nowadays, older people who need employment have to compete with younger

people. What problems do this cause? And what are the solutions?

改写：With the economic reform in the past few decades, stable jobs are becoming fewer and fewer. Therefore, some middle aged or even older people re-enter the job market to compete with younger job-seekers either for survival or better opportunities.

练习

针对 Part 5 的其他题目写出首段落

____

____

____

____

____

____

____

____

____

____

____

Step 5　主体段写作

根据 step 3 提纲中的主体段部分展开写作

- Paragraph 2：**主题句：对 younger people 和 older people 均产生影响甚至对家庭也有影响**

✓ 支持细节 1：younger people 找不到理想中的工作可能使他们失去发挥能力的机会，甚至会怀疑以前所受的教育

✓ 支持细节 2：older people 一旦在竞争中失败，可能会倍感压力，家庭生计也有可能受到影响

Such competition exerts great negative effect on both age groups or even their families.（主题句）For younger people, especially those fresh from college, lack of experience often becomes an excuse for companies to reject them, for training rookies takes quite a long time, which most small enterprises cannot afford.（年轻人求职失败原因）Thus, no matter how excellent they have been in college, they may lose the opportunity to put what they have learned to practice.（结果 1）Worse still, some may doubt the necessity to receive higher education, whose cost is a high burden for a poor family.（结果 2）（以上三句通过 cause and effect 的逻辑体现了支持细节 1）____________________

____

练习

请根据 Paragraph 2 提纲在以上横线部分完成支持细节 2

- Paragraph 3：主题句：解决方案必须在政府和企业层面做出

✓ 支持细节 1：政府应该提供再培训项目或提供小型创业项目等

✓ 支持细节 2：企业需要在招聘中消除年龄歧视，并发挥一定的社会责任感，加强创新以提供新的就业机会

支持细节 1：

To reduce these problems, major changes should be made by governments.（承上启下的主题句）For example, they should create some training programs for older workers, especially the laid-off ones, for they usually lack the IT-related skills necessary for today's new economy.（针对 older people 的解决方案）For young people who are creative but may lack working experience, the government can offer loans, which the ambitious young adults can rely on to set up some small businesses.

练习

请根据 Paragraph 3 提纲中的第二个支持细节再写一个段落

Step 6 结尾段写作

这里的例子依旧是承接上个步骤

- Paragraph 4：总结：可强调只有从企业、社会双方面加强努力才会将目前的负面影响降到最低

In summary, only through concerted efforts from the government and corporations can the problems brought by competition in the job market be reduced to the minimum.

练习：真题写作

针对 Step 2 里的真题进行文章写作

Section 3 Culture and Economy

Part 1 考什么

重点范围

全球化

(1) Should a country increase its business and cultural contact with others?

(2) Is it a good thing that a country loses its national identity?

(3) With increasing global trade, many daily necessities travel a long distance to another country. Is it a good thing?

(4) Should a country invite foreign companies to set up offices?

(5) What effects does a country with mixed cultures produce?

旅游

(6) What are the effects of international tourism?

(7) Does international travel make people more tolerant or prejudiced?

(8) What is the impact of tourism on the environment?

(9) What is the effect of air travel on the environment?

(10) What is the impact of tourism on the local culture?

(11) Why do people see increasingly similar sceneries around the world?

(12) Do you think it still necessary for us to travel in person since any information can

be obtained through the Internet?

(13) Should a historical and cultural attraction charge foreign and local visitors the same amount of money?

(14) Do you think space travel a positive or negative development?

次要范围

建筑

(15) Is it worthwhile for the government to spend money restoring old buildings?

(16) Do you prefer tall buildings or low buildings?

(17) Which is more important for a building, the intended use or the outer appearance?

(18) Why do buildings throughout the world look increasingly similar?

语言

(19) Do you think it necessary to learn a country's culture and lifestyle in order to learn its language well?

(20) Is it a positive development that English is taken as a global language?

(21) Should we invent a new language for international communication?

(22) Are there any languages that are increasingly used? Are there any languages that are being spoken by fewer and fewer people? What effects will be caused?

博物馆

(23) Do you think that a museum is important in cur life?

(24) What kind of role should a museum play, to entertain or to educate people?

(25) Is it reasonable to charge people for admission to a museum?

(26) How should we encourage people to pay more visits to museums?

Part 2 思考维度

文化和经济体现的也是精神生活和物质生活。精神和物质的对立性经常出现在雅思考题里，不管是少数民族语言、古建筑、历史景点、博物馆还是当地风俗，都是文化特性的一种体现，而经济全球化往往会破坏文化。旅游话题又是比较特殊的，既有商业化的一面也有促进文化保护的一面。所以以下给出的思考维度不是很多(也没必要太多)，但主要体现文化和经济在一个社会中孰轻孰重的关系。

(1) Which area should the government **focus on**, **economic development** or **cultural protection**? Does the decision depend on a nation's wealth?

(2) Is it unavoidable for a country to give up its **national identity** to **follow the trend of globalization**?

(3) What impact is made on local businesses by **economic globalization**?

(4) What **social impact** is made by the mixture of cultures?

(5) In your country, does **the boom of tourism** destroy or help to protect some **cultural heritage**?

(6) Can you give some examples to show people become **prejudiced** when facing **exotic cultures**?

(7) Do people often behave well when they travel?

(8) Will a high **admission fee** deter you from visiting **a historical site** or encourage you to visit it?

(9) Will the design of buildings affect human relationship?

(10) How close is a language related to a culture?

(11) How can high technology be integrated into museums to make the visit more interesting?

An Illustration 思考维度 1

(思考维度 1) 为了追求经济发展(**pursue economic development**),各国之间加强了经济合作(**strengthen economic cooperation**),例如发达国家到发展中国家建立工厂,充分利用当地的丰富的自然资源(**abundant natural resources**)和低廉的劳动力(**cheap labor**),但同时也带来了污染。随着国际商业交流的加强,城市里需要建造更多的摩天大楼(**skyscrapers**)以容纳跨国公司的总部和分公司(**to accommodate the headquarters and branch offices**)以及连锁酒店(**chain hotels**),与此同时有些古老的建筑被拆除了(**some ancient buildings have been demolished**),导致了文化特色(**cultural identity**)在一定程度上的丧失。幸运的是,有些政府已经意识到了文化保护的重要性(**realize the significance of cultural protection**)。他们采取有效的办法(**take effective measures**)来恢复(**restore/revive**)具有本土特色的生活方式(**indigeneous lifestyles**)和语言,使其成为旅游业的一大特色(**make them attractive to visitors**),因为只有不丧失民族特色的东西才能吸引世界的目光(**What bears unique national identity can attract the world attention**)。

通过以上的分析,是否可以部分回答"考什么 1、2、4、6、11、15"?

☺ 再看以下雅思考题,是否心中基本上有答案了?

(1) During the 20th century, contacts between different parts of the world developed quickly, thanks to the air travel and telecommunication. To what extent do you think societies benefit from increasing contact and closer relationships with foreigners brought by international tourism and business? (2014.8.21)

(2) Some people regard the increasing business and cultural contact between countries as a positive development. Others, however, believe that this would lead to the loss of national

identities. Discuss both views and give your own opinion. (2015.8.29)

Part 3 话题词汇补充

daily necessities	日用品
subsidiary	子公司
an inevitable trend	不可避免的趋势
international tourist	国际游客
book	预定
litter	垃圾
take a trip	去旅游
restore historical buildings	修复历史建筑
inextricable	分不开的
global language	世界通用的语言
recreational	娱乐性的
national identity	民族特性
benefit from ...	从……中获益
tourism	旅游业
multinational	跨国经营的
kill time	消磨时间
spread	传播
particular	特定的
learn about the world	了解世界
a thrilling experience	一次令人激动的经历
abstract	抽象的
concrete	具体的
move somebody to tears	使某人感动落泪
get relaxed and entertained	得到放松和娱乐
inspire	启迪
break with old customs	抛弃传统

续表

carry sth. down from generation to generation	代代相传
advocate a new lifestyle	倡导新的生活方式
determinate	限定的
eclipse	使……相形见绌
contribute to ...	对……有帮助
pastime	消遣
nurture imagination	培养想象力
meditate	沉思
instructive	有启发性的
arouse one's curiosity about something	引起某人对某事的好奇心
enrich one's knowledge	丰富某人的知识
tear down	拆除
preserve the cultural relics	保护文化遗产
reconstruct	重建
beautify our life	美化我们的城市
local customs and practices	风土人情
attract people's eyes	吸引人们的眼球

Part 4 句子翻译

使用给出的单词和词组，把下列中文句子翻译成英文，注意给定单词和词组的形式有可能在句中发生改变。

Example：

一些国家过于依赖于从其他国家进口日用品。(daily necessities)

Some countries are too dependent on importing daily necessities from other countries.

(1) 邀请外国公司来建立子公司的好处是这会为当地人带来更多的工作机会。(subsidiary)

____

(2) 现在安排一次旅行比以前更容易了因为人们可以在网上预订机票和酒店。(book)

____

(3) 一些旅行社雇佣会讲英语的导游来吸引国际游客。(international tourist)

---

(4) 旅游业可能会对环境产生负面影响因为一些游客会把垃圾扔在地上。(litter)

---

(5) 了解一个外国的文化的最好的方法之一就是去这个国家旅行。(take a trip)

---

(6) 有些人认为公款应当被花费在更重要的事情上,例如教育和医疗,而不是被花费在修复历史建筑上。(restore historical buildings)

---

(7) 我们在学习他国语言的时候也要学习这个国家的文化,因为语言和文化是密不可分的。(inextricable)

---

(8) 因为英语已经成为全球通用的语言,来自不同国家的人们可以更高效率地沟通了。(global language)

---

(9) 博物馆也应当有一些娱乐性来吸引参观者,否则人们可能会选择其他的活动来消磨时间。(recreational)

---

(10) 那些反对全球化的人争论到一个国家跟随全球化的潮流就可能会失去它的民族特性。(national identity)

---

(11) 当地政府通过向外国游客收取比本地游客更多的费用来获取利益。(benefit from ...)

---

(12) 在某种程度上,旅游业会不可避免地影响当地的生态系统。(tourism)

---

(13) 跨国公司会和本国公司争夺市场份额。(multinational)

---

(14) 现如今人们很少去博物馆了,因为有其他许多可以消磨时间的活动,例如看电影、玩电子游戏。(kill time)

---

(15) 跨国公司在全球范围内传播最新的、最先进的技术。(spread)

---

(16) 学习一种不同的文化的方法之一就是阅读由来自这种文化的作家们写的书。(particular)

Part 5 真题写作(混搭型问题)

在雅思写作考题中,观点类问题占了绝大多数,其次是 report 文体,还有一种类别是前两者的结合。来看一下以下真题:

2009 年 8 月 29 日真题

In the past, people used to travel to see the difference from their home country. However, the sceneries in places around the world seem similar nowadays. What are the causes of these similarities? Do you think that the advantages of this similarity outweigh the disadvantages? (原因 + 利弊讨论)

Give reasons for your answer and include any relevant examples from your own knowledge or experience.

Step 1 审题

题干中出现了今昔对比,然后让我们解释原因,显然原因应该是过去到目前这段时间发生的事情导致各地景色越来越像。这里的 scenery 应该是广义的,它不仅仅是自然风光,应该是你所到之处所看到的一切景象。在这里需要将 sceneries 进行具体化,有可能是充满高楼的城市面貌,也有可能是景点、建筑等等。而这一切应该都跟全球化有关。第二个问题是利弊讨论,一定要双边都涉及。由于是两个问题,对每一个都无须深入分析,反而降低了写作难度。

Step 2 构思

Similar sceneries:

(1) 现象:很多摩天大楼

原因:经济全球化导致容纳 business 的楼宇和酒店增加,由于空间的有限,有些古建筑遭到拆除;文化交流的增加也会导致建筑风格被模仿

(2) 现象:景点相似,如很多迪士尼

原因:旅游业的全球化,模仿以追求经济效益

Advantages:

(1) 便利,无须跑很远就能看到想看的景色

(2) 受到的文化冲击少

Disadvantages:

(1) 文化特色渐渐失去

(2) 旅游资源的丧失

Step 3 组织

对于有两个问题的考题,可以不必在首段直接给出答案(即原因和观点),大部分同学如果在首段给出了原因和观点,往往会觉得主体段的主题句就不是很好写了。当然如

果给出的原因是高度概括的、并且语言能力是特别强的,可以在首段先概述一下。现罗列如下。

- Paragraph 1: 题目改写
- Paragraph 2: 主题句: 全球化和追求利益是首要原因

✓ 支持细节 1: 建筑相似: 商业交流和文化交流的增加使得城市充满了高楼大厦,差异性减少。

✓ 支持细节 2: 景点相似: 旅游业的全球化,以增加经济效益为主要目的。

- Paragraph 3: 主题句: 这种趋势是弊大于利

✓ 支持细节 1: 表面上看方便了人群,处于国外所受的文化冲击变少了。

✓ 支持细节 2: 但是,文化特色的丧失是全人类的一种损失,也是宝贵的旅游资源的丧失,对旅游业的长期发展不利。

- Paragraph 4: 总结: 世界趋于相同主要是受全球化影响。虽然全球化给人们带来很多的物质上的便利、视野的开阔,但要警惕积淀千年的文化丧失。

Step 4　首段落写作

例子:

In the past, people used to travel to see the difference from their home country. However, the sceneries in places around the world seem similar nowadays. What are the causes of these similarities? Do you think that the advantages of this similarity outweigh the disadvantages?

改写: Unlike the past when people **enjoyed different views during travel**, **today witnesses great similarities among different countries.**

Step 5　主体段写作

根据 step 3 提纲中的主体段部分展开写作

- Paragraph 2: 主题句: 全球化和追求利益是首要原因

✓ 支持细节 1: 建筑相似: 商业交流和文化交流的增加使得城市充满了高楼大厦,差异性减少。

✓ 支持细节 2: 景点相似: 旅游业的全球化,以增加经济效益为主要目的。

In my opinion, globalization and pursuit of economic gains can explain this phenomenon. (主题句) With increasing international business contact, multinational corporations are spreading across the world, necessitating more highrise buildings to accommodate their headquaters and branch offices. Meanwhile, many old buildings, which were appealing to visitors, have been demolished to make room for these skyscrapers. (这两句解释了为什么很多城市充满高楼大厦) Furthermore, the appearance of buildings looks similar, probably because architectural styles are imitated due to frequent cultural exchange. (这一句以递进的关系解释了为什么高楼大厦的外观比较相似)(以上三句体现了支持细节 1) ____________________

练习

请根据 Paragraph 2 提纲在以上横线部分完成支持细节 2

● Paragraph 3：主题句：这种趋势是弊大于利

✓ 支持细节 1：表面上看方便了人群，处于国外所受的文冲击变少了。

✓ 支持细节 2：但是，文化特色的丧失是全人类的一种损失，也是宝贵的旅游资源的丧失，对旅游业的长期发展不利。

The assimilation among different countries produces more negative than positive effects.（主题句）Outwardly, unprecedented convenience is provided, for people don't have to travel far to see what they want to see and feel less cultural shock even if they are in a foreign country.（支持细节 1）

练习

请根据 Paragraph 3 提纲在以上横线部分完成支持细节 2

Step 6 结尾段写作

练习

请根据 Paragraph 4 提纲在以下横线部分完成结尾段写作

● Paragraph 4：总结：世界趋于相同主要是受全球化影响。虽然全球化给人们带来很多的物质上的便利、视野的开阔，但要警惕积淀千年的文化丧失。

练习：真题写作

(1) Some people regard the increasing business and cultural contact between countries as a positive development. Others, however, believe that this would lead to the loss of national identities. Discuss both views and give your own opinion. (2015.8.29)

(2) International travel makes people more prejudiced rather than broad-minded. Why? How to improve the understanding of countries they visit? (2015.8.13)

(3) Some languages are increasing in use, while the use of many others is declining. Do you think this is a positive or negative development? (2013.11.16)

(4) Some people think museums should be enjoyable places to attract and entertain young people. Other think the purpose of museums is to educate, not to entertain. Discuss both views and give your own opinion. (2009.4.30)

Chapter 9 Letters (General Training) — 1

G 类书信写作——1

Section 1 Introduction

Part 1 基本信息

G 类(移民类)小作文的第一篇与 A 类(学术类)小作文是不一样的,考生需要完成一封不少于 150 字的信件,时间限制也是 20 分钟。内容涉及投诉、建议、申请、咨询等各类跟生活有关的话题,旨在考查考生在交流信息、表达个人观点和情感等各方面能力。

例如:

> You should spend about 20 minutes on this task.
>
> *You recently visited a tourist destination and were very happy with the help given to you by the staff.*
>
> *Write a letter to the staff manager. In your letter*
>
> - give details of your visit.
> - describe how the staff helped you.
> - what do you want the manager to do?
>
> Write at least 150 words.
> You do NOT need to write any addresses.
> Begin your letter as follows:
>
> Dear . . . ,

如题可见，雅思书信写作的题目是由两个部分构成的：一是背景信息叙述，二是具体的写作任务。这就要求考生在充分了解写作背景信息的同时，必须对写作任务里面的每一点做出回应，遗漏任何内容都会导致一定程度的失分。

Part 2 写作格式

雅思书信写作通常包括三个部分：称呼、正文、落款。

1. 称呼

称呼是信件开头对收信人的称谓，雅思书信写作中的收信人都是在题目中拟定的，所以必须看清题目要求，了解收信人和写信人的关系，使用正确的称呼。

雅思书信写作中有以下三种常见的称呼：

(1) 如果收信人是不认识的个人、机构或团体时，通常用 Dear Sir or Madam, To whom it may concern 或者 Dear 加上头衔 Dear Professor/Director/Manager 等以示正式和礼貌；

(2) 如果收信人是认识但是交往一般或者属于日常业务来往的人，可以用 Dear Mr./Ms. +收信人的姓；

(3) 如果收信人是熟悉的人，如亲朋好友，则可以再 Dear 后直接加名字，若称呼全名或者只称其姓反而显得关系疏远。

2. 正文

正文部分根据信件功能和目的不同，可以分为投诉信、询问信、邀请信、求职信等。不同题材的书信，所使用的语气和用词都有所不同，收信人和写信人的关系也会影响到书信的内容，如和收信人比较熟悉，那么就没有必要用很正式的语言，甚至可以出现比较口语化的句子，内容方面也可以简单聊些家常；但如果不是非常熟悉，相对正式的语言就比较合适了，不然会给对方感觉过于随便，不够严谨和重视。

在格式方面，建议考生采用齐头式，即每段开头顶格，段与段之间空一行，从直观上给人层次分明、条理清晰的感觉，目前大多数商务书信和正式书信均采用这种格式。

3. 落款

最常见的落款是 Yours faithfully 或 Yours sincerely，前者多与 Dear Sir/Madam 一起出现，后者多与 Dear Mr. Smith etc. 一起出现。如是好友之间，则像 Bye for now/Cheers for now 这类相对随意的落款也是可以的。

署名可以随便写，不需要写自己的真实姓名，但是要注意与称呼相对应。在写给组织机构等的正式书信中，落款不建议写 Thomas 这种形式，最好写全名 Thomas Borne；但在写给朋友的书信中，前面的称呼是 George，那么后面的落款就应当是相应的 Thomas。这种常识性的东西最能反映一个人的写作修养，考生应当予以注意。

Part 3 写作风格

G 类写作的风格(writing style)可分为正式(如给公司写申请信)、半正式(如给同事写信)、非正式(如写信给家人或朋友)。确定写作风格是动笔前的第一步,这意味着我们该采用什么样风格的语言,而且通篇要做到前后一致。

练习:请将下面的表达式填入方框

(1) Hi Mum.

(2) I look forward to your reply

(3) Dear Mike

(4) Lots of love

(5) I'm afraid I won't be able to attend the meeting next week.

(6) Thanks for the parcel, it just arrived!

(7) Yours sincerely

(8) Dear Sir or Madam

(9) Kind regards

(10) I'm writing in response to your advertisement.

(11) I can't wait to see you next week.

(12) I'm looking forward to getting back to work.

	informal	semi-formal	formal
greeting			
opening statement			
closing statement			
ending			

Section 2 Letter of Complaint

Part 1 写作要点指导

投诉信(Letter of Complaint)是雅思写作中最常见的信件形式之一,涵盖范围较广,有反映产品质量的,有抱怨邻居宠物带来麻烦的,也有投诉账单出错的等。

此类书信一般都由三大部分组成:

(1) 自我介绍,说明投诉事由及与收件人的相关性,表明写作意图。

(2) 陈述投诉内容,可具体描述当时的情形,如时间、地点、人物等,指出具体问题所在，概括说明问题所产生的后果。

（3）提出解决方案或者特定要求，指明解决的时间期限，表达希望早日得到答复的愿望。

Part 2 范文解析

Writing Task

You should spend about 20 minutes on this task.

You have recently made a purchase from a department store in another town. However, when you arrived home, you found a fault with it.

Write a letter to the manager of the store. In your letter,

- **say what product you have bought**
- **explain what the problem is**
- **say what you would like to be done about it**

Write at least 150 words.

You do **NOT** need to write any addresses.

Begin your letter as follows:

Dear . . . ,

Sample letter

Dear Sir or Madam,①

I am writing to express my dissatisfaction about the purchase of an "SS" sweater from your department store last week. ②

I recently washed the sweater in cool water, as per the instructions on the label. However, the colour of the sweater faded heavily and even dyed other clothes. Now it looks like a used sweater rather than a new one. ③

I have tried to phone the store several times but the line is always busy. When the call got through, I spoke to a lady from your customer service department, who was really rude on the phone and informed me that I am not able to get a replacement sweater as it was washed. But from my understanding, it is a quality problem and the store should be responsible for it. Your store is a renowned one and I am disappointed to be treated in such a manner. ④

I would, however, be perfectly satisfied if you could kindly replace the sweater or refund my money, whichever is more convenient. ⑤

I understand you will give immediate attention to this matter and I look forward to hearing from you soon. ⑥

Yours faithfully, ⑦
Daniel Keaton

范文解析：

① 由于商场经理的性别未知，故称呼用 Dear Sir or Madam 或 Dear Manager 较为合适。

② 开头表明写信原因是反映商场购物问题，同时按照题目要求说明商品名称和购物时间。

③④ 具体说明情况，一方面是新买的衣服褪色严重，有品质问题；另一方面商场客服人员处理问题不当，态度欠佳。

⑤⑥ 提出解决方案，要求更换衣服或者退款，希望早日得到答复。

⑦ 落款参照称呼选用 Yours faithfully，由于是正式文体，故署名建议用全名 Daniel Keaton。

Part 3 句型练习

常用词汇句型点拨

(1) I am writing to **express my dissatisfaction about** . . .

(2) To be frank, in the first few weeks, **I got on well with** . . . . However, recently, I have discovered that . . .

(3) I am totally upset with . . . and can not **tolerate** anymore.

(4) Honestly, at the beginning. I was quite satisfied with your service. **To my great disappointment**, yesterday I found that . . .

(5) It is **inconceivable** and **out of my expectation** that it recurred again.

(6) To my great regret, they become **troublemakers** and affect my life seriously.

(7) To solve this problem, **some remedial actions** should be taken before things get worse.

(8) I shall be grateful if you could consider my situation and improve it **as soon as possible**.

句子翻译

☺ 使用给出的句型，把下列中文句子翻译成英文。

Example：

• 我写信来投诉我住的酒店房间的空调坏了。(make a complaint about . . .)

I am writing to **make a complaint about** the air-conditioner in my hotel room which stopped working.

(1) 我写信来表达我对这个产品的不满。(express my dissatisfaction about . . .)

____

(2) 一开始，我还和邻居们相处得挺好。(I got on well with ...)

____

(3) 我无法忍受他们白天黑夜一刻都不停地制造噪音。(tolerate)

____

(4) 我无法想象维修员竟然要求我支付如此高昂的维修费用。(inconceivable)

____

(5) 这家著名的五星级酒店的设施竟然如此简陋，这完全出乎我的意料。(out of my expectation)

____

(6) 这个导游是个惹事精，他总是给我指错路。(troublemaker)

____

(7) 我要求你们采取一些补偿措施。(some remedial actions)

____

(8) 请尽快派维修人员来我家。(as soon as possible)

____

文中句子翻译

把下列中文句子翻译成英文。

Dear Sir Madam.

(1) ____

(我写信来投诉你们公司在今年 5 月 1 日至 7 日组织的旅游。)

Although the hotel you arranged is rated as a four star, I found that the room was not cleaned on a daily basis and that my bed was made up only every three days.

In addition, the hot water was only supplied from 6:00 am to 10:00 pm, which means if I arrived back at the hotel late, it was impossible for me to take a shower with hot water.

(2) ____

(餐厅里的食物也同样让人失望。) Not only was it extremely overpriced, but the quality was very poor. Even after one lunch, I did not feel well due to bad stomach pains. I was forced to take sick leave the next day, and I enclose a copy of the doctor's note.

So, due to the discomfort and inconvenience, I request compensation for the doctor's fees to the amount of $316. I would also greatly appreciate a discount on my bill (receipt enclosed).

(3) ____

(我相信你会严肃处理我的投诉,并且将来会尽量提升你们的服务质量。) I look forward to hearing from you at your earliest convenience.

Yours faithfully,
Patrick Wilson

Part 4 真题练习

Exercise 1

Read the following writing task and underline the key words or phrases.

You should spend about 20 minutes on this task.

You just returned from a tour. However, you were dissatisfied with the service you received from the travel agency.

Write a letter to the manager of the agency. In your letter,

- **give the details of your tour**
- **explain why you were unhappy with the service**
- **say what you want the company do for you**

Write at least 150 words.

You do **NOT** need to write any addresses.

Begin your letter as follows

Dear . . . ,

Exercise 2

Do the following writing task.

You should spend about 20 minutes on this task.

You eat at your company cafeteria every lunchtime. However, yon think there are some serious problems which need to be improved immediately.

Write a letter to the manager of the cafeteria. In your letter,

- **introduce yourself**
- **say what is wrong with the cafeteria**
- **suggest how it could be improved**

Write at least 150 words

You do **NOT** need to write any addresses

Begin your letter as follows

Dear . . . ,

Section 3 Letter of Inquiry

Part 1 写作要点指导

询问信(Letter of Inquiry)在雅思写作中非常常见,主要目的是寻求所需信息,如询问展览会详细情况、了解如何加入健身俱乐部、询问如何租用场地搞活动等。

此类书信一般都有三大部分组成:

(1) 开门见山,说清楚是要询问哪方面的信息。

(2) 提供背景情况(如从何种渠道了解到相关信息和联系方式),表明写信原因,具体询问相关事宜。

(3) 希望早日收到回复,同时感谢对方帮助。

Part 2 范文解析

Writing Task

You should spend about 20 minutes on this task.

You are considering immigrating to an English-speaking country and find an advert of IELTS training course in the newspaper.

Write a letter to the training centre. In your letter,

- **introduce yourself**
- **explain why you contact the centre**
- **ask for any relevant information you want to know about the course**

Write at least 150 words.

You do **NOT** need to write any addresses.

Begin your letter as follows:

Dear . . . ,

Sample letter

Dear Sir or Madam, ①

I would like to obtain some useful information on the IELTS training course in your centre. ②

I am a businessman and plan to immigrate to Australia for developing my career, which means I have to pass the IELTS examination with a qualified score. ③ I saw your advert in the City Daily last Friday and the IELTS training course mentioned in the advert might be suitable for me. ④

Therefore, I am interested to know when the course starts and how long it lasts. Do you offer any one-month training course starting before or, at the latest, at the end of this month? Is there a limit on the number of students in one class? How about the charges involved? Could you send me some materials about the course introduction, the teaching staff and the possible schedule for the course? ⑤

Thank you for your assistance and I am looking forward to receiving your reply soon. ⑥

Yours faithfully, ⑦
Allen Zhang

范文解析

① 由于收信人是不认识的组织结构,故称呼用 Dear Sir or Madam 较为合适。

② 开门见山,表明所需询问的内容是雅思培训课程方面的信息。

③ 简单介绍自身情况,表明是为了出国移民才需要参加雅思培训的。

④ 解释信息来源,是从上周五的报纸广告中获知相关课程内容的,当然也可以是网络或者朋友推荐。

⑤ 提出关于雅思培训课程的具体问题,如开班时间、周期、学生人数、费用等。

⑥ 对收信人能提供帮助表示感谢,体现礼貌原则,同时表明获取信息的急切心情。

⑦ 落款参考称呼选用 Yours faithfully,由于是正式文体,故署名建议用全名 Allen Zhang。

Part 3 句型练习

常用词汇句型点拨

(1) I want to know if it is possible for you to **provide me with information regarding** ...

(2) I **take great interest in** ...

(3) I would like to **get more details of** ...

(4) It would **be highly appreciated** if you could inform me what I have to do to ...

(5) I **am** also **greatly concerned about** ...

(6) Thank you for your **time and consideration**.

句子翻译

使用给出的句型,把下列中文句子翻译成英文。

Example:

我对你们公司举办的展览很感兴趣。(... has aroused my great interest.)

- The exhibition held by your company has aroused my great interest.

(1) 我想知道你是否能提供给我一些关于这次演出的信息。(provide me with information regarding ...)

____

(2) 我对这个国际交换生的项目非常感兴趣。(take great interest in ...)

____

(3) 你是否能多告诉我一些申请住宿方面的细节?(tell me more details of ...)

____

(4) 如果你能发给我一张希腊地图,我会非常感谢你。(be highly appreciated)

____

(5) 我十分关心保险公司是否会赔偿我的损失。(be greatly concerned about ...)

____

(6) 感谢您花时间读我的信,感谢您的关心。(time and consideration)

____

文中句子翻译

把下列中文句子翻译成英文。

To whom it may concern,

(1) ______________________________

(我想知道一些关于你们博物馆即将举办的清代文化展览会的信息。)

I am presently studying for a degree in ancient Chinese Literature and (2) ______________________________ (对这个时代特别感兴趣). Indeed, I shall soon begin writing my dissertation focusing on how much the literature tells us about the way in which ordinary people of the time lived. I am therefore interested to know if your exhibition focus on all sectors of Qing Dynasty society, or whether it is mainly concerned with the monarchy.

(3) ______________________________

(我还想知道在你们的档案里是否有关于这个时期的文字记录。) And if so, would I be allowed to review any of the material?

I look forward to hearing from you soon.

Yours faithfully,
Aron Stanford

Part 4 真题练习

Exercise 1

Read the following writing task and underline the key words or phrases.

You should spend about 20 minutes on this task.

Your local museum is advertising an exhibition that you are interested in going to see.

Write a letter to the museum. In your letter,

- **introduce yourself**
- **explain why you want to visit**
- **ask for any relevant information you want to know about the exhibition**

Write at least 150 words.

You do **NOT** need to write any addresses

Begin your letter as follows:

Dear . . . ,

Exercise 2

Do the following writing task.

You should spend about 20 minutes on this task.

Your community has no sport facilities but you find a health club nearby.

Write a letter to the club. In your letter,

- **introduce yourself**
- **describe facilities or service you want**
- **inquire about the details of membership**

Write at least 150 words.

You do **NOT** need to write any addresses

Begin your letter as follows:

Dear . . . ,

Section 4 Letter of Advice

Part 1 写作要点指导

建议信(Letter of Advice)是对收信人就某一问题提出建议和忠告。建议信有可能是写给组织或机构,就改进某些问题提出建议,也有可能是写给个人,就某件事情提出自己的观点和看法。

此类书信大致可分为三个部分:

(1) 开头部分可简要介绍自己,并表明写作意图。

(2) 主体部分根据题目要求,可先肯定优点,再提出需要改进的地方或是先分析状况和原因,再给出建议。

(3) 结尾部分可总结建议或表明原意进一步协助的态度。

TIPS:

注意建议信不是投诉信,因此语气要礼貌当先,让收信人感觉到这是一种交流,是善意地给出建议,而非恶意地宣泄情绪。同时,提出的观点和看法要合情合理,具有可行性,不要夸夸其谈,不切实际。

另外,根据收信人的身份不同,文体风格也是有所差异的,如果是写给组织机构的建议信,则为正式文体,故用语气当正式严谨;而给熟悉的人或者朋友提出建议时,用语气就可相对轻松随意些,不然反而像是在说教,产生陌生感和距离感。

Part 2 范文解析

Writing Task

You should spend about 20 minutes on this task.

You are studying at university and one of your lecturers has asked his students to write and suggest ways in which he could improve his teaching.

Write a letter to the lecturer. In your letter,

- **tell the reason for writing**
- **say what you enjoy about his lectures**
- **suggest how they could be improved**

Write at least 150 words.

You do **NOT** need to write any addresses.

Begin your letter as follows:

Dear ...,

Sample letter

Dear Dr Burton, ①

I am Tyler Fog, one of your students. Last week, you asked us to write and give you feedback on your lectures. Therefore, I have outlined my thoughts below. ②

In general, your lectures are very informative and inspiring. You are good at incorporating your personal experiences into the class teaching and I particularly like the way you demonstrate complex issues with the use of simple drawings indeed. This makes your lessons both interesting and memorable. ③

However, I do feel that you could provide us with more handouts, as I often don't have time to take down all the important points. I would also like to see more discussion work, as I find this method the most suitable way to clarify and deepen my understanding of the subject content. ④

I would like to thank you for the interest you are taking in your students and look forward to your next lecture. ⑤

Yours sincerely, ⑥
Tyler Fog

范文解析：

① 因为是写给确定且熟悉的人，所以称呼可以用 Dear Dr Burton。
② 表明写信人的身份是学生以及写信的原因是提供反馈建议信息。
③ 充分肯定教师在授课方面的优点：深入浅出，结合个人经历，令人印象深刻。
④ 提出合理的建议：提供更多的讲义以及组织讨论活动。
⑤ 再次肯定教师的表现，体现礼貌原则。
⑥ 落款参考称呼选用 Yours sincerely，署名用全名 Tyler Fogy 以示尊重。

Part 3 句型练习

常用词汇句型点拨

(1) I am writing **in reply to** . . .
(2) I would like to express my **views concerning** . . .
(3) I would like to **see more improvements in** . . .
(4) You may **consider doing** . . .
(5) **If I were you, I would** . . .
(6) I hope you will **find** these suggestions **helpful**.
(7) Please contact me if I can **be of any assistance**.

句子翻译

使用给出的句型，把下列中文句子翻译成英文。

Example：

我觉得如果我们能为那些付不起学费的孩子们筹款，那将是非常好的。(it would be beneficial if . . .)

• I feel that it would be beneficial if we could raise money for children who can't afford their tuition.

(1) 我写信来答复你的请求。(in reply to . . .)

____

(2) 我想表达一下我对这个项目的一些看法。(views concerning . . .)

____

(3) 我希望你们能改善你们的菜谱。(see more improvements in . . .)

____

(4) 你可以考虑一下重新设计这个网站。(consider doing . . .)

____

(5) 如果我是你的话,我会招聘一名销售人员。(If I were you, I would . . .)

____

文中句子翻译

把下列中文句子翻译成英文。

Dear Catherine,

I'm delighted that you are coming to Valencia next month. (1) ____

(如果你能和我以及我的家人住在一起那就太好了), who send you their best wishes. Otherwise, if you prefer, I can easily book you a cheap but comfortable hotel near the beach — so that you can be more independent.

There are lots of things to do in my city. (2) ____

(如果我是你的话,我会花几天时间在沙滩上休息,然后再花一到两天时间在城市观光。) There are several interesting museums and art galleries which I'm sure you will enjoy. One place you really should visit is an enormous aquarium called the Oceanographic Park, where you'll want to spend the whole day. Also,

(3) ____
(你应该去我们这儿一个很棒的主题公园,离这儿大概一小时的车程。) You don't need to bring a lot of clothes since the weather is normally warm and sunny at this time of year. In the evening it's a bit cooler, so you may need a jersey and a jacket.

Please let me know exactly when you're coming so that I can meet you at the airport. It'll be great to see you again so we can get up-to-date with all our news!

Love
Billy

Part 4 真题练习

Exercise 1

Read the following writing task and underline the key words or phrases.

You should spend about 20 minutes on this task.

An English-speaking friend wants to spend a two-week holiday in your region and has written asking for information and advice.

Write a letter to your friend. In your letter,

- **offer to find somewhere to stay**
- **give advice about what to do**
- **give information about what clothes to bring**

Write at least 150 words.

You do **NOT** need to write any addresses.

Begin your letter as follows:

Dear . . . ,

Exercise 2

Do the following writing task.

You should spend about 20 minutes on this task.

You are not satisfied with the traffic condition in your city.

Write a letter to the local authority. In your letter,

- **describe the traffic situation now**
- **explain the causes of these problems**
- **give your opinion on how to solve these problems**

Write at least 150 words.

You do **NOT** need to write any addresses.

Begin your letter as follows:

Dear . . . ,

Section 5 Letter of Application

Part 1 写作要点指导

求职信写作策略

求职信(Letter of Application)是写信人就某一招聘广告或就业信息写信前去应聘,对于移民类考生而言,掌握此类书信的写作技巧是非常必要的。

此类书信通常可分为三个部分:

(1) 开头部分表明求职意图,并告知招聘信息获取渠道。

(2) 主体部分主要介绍个人情况,包括教育背景、工作经历等,强调与应聘职位相关的信息,同时说明应聘该职位的动机和理由。

(3) 结尾部分希望对方能考虑自己的申请,给予考虑,并表达谢意。

TIPS:

此类书信属正式文体,故需注意用语正式、严谨、礼貌。求职意图明确,相关信息详实,切记模棱两可,职位定位不明。强调资深经历和优点的同时,也要把握尺度,适可而止,避免海阔天空,夸夸其谈。

Part 2 范文解析

Writing Task

You should spend about 20 minutes on this task.

You have seen a job advertised in your local newspaper.

Write a letter to the personnel manager. In your letter,

- **introduce yourself**
- **outline your experiences and qualifications**
- **say why you would like the job**

Write at least 150 words

You do **NOT** need to write any addresses.

Begin your letter as follows:

Dear . . . ,

Sample Letter

Dear Mr. Anderson, ①

I am writing in response to the advertisement you placed in the Manchester Evening News for a librarian. ②

I graduated with a Master's degree in Librarian Studies in 1990 and began my career in Guildford Public Library. In 1995 I moved to Central Library, London and in 1998 was promoted to subject specialist in the humanities department. ③

During the past ten years. I have also been actively involved in academic research and have published several articles in "Librarian Now", "Library Matters" and "Librarian Daily". I also teach librarian studies on a part-time basis at the University of London. ④

However, my husband has recently been re-located to Manchester by his company and I am therefore seeking a position in the same area. ⑤

I have enclosed my resume that outlines in detail my qualifications and experiences well as an open letter of recommendation from London Central Library. ⑥

Thank you for considering my application and I look forward to hearing from you soon. ⑦

Yours sincerely, ⑧
Sarah Simmons

范文解析

① 通常招聘信息都会提供具体的联系人,一般为人事管理人员。
② 表明应聘职位为"librarian",信息来源为"Manchester Evening News"。
③④ 介绍个人教育背景和相关工作经验,以及学术研究情况。
⑤ 说明调整工作的原因是家庭问题。
⑥ 提供先关补充材料,如证书、推荐信等。
⑦ 表示感谢和期待。
⑧ 落款参考称呼选用 Yours sincerely,署名用全名 Sarah Simmons 以示尊重。

Part 3 句型练习

常用词汇句型点拨

(1) I am writing **in response to** your advertisement in . . .

(2) I would like to **apply for the position of** . . .

(3) I **graduated from** . . . with a . . . degree in . . .

(4) I have been working in . . . since my graduation and have therefore **attained a fair knowledge and experience** in this field.

(5) I am a **rational** and **diligent** young man with good **interpersonal skills**.

(6) I am used to **working under pressure.**

(7) I am **experienced in** . . . , which I believe **qualifies** me **for** the position of . . .

(8) I hope you would consider my application favourably and **grant** me **an interview**.

(9) I have enclosed my resume that outlines **in detail** my qualifications and experiences.

(10) Your **favorable consideration** of my application will be highly appreciated.

句子翻译

☺ 使用给出的句型,把下列中文句子翻译成英文。

Example:

我写信来想问问你们这里有秘书的职位空缺吗?(an opening for . . .)

• I write to inquire if you still have an opening for secretary?

(1) 我写信来对您在《上海日报》上刊登的广告做出回复。(in response to . . .)

____

(2) 我想应聘咖啡师这个职位。(apply for the position of . . .)

____

(3) 我从利兹大学毕业,并且持有建筑学硕士学位。(graduated from . . .)

____

(4) 我毕业之后就开始从事金融业,因此我具有和这个领域相关的知识和经验。(attained a fair knowledge and experience . . .)

____

(5) 我在工程学方面非常有经验,我相信这使我能够胜任高级工程师这个职位。(experienced in . . . , qualifies . . . for . . .)

____

文中句子翻译

把下列中文句子翻译成英文。

Dear Sir/Madam,

I am a Chinese national from Shanghai and at present I am studying for a Master's degree in Business Administration here at the University of Bath, where I have been for the last two months.

(1) ____
(我在找一份兼职工作,我想知道您是否能帮我。) Preferably, I would like an office job, perhaps working as a secretary or office administrator. I can only work during afternoons and at weekends as my university studies occupy most of the day.

As you can see from my curriculum vitae, I have a degree in Marketing from the University of Tongji and (2) ____
(我能够在团队协作的环境下工作。) Also, I am a competent computer-user and can speak Chinese, English and French fluently. While I was studying for my degree, I worked as a part-time office manager for an import-export firm in recent years, I have also had temporary summer jobs as a hotel receptionist in Shanghai, China. (3) ____________________
(我已经准备好马上就可以开始工作。)

I look forward to hearing from you.

Yours faithfully,
Vivian King

Part 4 真题练习

Exercise 1

Read the following writing task and underline the key words or phrases.

You should spend about 20 minutes on this task.

You are looking for a part-time job.

Write a letter to an employment agency. In your letter,

- **introduce yourself**

- **explain what sort of job you would like**
- **say what experience and skills you have**

Write at least 150 words.

You do **NOT** need to write any addresses.

Begin your letter as follows:

Dear . . . ,

Exercise 2

Do the following writing task.

You should spend about 20 minutes on this task.

You noticed an advertisement on the Internet and want to apply for the job. Write a letter to the company. In your letter,

- **introduce yourself**
- **describe your qualifications**
- **explain the reasons why you think you are suitable for the job**

Write at least 150 words.

You do **NOT** need to write any addresses.

Begin your letter as follows:

Dear . . . ,

Chapter 10 Letter (General Training) —2

G 类书信写作——2

Section 1 Letter of Apology

Part 1 写作要点指导

道歉信(Letter of Apology)是雅思写作中常见的信件形式之一。写信人要为给对方带来了麻烦而表达歉意,然后提出弥补的措施,并询问对方是否接受这些补偿措施。

此类书信通常可分为三个部分:

(1) 开头部分明确说明为何事而道歉,并表达歉意。

(2) 解释当时的情况,为何会对对方造成麻烦、困扰或不便。

(3) 提出弥补的措施,再次表达歉意,并希望对方能够理解或原谅。

写道歉信时,语气要礼貌,要让对方感到写信人的诚意。写信人提出的补偿措施也应当符合实际情况、具有可行性,并且尽量能最大程度上弥补对方的损失。

Part 2 范文解析

Writing Task

You should spend about 20 minutes on this task.

You are staying in rented accommodation. You recently held a party to celebrate your birthday. Several neighbours have complained about the noise to your landlord.

Write a letter to your landlord. In your letter:

- **apologise for the disturbance**
- **explain the situation**
- **say how you will remedy the situation**

Write at least 150 words.

You do **NOT** need to write any addresses.

Begin your letter as follows:

Dear . . . ,

Sample letter

Dear Mr Jones,①

I am writing to apologise for the incident last week when some of my neighbours complained to you. I am so embarrassed about this, because I am normally a quiet person and I do respect the privacy of my neighbours. ②

The main reason for the excessive noise was that it was my 29th birthday party and my girlfriend threw a surprise party for me. She had invited around 30 of my friends to help me celebrate the big day and perhaps she did not realise how much noise would be made by the travelling disco she had hired. ③
I would also explain that after I had got over the shock, I did knock on the door of my immediate neighbours to ask if they wanted to come round and offered to turn the music down after 11 o'clock. ④
Unfortunately, I did not think of inviting the other residents of the block. ⑤

Once again, please accept my apologies and I assure you that this situation will not be repeated. ⑥ I have personally apologised to my neighbours, who were all very understanding. ⑦

Yours sincerely
Tom Bridge⑧

范文解析:

① 收信人是房东,所以称呼为 Dear Mr Jones 较为合适。

② 开头表明写信原因是向房东和邻居们道歉,并表示自己不是故意打扰邻居们的。

③ 解释事情的起因是因为女友举办了 surprise party,没有考虑到音乐的声音会太响,而我一开始并不知情。

④ 继续解释说我了解了情况之后,询问了隔壁的邻居是否想要我减低音乐的音量。

⑤ 但是我没有想到去问问别的邻居。

⑥ 再次表达歉意,并保证以后不会再发生这样的事了。

⑦ 表示我已经亲自向邻居们道歉了,而且邻居们也都表示谅解。

⑧ 落款称呼选用 Yours sincerely,由于是正式文体,故署名建议用全名 Tom Bridge。

Part 3 句型练习

常用词汇句型点拨

(1) I am writing to **show my sincere apology for** ...

(2) **Considering/Given sth./doing/that clause**

(3) **To remedy this unpleasant matter**, I wish to ...

(4) **The main reason for/why ... was that ...**

(5) She **did not realise** how much noise would be made.

(6) **I would also explain that ...**

(7) A **happened to be** B

(8) Once again, **please accept my apologies** and **I assure you that ...**

句子翻译

使用给出的句型,把下列中文句子翻译成英文。

Example:

- 我写信来为我给您带来的麻烦而道歉。(apologise for ...)

I am writing to **apologise for** the trouble I brought you.

(1) 我写信来为我没能参加你上周天举办的派对而表达歉意。(show my sincere apology for ...)

____

(2) 我面试的那天碰巧正好是你举办派对的那天。(... happened to be ...)

____

(3) 考虑到这次面试是一生中难得遇到的机会,我不得不错过你的聚会。(Considering ...)

____

(4) 为了弥补这件不愉快的事情,我的朋友们提出由他们来打扫您的公寓。(To remedy this unpleasant matter, ...)

____

(5) 我面试迟到的主要原因是我遇到了交通堵塞。(The main reason why ... was that ...)

____

(6) 我没有意识到我请来的爵士乐队会制造出那么大的噪音。(did not realise ...)

____

(7) 我还要解释的是,我给房东打过电话想要解释这个情况,但他一直没有接我的电话。(I would also explain that ...)

____

(8) 请接受我的道歉,我向您保证我明天一定准时到。(please accept my apologies, .../I assure you that ...)

____

文中句子翻译

把下列中文句子翻译成英文。

Hi Kate,

(1) ____（对于昨天我们没能够见面，我感到极其抱歉。）I really wanted to come, but I was not in town.

(2) ____（让我解释一下发生了什么事。）An uncle who used to work with my dad when we were in Iceland turned up in the morning. I had to take him on a sightseeing trip. I thought that we would be back by 4 pm and in that case, I could have come to your place at 6.

(3) ____（不幸的是，我们的行程有了一些变动，结果我们迟到了。）When I realized that I wouldn't be able to make it on time, I tried to call you but I guess we were outside the mobile coverage area. I tried again after some time, but still I couldn't get through to you. I am really sorry about this.

I really want to meet you before you leave for London on Saturday. Would it be alright if I came to your place on Friday in the afternoon? I am free on that day.
Hope to hear from you soon.

Best
Cecelia

Part 4 真题练习

Exercise 1

Read the following writing task and underline the key words or phrases.
You should spend about 20 minutes on this task.

Your neighbours have recently written to you to complain about the noise from your house/flat.

Write a letter to your neighbours. In your letter

- **explain the reasons for the noise**
- **apologise**
- **describe what action you will take**

Write at least 150 words.
You do **NOT** need to write any addresses.
Begin your letter as follows:
Dear . . . ,

Exercise 2

Do the following writing task.

You should spend about 20 minutes on this task.

Write an apology letter to a friend from overseas that it will be impossible for him or her to stay with you.

In your letter,

- **tell why it is not possible**
- **give him alternative choice to live**
- **invite him or her to come in the future**

Write at least 150 words.

You do **NOT** need to write any addresses.

Begin your letter as follows:

Dear . . . ,

Section 2 Letter of Gratitude

Part 1 写作要点指导

感谢信(Letter of Gratitude)是雅思写作中常见的信件形式之一,写作目的是感谢他人的帮助,有写给朋友的,也有写给组织机构的。

此类书信一般都由三大部分组成:

(1) 介绍写作目的,阐明为什么表示感谢,阐明收信人提供了什么样的帮助,以及最终取得了什么样的良好的结果。

(2) 详细描述事情的经过,可具体描述当时的情形,如时间、地点、人物等。

(3) 再次表达谢意,并根据题目要求提出答谢的方式,如邀请对方来家里玩,等等。

TIPS:

注意收信对象的身份不同,文章的风格也不一样。如果收信人是酒店经理、商店工作人员、组织机构等,就应该使用正式的文体,用词严谨、大方。如果收信人是老同学、朋友或熟人等,则为非正式的文体风格,语气可以相对轻松随意。

Part 2 范文解析

Writing Task

You should spend about 20 minutes on this task.

You celebrated your birthday with friends and family in a restaurant last week. It was a great success.

Write a letter to the restaurant to thank them. In your letter,

- **Mention the food and the service**

- **Explain that you really enjoyed the atmosphere**
- **Suggest any improvements to make things better**

Write at least 150 words.
You do **NOT** need to write any addresses.
Begin your letter as follows:
Dear . . . ,

Sample letter
Dear Sir/Madam,①

I celebrated my 25th birthday with my friends and family in your restaurant last week and I am writing to thank you for making it a grand success. I really appreciate the excellent service provided by your people. ②

My friends and family enjoyed every aspect of the party. ③ We, in particular, loved the food. It was mouth-watering to say the least. The perfect service complemented the food and made it even tastier. All of my guests absolutely loved the North Indian and the Italian foods served at the party. ④ I must also mention the kind service provided by your staff. They were extremely polite and went out of their way to ensure that we were comfortable. ⑤ The ambiance was quite relaxing and the decoration beautiful. In fact, the flowers and the scents used for the party were my favourites. ⑥

I have absolutely no complaints about the food or the service, but I feel that it would be great if you could add more parking space to the restaurant. ⑦

Once again, thank you so much for the best service.

Yours sincerely
Oliver Burkeman⑧

范文解析

① 由于收信人是不认识的酒店管理人员,故称呼用 Dear Sir/Madam 较为合适。

② 开门见山,表明写信来是为了赞扬酒店提供的服务,并对酒店工作人员表示感谢。

③ 首先表示总体感受是对酒店承办的聚会的各个方面都很满意,接下来具体从三个方面解释为什么很满意。

④ 详细描述了聚会上的食物非常美味,大家都很喜欢。

⑤ 表扬了酒店的工作人员,称赞他们的服务非常到位。

⑥ 表示很欣赏酒店的优美环境,如:装修风格、鲜花和香味。

⑦ 根据题目要求,提出对酒店的建议,即希望可以多增加几个停车位。

⑧ 落款参考称呼选用 Yours sincerely,由于是正式文体,故署名建议用全名 Oliver Burkeman。

Part 3 句型练习

常用词汇句型点拨

(1) **I sincerely appreciate** your help during my stay.

(2) I am writing to thank you for **your kind assistance/generous help.**

(3) **I must also mention** the kind service provided by your staff.

(4) I **am also very much grateful to** Mr. Clark **for** taking good care of me when I was sick.

(5) We, **in particular, were satisfied with** the food and the service.

(6) I **was** similarly **impressed with** the large variety of local and International wines available.

(7) **If** you **hadn't pushed** me, I **would have been hit** by the car.

(8) **Once again, thank you so much for** the best service.

句子翻译

使用给出的句型,把下列中文句子翻译成英文。

Example:

我写信来感谢您为我提供了舒适的家具。(I am writing to thank you for ...)

● I am writing to thank you for providing me with the comfortable furniture.

(1) 对于您在过去三个月以来对我的协助,我向您表达诚挚的感谢。(I sincerely appreciate ...)

____

(2) 如果没有你的慷慨的帮助,我就不可能成功。(your generous help)

____

(3) 我还必须提一下李大厨准备的美味可口的炖牛肉。(I must also mention ...)

____

(4) 我还想为您给了我这么好的建议向您表示感谢。(be also very much grateful to ... for ...)

____

(5) 我们尤其对家具和装饰非常满意。(We, in particular, were satisfied with ...)

____

(6) 你们的菜单上有非常多的选择,从中餐到日料到意式匹萨,给我留下了深刻的印象。(... was impressed with ...)

____

(7) 如果你没有提醒我交电费,我很可能会忘记这件事。(If ...)

____

文中句子翻译

把下列中文句子翻译成英文。

Dear Sir or Madam,

(1) ____
(我最近在新加坡旅行时接受了你们的员工的良好服务,我写信来对此表示诚挚的感谢。) This was my first trip to Singapore. Actually, it was my very first trip to a foreign country, so I was a bit nervous. I felt relieved when Justin, one of your staff members, received me at the airport with a warm smile. He not only took me to the hotel but also kept me entertained and relaxed during the journey by talking about various tourist attractions along the way. He was very polite and generous. Better still, he has a great sense of humour.

(2) ____
(还让我十分欣赏的是你们的员工都是知识丰富的人。) They seem to know everything about Singapore. Although I was in Singapore for only two days, your staff members made sure that I visited all places of interest.

People like them are an asset to any organisation and I must tell you that you are fortunate to have them on your payroll. (3) ____
(请告诉他们我有多么感谢他们友好的服务。)

Best regards
Robin Chinning

Part 4 真题练习

Exercise 1

Read the following writing task and underline the key words or phrases.
You should spend about 20 minutes on this task.

You have worked for a company for a short time during your college course. Write a letter to the head of department expressing your gratitude. In your letter,

- **thank the head of department**
- **explain how this has helped you**

- **say what your future plans are**

Write at least 150 words.

You do **NOT** need to write any addresses.

Begin your letter as follows:

Dear . . . ,

Exercise 2

Do the following writing task.

You should spend about 20 minutes on this task.

Write a thank you letter to the public transport authority about the manager who helped you to find something you lost and say

- **what did you lose?**
- **why was it so important to you?**
- **how did the manager help you find it?**

Write at least 150 words.

You do **NOT** need to write any addresses.

Begin your letter as follows:

Dear . . . ,

Section 3 Letter of Explanation

Part 1 写作要点指导

解释信(Letter of Explanation)是雅思写作中最常见的信件形式之一,涵盖范围较广,有请管理员帮忙的,有遗落物品请朋友归还的,也有指导朋友住宿的,等等。

此类书信一般都由三大部分组成:

(1) 先简要阐明主要情况,让对方了解大概是什么样的情况。

(2) 做具体的解释,详细说明为什么会有这样的情况,让对方对事情的细节有一定的了解。

(3) 提出解决方案,给对方一些建议或指导,也可以提出一些要求。并希望早日得到对方的回复。

Part 2 范文解析

Writing Task

You should spend about 20 minutes on this task.

You live in a room in college which you share with another student. However, there are many problems with this arrangement and you find it very difficult to work.

Write a letter to the accommodation officer at the college. In the letter,

- **describe the situation**
- **explain your problems and why it is difficult to work**
- **say what kind of accommodation you would prefer**

Write at least 150 words.

You do **NOT**need to write any addresses.

Begin your letter as follows:

Dear . . . ,

Sample letter

Dear Sir or Madam①

I would like to bring this problem to your immediate attention. I have been living in a shared room for two months. My roommate recently returned from his holiday and has been acting strangely. He refuses to cooperate with me and doesn't clean the room. ②

I am in the final year of my bachelor's program and I have to study a lot. My roommate likes to watch the television all the time and he keeps the volume high. This disturbs me and hence I cannot prepare well for my examination. ③ I have time and again asked him to reduce the volume, but he doesn't listen to me. ④

My roommate also doesn't like to clean the room. I have prepared a cleaning routine, but he does not stick to it. He always leaves his rubbish on the table that he shares with me. In addition, sometimes he forgets to put the leftover food in the garbage bin. For these reasons, the room smells bad. ⑤ On some days, especially at midnights, he uses his mobile phone and speaks loudly with his friends. This disturbs my sleep and makes it impossible for me to concentrate on my studies the next day. ⑥

I really want to move out of this room as soon as possible. I believe that it will benefit both parties. I am looking for a single room with kitchen and bathroom facilities. It would be really helpful if you could arrange one near my campus. ⑦

I am looking forward to hearing from you soon.

Thank you for your time and support.

Yours sincerely
Alma Willis⑧

范文解析：

① 首先开门见山地大致介绍了自己遇到了什么样的问题。

② 具体描述了室友看电视声音太大影响自己学习。

③ 解释了我曾经与室友沟通，但是效果并不好。

④ 解释了另一个情况是室友不注意卫生，给我造成了困扰。

⑤ 室友常常半夜大声打电话，使我睡不着觉。

⑥ 提出请求，希望对方能够给自己重新安排一间宿舍。

⑦ 落款参考称呼选用 Yours sincerely，署名用全名 Alma Willis 以示尊重。

Part 3 句型练习

常用词汇句型点拨

(1) I would like to **bring** this problem **to your immediate attention**.

(2) **In addition**, ...

(3) **For these reasons**, ...

(4) **I am wondering how to** return this T-shirt to you.

(5) **I can either** ship it to you by post **or** return to you in person when you fly back home in winter. **It is your call**.

(6) **I believe that it will benefit both parties**.

(7) **It would be really helpful if** you **could** arrange a room near my campus.

(8) **Thank you for your time and support**.

句子翻译

使用给出的句型，把下列中文句子翻译成英文。

Example:

那天我将不能来接机场你了，因为我要加班。(I won't be able to ...)

- I won't be able to fetch you from the station as I have to work late that day.

(1) 我希望这件事能立即得到您的关注。(bring ... to your immediate attention)

____

(2) 除此之外，我的室友听音乐时还不喜欢戴耳机，这对我来说是一种干扰。(In addition, ...)

____

(3) 因为这些原因，我希望你能尽快退款给我。(For these reasons, ...)

____

(4) 我不知道如何将设备运送给你。(I am wondering how to ...)

____

(5) 我既可以开车送你去机场，也可以给你预定一辆出租车。随你决定。(I can

either . . . , or . . . . It's your call.)

____

(6) 如果你能寄给我一份旅游指南，那对我来说会很有帮助。(It would be really helpful if . . . could . . .)

____

文中句子翻译

把下列中文句子翻译成英文。

Dear Lena,

I am very happy to hear that next week you are coming to my place and staying with me for three weeks. (1) ______________________________
(不幸的是，我没办法来车站接你了，因为那天我要开会。) But don't worry. I will give you the directions, so you will have no difficulty finding my place.

After getting off the train at the Queen's Street train station, walk to the bus stand which is just 5 minutes from there. Wait on platform 2 for the bus number 12. It will take you to my home through the inner streets of the suburb. As you enjoy the journey through the suburbs, look out for the old heritage church in Sydney Park. You have to get off the bus at the next stop. Then take the Euston road which is opposite the bus stop.

I'll leave the keys under the door mat. Get inside and make yourself comfortable. I will be back home by 5:30 pm. (2) ______________________________

____
(然后我们去城里，去哪家餐厅由你来决定。)

(3) ______________________________
(我等不及想要见你了。注意旅途安全。)

Love,
Renee

Part 4 真题练习

Exercise 1

Read the following writing task and underline the key words or phrases.

You should spend about 20 minutes on this task.

You have just spent a weekend at a friend's place. When you returned home, you

discovered that you have left a coat containing some belongings in his house.

Write a letter to your friend. In your letter,

- **tell him that you left the coat behind**
- **explain what the coat looks like**
- **make some suggestions about how to get the coat back**

Write at least 150 words.

You do **NOT** need to write any addresses.

Begin your letter as follows:

Dear . . . ,

Exercise 2

Do the following writing task.

You should spend about 20 minutes on this task.

A family member is coming to stay with you. He/She will be arriving by train in the morning, but you won't be home until the evening.

Write a letter to your relative. In your letter,

- **explain arrangements you have made for them to have keys and get into the house**
- **tell your relative how to get from the train station to your house**
- **say when you will be home and suggest what you could do together that evening**

Write at least 150 words.

You do **NOT** need to write any addresses.

Begin your letter as follows:

Dear . . . ,

Section 4 Letter of Request

Part 1 写作要点指导

请求信(Letter of Request)是雅思写作中常见的信件形式之一,通常是写信给他人,请求他人帮助,通常是请求朋友代为照顾自己的宠物,请朋友帮助自己找工作,等等。因此,语气要礼貌客气。

此类书信一般都由三大部分组成:

(1) 介绍写作目的,描述自己遇到怎样的情况,或者自己面临怎样的问题。

(2) 表示自己需要对方的帮助,并希望对方同意。

(3) 详细解释说明对方如何才能帮助自己。

Part 2 范文解析

Writing Task

You should spend about 20 minutes on this task.

A friend has agreed to look after your house and pet while you are on holiday.

Write a letter to your friend. In your letter,

- **give contact details for your friend when you are away**
- **give instructions about how to care for your pet**
- **describe other household duties**

Write at least 150 words.

You do **NOT** need to write any addresses.

Begin your letter as follows:

Dear . . . ,

Sample Letter

Dear Joan,

Thank you so much for honouring my request to take care of my place while I am away. I really appreciate your kind gesture. ①

I am writing to brief you about the main chores you will have to do in my absence. As you probably already know, I keep an aquarium at home. So your most important task is to take care of my fish. They mean a lot to me! Basically, all that you need to do is to feed them and clean their water filter. As for the food, just fill up the feeder every other day. It is located at the top right of the aquarium; you can't miss it! As for the filter, you need to clean it once every 3 days. ②

Other than that, there isn't much to do. It would be great if you could keep the place clean. There are two trash bins in the kitchen. Put the leftover food and other waste in the blue bin and recyclable items in the green one. The garbage man will come and collect them every day. ③ If you have any other questions, please don't hesitate to contact. I will be available via email or phone. ④

Many thanks,

Ruby⑤

范文解析

① 介绍写信的背景是对方答应了自己的请求,并对此表示感谢。

② 根据题目要求，请求对方照顾自己的宠物。

③ 详细介绍了其他的一些家务活。

④ 向对方说明，有问题可以随时联系自己。

⑤ 由于是朋友之间的通信，属于非正式的信件，因此落款参考称呼选用 Many thanks，署名不必用全名。

Part 3 句型练习

常用词汇句型点拨

(1) **I am writing to brief you about** the main chores you will have to do in my absence.

(2) **As you probably already know**, I keep an aquarium at home.

(3) **All that you need to do is to** feed them and clean their water filter.

(4) **As for** the food, just fill up the feeder every other day.

(5) **Other than that,** there isn't much to do.

(6) **It would be great if** you **could** keep the place clean.

(7) They would pass their time watching TV or playing video games. So **you should have no trouble** keeping them busy throughout the day.

(8) In the morning, **you could perhaps** let him have a bowl of cereals.

(9) **If you have any other questions, please don't hesitate to contact.**

(10) **I will be available via email or phone.**

句子翻译

☺ 使用给出的句型，把下列中文句子翻译成英文。

Example:

我写信来向你简要描述我想找的工作。(I am writing to brief you about . . .)

• I'm writing to brief you about the kind of job I am looking for.

(1) 也许你已经知道了，我将出发去夏威夷度过一个为期两周的假期。(As you probably already know, . . .)

____

(2) 你需要做的全部事情就是每天早上遛我的贵宾狗(poodle)，为了能让它保持健康。(All that you need to do is to . . .)

____

(3) 至于草坪，你需要每隔两至三天给它浇一次水。(As for . . .)

____

(4) 除此之外，你只需要照看女孩儿们并保证她们安全。(Other than that, . . .)

____

(5) 如果你能为我说几句好话，那就太好了。(It would be great if . . .)

____

(6) 你和我的室友交流应该没有问题,因为他英语讲得还不错。(You should have no trouble doing . . .)

____

(7) 你可以给他讲一些睡前故事来安慰他。(You could perhaps . . .)

____

文中句子翻译

把下列中文句子翻译成英文。

Dear Annie,

Thanks very much for your last letter — it was great to hear from you and to hear all your news. You seem to be enjoying your time off work.

I am busy as usual. In fact, I am going on a six day business trip next Sunday. Do you think you could take care of my boys while I am away? I am not exactly comfortable about leaving them in a day care centre. That's why I am asking your help. If you think you could babysit, I will drop them at your place on Sunday morning.

They are very easy-going and get on well with everybody — they are particularly fond of you. (1) ____
(至于他们的饮食习惯,他们不太喜欢蔬菜,但他们的确会吃水果和麦片。) So you should have no trouble keeping them full throughout the day. You also don't have to worry about keeping them busy. They would pass their time watching TV or playing video games.
(2) ____
(晚上你或许可以带他们散步。)I will be back in town on Thursday evening and pick them up from your place on my way home from the airport.

(3) ____(我希望你不介意为我做这件事。)

Hope to hear from you soon.

Many thanks

Marina

Part 4 真题练习

Exercise 1

Read the following writing task and underline the key words or phrases.

You should spend about 20 minutes on this task.

You are going to another country to study. You would like to do a part-time job while you are studying, so you want to ask a friend who lives there for some help.

Write a letter to this friend. In your letter,

- **give details of your study plans**
- **explain why you want to get a part-time job**
- **suggest how your friend could help you find a job**

Write at least 150 words.

You do **NOT** need to write any addresses.

Begin your letter as follows:

Dear . . . ,

Exercise 2

Do the following writing task.

You should spend about 20 minutes on this task.

You are planning to organize an event in the countryside.

Write a letter to your friend asking him/her to help you with your arrangements. In your letter you have to explain:

- **the reason for organizing the event**
- **the arrangements you have already made**
- **what your friend can do to help you**
- **what activities you have decided on**

Write at least 150 words.

You do **NOT** need to write any addresses.

Begin your letter as follows:

Dear . . . ,

Section 5 Letter of Invitation

Part 1 写作要点指导

邀请信(Letter of Invitation)是雅思写作中常见的信件形式之一。涵盖的范围比较广泛,有写给朋友的非正式的信件,如:邀请朋友来家里玩,邀请朋友和自己一起旅游,等等。也有正式的信件,如:邀请教授来做演讲,等等。

此类书信一般都由三大部分组成:

(1) 开门见山,写明邀请对方来做什么事,也可以写邀请对方的原因。

(2) 根据具体的题目要求,描述一些细节。

（3）确定行程安排，并询问对方是否同意。

Part 2 范文解析

Writing Task

You should spend about 20 minutes on this task.

You have recently moved to a different house.

Write a letter to an English-speaking friend. In your letter,

- **explain why you have moved**
- **describe the new house**
- **invite your friend to come and visit**

Write at least 150 words.

You do **NOT** need to write any addresses.

Begin your letter as follows:

Dear . . . ,

Sample Letter

Dear Jamie,

Sorry, I haven't written to you for so long. I have been quite busy over the last few months. How are you doing? I hope everything is okay. ①

We just moved to our new home. As you probably know, I had been searching for a new home for a while. My old home was a long way away from my office. In fact, the daily commute used to take nearly two hours. Now that my wife has also started working, we decided to buy an apartment in the suburb. ②

It is a spacious apartment with two bedrooms and a balcony. Also it is only a 5 minutes' walk from our offices. Of course, the best thing about this home is its balcony. We can host small parties there. Also it is a great place to unwind after spending a stressful day at work. ③

Well, why do I have to rant on and on about my new residence? Can't you visit us over the weekend and see it for yourself? It would be fun to have you here. ④

Looking forward to your visit.

Best

Arthur⑤

范文解析

① 开头可以先向对方问好,并告诉对方自己的近况。

② 告诉对方自己最近搬家了,并解释了搬家的理由。

③ 描述了自己的新家。

④ 按照题目要求,邀请对方来自己的新家玩。

⑤ 由于是朋友之间的通信,属于非正式的信件,因此落款参考称呼选用 Best,署名不必用全名。

Part 3 句型练习

常用词汇句型点拨

(1) I am writing to invite you to . . .

(2) Now that . . .

(3) You are the ideal person to . . .

(4) The best thing about . . . is . . .

(5) to see it for yourself

(6) be scheduled

句子翻译

使用给出的句型,把下列中文句子翻译成英文。

Example:

我写信来邀请您在我们的年度慈善捐款会上发表演讲。(I am writing to invite you to . . .)

- I am writing to invite you to make a speech at our annual charity donation meeting.

(1) 既然我已经定居下来了,那么你在造访纽约期间,为什么不和我住在一起呢?(Now that . . .)

____

(2) 您有着国际声誉,并且在年轻人中有积极的影响力,您是理想的人选来鼓励年轻人将他们能负担得起的钱款捐给慈善机构。(You are the ideal person to . . .)

____

(3) 去瑞士阿尔卑斯山的旅程的最好的一部分就是我们可以滑雪。(The best thing about . . . is . . .)

____

(4) 也许下周四你可以和我一起去画廊,你自己看看,这样你就可以对这些画的细节有一些确切的了解。(to see it for yourself)

____

(5) 你的航班被安排在周二下午三点,我们会在中午十二点左右来你的住处接你。

(be scheduled)

文中句子翻译

把下列中文句子翻译成英文。

Dear Paul,

I've got some really exciting news to share with you. Guess what? I've won a holiday for two people in a competition. (1) ________________________________
(我确实希望你能和我一起去。)
All I had to do to win the competition was to write a slogan for a local travel agency. My winning submission was "Fly LTC and see the world". As I said, my prize is a holiday and it is a cruise around the Mediterranean for a fortnight. The ship is the latest luxury liner and has all sorts of entertainment facilities including a swimming pool, a cinema complex and onboard tennis courts. (2) ________________________________
(这听上去似乎应该会十分有趣。)

(3) ________________________________
(我真的很希望你今年暑假有空。) I'd love it if you could come with me, as it sounds just your cup of tea and you could always act as an interpreter for me when we get to Spain!

I need to book the cruise quite soon, so just drop me a line if you are free.

All the best
Ann

Part 4 真题练习

Exercise 1

Read the following writing task and underline the key words or phrases.
You should spend about 20 minutes on this task.

Writing a letter to invite one of your friends to attend a large celebration at your home.

In your letter,

- **state the reason why the celebration is held**
- **state all details about the celebration**
- **also, ask your friend to do a favor for you**

Write at least 150 words.

You do **NOT** need to write any addresses.

Begin your letter as follows:

Dear . . . ,

Exercise 2

Do the following writing task.

You should spend about 20 minutes on this task.

You won a competition and received a vacation for two as a prize. Write a letter to a friend to ask him/her to go on holiday with you.

In your letter, you should:

- **tell him/her about the competition you won**
- **state what kind of vacation it is**
- **explain why you would like him/her to go on holiday with you**

Write at least 150 words.

You do **NOT** need to write any addresses.

Begin your letter as follows:

Dear . . . ,

Section 6 Letter from a Friend

Part 1 写作要点指导

友情信(Letter of Friendship)是雅思写作中常见的信件形式之一。涵盖的范围比较广泛,如:为朋友安排旅程,就朋友的某个个人问题提出建议,约定下次碰面的时间,等等。由于是写给朋友的非正式的信件,故写作风格可以相对轻松。

此类书信一般都由三大部分组成:

(1) 开头可以先向对方问好,问问对方的近况,也可以向朋友简单地介绍一下自己的近况。

(2) 根据具体的题目要求,交代写信的主要目的。

(3) 描述一些细节,可以给出一些建议、提醒,等等。

Part 2 范文解析

Writing Task

You should spend about 20 minutes on this task.

During a recent visit to your home, your friend forgot something at your place. Write a letter to your friend explaining the situation. In your letter you have to mention:

- **what your friend forgot**
- **where the item is now**

- **a proposed arrangement to return the item**

Write at least 150 words.

You do **NOT** need to write any addresses.

Begin your letter as follows:

Dear . . . ,

Sample Letter

Dear Gina

Thanks a lot for a great weekend. We really enjoyed your company. It brought back a lot of fond memories of our college days when we would spend alternate weekends at each other's place. ①

There is yet another reason for writing this letter. I don't know if you have already noticed it, but you have left a few books behind. They are still sitting on the coffee table where you left them. ②

I know you are an avid reader and carry your books wherever you go. I was wondering if you would need them urgently. ③ In that case, we will have to arrange a time to meet. You can visit our place any time. Although I will be in the office, you will be able to collect the books from my wife. ④ Now in case you are busy, we can send them to your place. ⑤ Let me know which arrangement suits you better. ⑥

See you soon, I hope. Thanks again.

Best

Antony⑦

范文解析

① 交代写作背景,是和对方一起度过了一个愉快的周末。

② 交代写这封信的主要目的是告诉对方她有一些书落在自己家里了。

③ 询问对方是否急需这本书。

④ 表示对方可以来自己家里取这本书。

⑤ 表示如果对方很忙,没有时间来取书的话,自己也可以将书寄给对方。

⑥ 请对方告知自己哪种安排更合适。

⑦ 由于是朋友之间的通信,属于非正式的信件,因此落款参考称呼选用 Best,署名不必用全名。

Part 3 句型练习

常用词汇句型点拨

(1) **I am so happy to learn that** you are coming to New York for the coming holiday.

(2) **I regret to tell you that** I will not be able to stay with you while you are here.

(3) **I was wondering if** you **would** need them urgently.

(4) **In that case**, we will have to arrange a time to meet.

(5) **In case** you are busy, we can send them to your place.

(6) **I suggest that** ... **should do** ...

(7) Finally, **a kind reminder —** as the weather in Bombay is getting hotter, you had better bring your sunglasses and sunblock with you.

句子翻译

使用给出的句型,把下列中文句子翻译成英文。

Example:

我很高兴我赢得了两张飞往洛杉矶的机票。(I am so happy to learn that ...)

- I am so happy to learn that I've won two tickets to Los Angles.

(1) 我很遗憾地告诉你我不能来机场接你了,因为那天我和我的牙医有约。(I regret to tell you that ...)

____

(2) 我想知道你是否能在我不在城里的时候送我的儿子 Ian 去上学。(be wondering if ... would ...)

____

(3) 在那样的情况下,我会需要你带一些食物来聚会。(In that case, ...)

____

(4) 假使你到达时我正好不在家,你可以在门垫下面找到钥匙。(In case ...)

____

(5) 我建议你明天去看医生。(I suggest ... should do ...)

____

(6) 最后,友情提示——由于明天可能会有交通堵塞,你最好早一点儿离开酒店。(a kind reminder-)

____

文中句子翻译

把下列中文句子翻译成英文。

Dear Lilian,

I hope this letter finds you in good spirits. Sorry I haven't written to you for so long. I've

been quite busy over the last year. (1) ______________________________
(既然我已经完成了我的学业,我可以说闲了下来。)

(2) ______________________________
(我写这封信的原因是想请你帮个小忙。)I've just discovered that there is a vacancy for an mechanical engineer in your company. I saw the advertisement in the newspaper. I'm interested in this position. As you know, I've always been into mechanics and that was the reason I decided to study mechanical engineering at university. I've got the necessary qualifications, so I guess I'm a deserving candidate.

Since you've been working with them for well over two years, I thought you'd be able to help me with the application process. Would you be willing to serve as a positive reference for me?

I hope you don't mind doing this for me. I don't know any other person who works at your company, so (3) ______________________________
(如果你能推荐我做这份工作,我会非常感激。)

I hope to hear from you soon.

Many thanks

Renee

Part 4 真题练习

Exercise 1

Read the following writing task and underline the key words or phrases.

You should spend about 20 minutes on this task.

You will leave the country you are living now and go back to your home country soon.

Write a letter to your sports centre team mates to say goodbye. In your letter,

- **explain why you have to go back to your home country**
- **say what you enjoyed with them in sports centre**
- **tell them when and how you will meet them again**

Write at least 150 words.

You do **NOT** need to write any addresses.

Begin your letter as follows:

Dear ...,

Exercise 2

Do the following writing task.

You should spend about 20 minutes on this task.

Your friend will visit you. Someone has given you two sport tickets.

Write a letter to your friend. In your letter,

- **present where you got those tickets and who gave them to you**
- **what is the sport event**
- **invite your friend to go with you**

Write at least 150 words.

You do **NOT** need to write any addresses.

Begin your letter as follows:

Dear . . . ,

Answer 答案

Chapter 1

Section 2

Part 1

练习 1

Overview：North America，Oceania，Latin America：Net Exporters

Europe，Near East，Africa，Far East：Net Importers

Key features：在 net exporters 中，北美的数据最大，超过 Oceania 和 Latin America 的总和，而后两者非常接近；在 net importers 中，欧洲居首位，Far East 局末位。

练习 2

Key words：moral obligation，aid money，poor

Part 2

练习 1

（1）表因果：in that，owing to，attributable to，since，as，for

（2）表转折：while，in spite of，despite，nevertheless，nonetheless

（3）表递进：what's more，in addition，in addition to，besides，apart from

（4）表类比：equally important，likewise，by the same token

（5）表对比：on the other hand，in contrast to，whereas，while，instead

（6）表举例：for instance，a case in point，as an illustration，to illustrate，take ... for example

（7）表强调：as a matter of fact，certainly，of course

（8）表解释：put another way，to put it another way，I mean，which means

（9）表条件：on the condition that，unless，in case，in the event that

（10）表目的：to the end that，for fear that，lest

（11）表总结：to conclude，in conclusion，in summary，all in all，in a word

练习 2

	conj.	prep.	adv.	verb phrase
cause	because since as	due to thanks to as a result of		result in lead to give rise to
effect	so so that		therefore as a consequence accordingly	result from be attributable to be credited to

(1) The air is severely polluted. Accordingly, people wear masks when they go out.

(2) Due to population explosion, the natural resources on earth have rapidly diminished.

(3) His facility for dealing with interpersonal relations resulted in his promotion to the position of Human Resources Manager.

(4) There might be a traffic jam, so I started an hour earlier.

练习 3

(1) preschoolers (上下义)

(2) economic development (词性转换)

(3) save energy (反义替换)

(4) a distant region (同义替换)

Part 3

练习 1

(1) novelty

(2) envious

(3) irritable

(4) intensify

(5) cancellation

(6) investigation

(7) pleasure

(8) memorable

(9) grieved

(10) precariously

练习 2

(1) make contributions to

(2) make progress in

(3) I remember clearly that

(4) The lions are roaring.

Chapter 2

Section 2

Part 1

练习 2

(1) Chinese people consume more tea than Americans. (SVO)

The consumption of tea in China is larger than that in America. (SVP)

(2) Boys spend more time watching sports programmes than girls. (SVO)

The time spent in watching sports programmes by boys is longer than that by girls. (SVP)

(3) In this company, more females than males possess a master's degree. (SVO)

In this company, the number of females who hold a master's degree is larger/greater than that of males. (SVP)

There are more females with a master's degree than males in this company. (There be 句型/SV)

(4) Women spend more money on cosmetic products and clothes than on electronic products. (SVO)

Women's expenditure on cosmetic products and clothes is higher/larger than that on electronic products. (SVP)

(5) Generally, Japanese men work longer than Chinese men. (SV)

Generally, the time spent on work by Japanese men is longer than that by Chinese men. (SVP)

3. 表格

Small difference: slightly, a bit, a little

Big difference: much, a lot, considerably, far

补充: Small difference: marginally

Big difference: remarkably, noticeably, significantly

练习 3

(1) Coffee in the UK is far more expensive than that in France.

(2) The cost of a coffee in Spain is slightly lower than that in France.

Part 2

练习 1

(1) French fries are not as expensive as hamburgers.

(2) Majorca is not as hot as Castellon.

(3) Northern trains are not as fast as southern trains.

练习 2

(1) The number of boys who love playing football is roughly 5 times as large as that of girls.

(2) The output of coffee in South America is approximately 3 times as large as that in Asia.

(3) Shipping companies gain over twice as much profit as retailers.

(4) The number of people with permanent jobs is 3 times as large as that of people with temporary jobs.

(5) The Britain residents' expenditure on food is around 4 times as high as on entertainment.

Part 3

练习 1

(1) The average price of a house in Sloane Square is around a fifth higher than that of a house in Notting Hill, at £620,000 and £500,000 respectively.

(2) Hip-hop music is around three times as popular as jazz music among 20 – 30-year-olds, at 35% and 11% respectively.

(3) Newark Airport was much less busy than JFK Airport in March, with 1.9 million and 2.9 million users respectively.

Part 6

(1) a: 2　b: 3　c: 5　d: 6　e: 4　f: 7　g: 1

(2) 20%: a fifth of/one in five/one out of five/one out of every five
25%: a quarter of/one in four/one out of four/one out of every four
50%: half of/one in two/one out of two/one out of every two

Part 7

练习 1

(1) place
(2) list
(3) one
(4) list
(5) place

Section 3

Part 1

Key Points

(1) The two bakeries, the 8 items sold
(2) 8 items
(3) Sales

(4) Bernie's Buns sold more items than Lovely Loaves. Doughnuts were the most popular while toasted sandwiches were the least.

(5) The sale of Bernie's Buns was better than that of Lovely Loaves in all except fresh loaves and salads.

(6) Sweet snacks and savoury snacks

(7) Bernie's Buns first, Lovely Loaves second; or in order of sales of items.

(8) Sales: sold, sell, buy, purchase, etc.

Part 4

练习

(1) The table given illustrates how the proportion of families living in poverty varies with family types in Australia in 1999.

(2) The first pie graph provides the information about energy use in an ordinary Australian family and the second demonstrates the resulting greenhouse gas emissions.

(3) The bar chart indicates that adults study for 8 different purposes and the pie chart shows the division of education cost among three parties.

Chapter 3

Section 2

Part 1

练习 1

表示"上升/增加"	表示"下降/减少"	表示"大幅度上升/增加"	表示"大幅度下降/减少"
rose went up grew improved increased	declined dropped fell went down decreased	rocketed shot up jumped soared surged doubled	halved plummeted plunged

练习 2

(1) considerably; drastically; dramatically; remarkably; sharply; significantly; strikingly

(2) marginally; slightly; negligibly

(3) modestly; moderately

(4) rapidly

(5) gradually

(6) steadily

练习 3

(1) a rise

(2) a fall

(3) a levelling-off

(4) a decline

(5) a soar

(6) a plummet
(7) an increase
(8) a drop
(9) a fluctuation
(10) a plunge
(11) a decrease
(12) a dip
(13) a recovery
(14) a jump
(15) a surge
(16) growth

练习 4

(1) dramatic
(2) considerable
(3) steady
(4) negligible
(5) remarkable

练习 5

(1) at
(2) at
(3) until
(4) to
(5) by
(6) from
(7) to
(8) at
(9) between
(10) to
(11) at
(12) at

练习 6

If we look at Bernie's Buns, income started **at** £20,000 in 2000, and then there was a slight rise **to** £25,000 in 2001. At this point, the figure fell back **to** just over £20,000, followed by a slight increase **to** just under £40,000. Earnings then levelled off **at** £39,000, and then fell marginally **to** £38,000. Income then rose **by** £23,000, **from** £38,000 **to** £61,000. In the next two years there was a gradual rise **to** around £62,000, and then the figure peaked **at** around £65,000.

练习 7

(1) that considerably more people were employed in it than in the other sectors of the

economy.

(2) the peak percentage of employment over the whole period.

(3) to just under 50%.

(4) that a significantly lower percentage of people were employed in it than in the other sectors of employment.

Part 2

练习 1

(1) The graph shows data about the number of DVDs which were sold in the UK and the USA between 2005 and 2008.

(2) The graph shows information about how much chocolate was produced in Colombia from 1997 to 2007.

The graph shows data about the amount of chocolate which was produced in Colombia between 1997 and 2007.

衔接手段

先后顺序: Following this, after which, At this point, Next, this was followed by, Subsequently

练习 2

(1) Income began at just over £80,000 and then it went up slightly to £95,000 in 2001.

(2) There was a steady fall to £80,000, after which income recovered to £90,000 in 2004.

(3) Earnings dropped sharply to just over £60,000. At this point, there was a slight dip.

(4) There was a slight rise to just under 60,000. Subsequently, the figure went down considerably.

(5) Income fell significantly to £40,000. Next, the number levelled off.

练习 3

(1) With respect to the income of Robbie's Bakery, it began at just under £60,000.

(2) If we look at the amount of money which was earned by Bernie's Buns in 2000, it was £20,000.

(3) As for the earnings of Robbie's Bakery, they remained stable during the first five years of the graph.

(4) Regarding the income for Lovely Loaves, it fluctuated considerably between 2000 and 2005.

Section 3

Part 1

Key Points

(1) time

(2) the size of land for organic food

(3) kept on increasing until 1995, and then remained relatively stable

(4) kept on increasing until 2000 and then remained relatively stable before an abrupt decrease since 2005.

(5) Between 1985 and 1995, the trend was similar and the figure in 2010 was similar.

(6) 25 thousand hectares in 1985, 170 thousand hectares in 1995 and around 150 thousand hectares in 2010, which showed similarities. 180 thousand hectares and 280 thousand hectares in 2000, which showed the peak

(7) first, the information of the period from 1985 to 1995, which showed the similarities between the two countries, and then the rest years, which showed the differences.

(8) size: area, (how much) hectares

Chapter 4

Section 1

Part 2

(一)

练习 1

(1) Canada is in the north of North America.

(2) Hainan Island is to the south of Guangdong Province.

(3) Texas is in the south of the US.

练习 2

(1) Ohio lies on the west of Pennsylvania.

(2) Germany is located on the east of France.

(3) Britain lies to the west of the European Continent.

练习 3

(1) The shed is on the border of the national park.

(2) An expensive department store is located in the center of London.

(3) The factory is situated on the border of the town.

(4) The library lies on the edge of the campus.

(5) The gym is located in the middle of the neighborhood.

练习 4

(1) The swimming pool lies in the vicinity of the yard.

(2) The drug store is located in the proximity of the hospital.

(3) My neighbor's yard is adjacent to ours.

练习 5

(1) In the vicinity of the museum lies a small shop, where visitors can buy a variety of souvenirs.

(2) In the proximity of the greengrocer's is a seafood market with fresh oysters and lobsters available.

练习 6

(1) The pavement is parallel to Lane Crawford.

(2) The two roads intersect near the fountain.

(3) Marbury Road is parallel to Orchard Street.

练习 7

(1) The coach can hold 20 passengers at most.

(2) The hospital wards have a capacity of 60 patients.

(3) There are enough rooms to accommodate 80 travelers in the hotel.

(二)

练习 1

(1) After the reconstruction, the number of the guest rooms rose to 15.

(2) The number of bus stations reduced by 5% in three years.

(3) The hotel rooms have been doubled to accommodate more travelers.

练习 2

(1) The narrow path was expanded into a wide road.

(2) My neighbor has enlarged his lawn.

(3) Now there is a better working environment with an enlarged office.

练习 3

(1) The size of the town center shrunk greatly in 2005.

(2) The tropical rain forest has reduced by half in the past ten years.

(3) The lounge has been halved to make room for the new duty-free shop.

练习 4

(1) A bookshop appeared in the vicinity of the primary school two years later.

(2) A cloakroom emerged beside the stairs.

练习 5

(1) There is a great change in the campus. The canteen has disappeared.

(2) The shopping mall, together with its parking lot, has vanished.

练习 6

(1) The stadium has been moved to the city center.

(2) They decided to relocate the factory in the countryside.

Section 2

Part 2

练习 1

动词	过去分词	动词	过去分词
grow	grown	hold	held
sow	sown	grind	ground

续表

动词	过去分词	动词	过去分词
sell	sold	put	put
take	taken	cut	cut
wrap	wrapped	weave	woven

练习 2

(1) Oranges are exported from Spain to colder countries in Europe.

(2) Coffee beans are ground in a machine in order to be made into coffee powder.

(3) Rice is put into bags and then delivered to supermarkets.

(4) Bars of chocolate are wrapped in silver paper and put into boxes.

练习 3

Next	The first stage is	The last stage is
Then Subsequently After that At this point The next step is that Following this The following step is that and then after which	First of all The first step is that To begin with Initially	Finally The last step is

练习 4

(1) Once the tea leaves have been picked, they are then put in the sun to dry.

(2) After the tea leaves have been picked from the tea plants, they are (then) packed into boxes.

(3) When the boxes have been loaded onto a lorry, they are then taken to supermarkets.

(4) Once you have put the tea bag in the cup, you can then pour hot water into it.

练习 5

(1) The fruit is sent to a factory, where it is put into cans.

(2) The biscuits are put in the oven in order to be cooked.

(3) The farmer waters the plants, which makes them grow more quickly.

(4) The mushrooms are stored in a dark room, so that they stay fresh.

Chapter 5

Section 1

Part 4

(1) He is a selfish person without any consideration for others.

(2) Children could learn self-control and discipline in group activities.

(3) It is the basic requirement for students to have respect for teachers and obey school rules.

(4) Schools offer a space for children of a similar age to interact with each other, to make friends and to learn how to get on with each other.

(5) For many students, graduating from high school means being economically independent and coping with the challenge all by themselves.

(6) Nowadays, when choosing staff, we not only emphasize the academic qualifications of a person, but also his practical ability.

(7) Children acquire their mother tongue on the basis of knowledge and experience.

(8) Linguists have studied the way children pick up a language, and found something useful for adults.

(9) People studying aboard have a boarder view of life and better personal resources to draw on.

(10) Everyone should invest some time in community service.

(11) You can achieve nothing without enthusiasm.

(12) She has a good command of French.

(13) Math is a compulsory subject for many college students.

(14) Lifelong learning is essential for employability.

(15) Our only choice is whether to be a good role model or a bad one.

(16) Teachers should teach their students not to bully others.

(17) Universities often require their graduates to pursue knowledge for life at the graduation ceremony.

(18) I hope to do a chemistry degree.

(19) There are only 5 students who have enrolled in this course.

(20) He secured a position in a store at US $400 a week.

(21) Many people suffered from cultural shock when they went abroad.

(22) Students must have access to a library.

(23) We will have some vocational training before graduation.

Part 5

Step 1 练习

(1) 关键词：in group, alone, benefits, more effective

逻辑：观点对比

(2) 关键词: college, university, best, leave school as soon as possible, through work experience

逻辑: 观点对比

(3) 关键词: evaluate, criticize, improve the quality, loss of respect

逻辑: 观点对比

(4) 关键词: difficult, concentrate, pay attention, reasons, solve

逻辑: 现象+原因+解决方法

(5) 关键词: difficult, concentrate, pay attention, reasons, solve

逻辑: 现象+观点

Section 2

Part 4

(1) Most old people are computer illiterate, so we need to encourage them to learn computer knowledge.

(2) The biggest benefit of face-to-face teaching is that it can facilitate communication.

(3) Significant breakthroughs have been made since the Industrial Revolution.

(4) Students spend most of their spare time surfing the Internet.

(5) Being indulged in the cyber world would deprive students of interest in study.

(6) Radiation from electronic products causes a negative effect on people's health.

(7) The use of security cameras in shops prevents shoplifting to a great extent.

(8) The advanced science and technology have opened door for rural women to become rich.

(9) Scientific inventions can benefit mankind; on the other hand, they sometimes bring disasters.

(10) When some people upload other people's photographs onto social network sites, they do not realize their actions have invaded others' privacy.

(11) The police have been keeping him under surveillance.

(12) New development in technology helps make life easier.

(13) Discovering a cure for AIDS would be a major medical advance.

(14) All new medical advances are potentially unsafe, and no progress would be made if safety alone were the issue.

Chapter 6

Section 1

Part 4

(1) We find ourselves surrounded by all kinds of advertisements.

(2) The government should impose strict restrictions on advertisements.

(3) It is extremely costly to run an advertisement.

(4) Advertising boosts the sales of goods and it encourages people to buy things that

they don't really need.

(5) They cannot be swayed by those advertisements.

(6) An overwhelming number of advertisements regard children as the target group.

(7) It is undeniable that the modern mass media has a huge impact on our daily life and society.

(8) It seems that bad news dominates the headlines of all kinds of media.

(9) It is no doubt that the juveniles who read these magazines will have a wrong worldview.

(10) Much detailed crime coverage is biased or exaggerated.

(11) The principle purpose of reporters covering criminal acts is to boost newspaper circulations or television rating.

(12) If such reports continue to go uncontrolled, they will exert even more baneful influence on individuals.

(13) People can learn about what is happening around the world simultaneously by watching TV.

(14) Youngsters will imitate the scenes and actions of violence and crimes in TV programs, thus becoming criminals.

(15) TV programs can cultivate children's creativity and ability to tackle difficulty.

Section 2

Part 4

(1) He's been released from prison.

(2) Teenagers sometimes fail to make accurate judgments due to their immaturity.

(3) Teenagers are liable to imitate the violent scenes on TV and in movies.

(4) When teenagers become addicted to playing computer games, they need a great amount of money to support this.

(5) Indulging in the unreal world, teenagers are likely to become increasingly isolated from others.

(6) Parents are so engaged in their work that they spend little time with their children.

(7) Actions, such as strict censorship on the press, should be taken for the sake of preventing teenagers from committing crimes.

(8) However, adolescents are quite rebellious and unwilling to follow their parents' will.

(9) An increasing number of people have begun to challenge against the existing practice of capital punishment.

(10) The record of crime rate has been constantly renewed.

(11) We should retain the practice of putting criminals into prison.

(12) The juvenile delinquency can be attributed to the rising divorce rate and family violence.

Chapter 7

Section 1

Part 4

(1) Climate change not only has a severe impact on human, but also devastates the natural world and leads to the extinction of endangered species.

(2) We have already seen in many parts of the world that soil erosion has led to food shortages .

(3) *It should not be forgotten that* illegal logging *in the Amazon Basin is still a major factor for* deforestation.

(4) Individuals can make a small contribution to the environmental protection by reducing the use of fossil fuels.

(5) *It is no longer possible to say that* human activity *does not affect weather conditions.*

(6) *An obvious solution is to* employ more wind and solar power.

(7) *Wind energy and other sources of renewable energy* will help to reduce carbon dioxide emissions to an acceptable level.

(8) It isn't difficult to improve the energy efficiency of your home.

(9) *Investment in renewable resources will help* avert the impact *of the carbon dioxide emissions.*

(10) Non-biodegradable material does not decay or dissolve awaynaturally.

(11) Environmental protection has been caught in a vicious circle in some places.

(12) Scientists are wondering what effects global warming will have on the biosphere.

(13) Major efforts are being made to protect the endangered species.

(14) The environment may be permanently damaged because of air pollution.

(15) Accelerated soil erosion may affect the environment in agricultural areas.

(16) They pursue profit at the cost of the environment.

Section 2

Part 4

(1) In many developed countries, education and health care are funded by the government.

(2) It is widely believed that the authorities should be responsible for the gap between the rich and the poor.

(3) Many people doubt whether it is worth investing in art.

(4) They think preserving historic buildings is a complete waste of public money.

(5) I spent two months doing volunteer work in a small village in West Africa.

(6) NGOs should be encouraged to spend money on humanitarian projects.

(7) Compared with developed countries, developing countries rely more on agriculture.

(8) It took years to recover from economic crisis.

(9) Industrialization can have negative effects such as environmental pollution.

(10) It is a matter of utmost importance for them to find their way out of poverty.

(11) It is obviously impossible for an impoverished country to sponsor artists while the majority of people are living under the poverty line.

(12) As the poverty problem has been solved, it is time to raise the living standard.

(13) Governments ought to take practical actions to satisfy the basic needs of people from all walks of life.

(14) Many industrialized countries give help to their poor counterparts regularly.

(15) In face of severe fiscal problems, they had to seek help from other countries.

Chapter 8

Section 1

Part 4

(1) In this case, a woman may not have much time for work since she has to bring up her child all by herself.

(2) Parenting can be more stressful for single parents.

(3) Sibling rivalry often causes parents anxieties.

(4) The importance of nuclear families is replacing that of extended families, which is a great social change.

(5) Labor unions should be independent from the government.

(6) No matter what they major in, most graduates hope to work in an office. In other words, they want to be white-collar workers.

(7) People go to night schools in an attempt to better themselves.

(8) Those who lack related experience are likely to encounter difficulties when hunting for a job.

(9) Surveys show that most job-hoppers agree that money is the prime concern.

(10) The high income of sports stars can be justified since their career life-span is relatively short.

(11) Some people assert that the price of daily necessities should remain stable.

(12) People are swarming into big cities for the sake of better job opportunities.

(13) In the past few years, cities have been expanding at an unprecedented rate.

(14) Individuals should pay a higher proportion of their medical cost to ease the financial burden of the government.

(15) Feasible measures should be taken to prevent overpopulation.

(16) Studies show that overwork can lead to stress-related illness, such as insomnia.

Section 2

Part 4 句子翻译

(1) There must be equal opportunities for boy and girl students in college education.

(2) Engaging in school activities allows students to learn to cooperate and compromise.

(3) Some educators believe that young children should be sent to school earlier so that they won't be too reliant on their parents.

(4) There is an increasing trend for parents to send their children to study abroad in order to broaden their horizons.

(5) Even those who have been in the industry for years have to take the on-the-job training to keep their skills fresh and up-to-date.

(6) To balance entertainment and study doesn't mean that students should give up watching TV completely.

(7) With the increase of aging population, the government is having difficulty in paying pensions.

(8) Age discrimination must be eliminated in the labor market.

(9) The use of smart phones, laptops and other electronic devices can distract students from study.

(10) As the young population is exploding, the government needs to create more job opportunities.

(11) Young children need their parents' supervision since they do not have strong self-control.

(12) It is not true that all TV programs have an adverse impact on children for some of these programs are edifying.

(13) Now entertainment stars and sports starts are becoming more and more influential in our society.

(14) Peer pressure can be one of the reasons for children's bad behavior at school.

(15) Both husbands and wives ought to take the responsibilities of doing housework and looking after their children.

(16) There is growing concern over children who are addicted to video games.

(17) Most elderly people are computer illiterate, so we should encourage them to learn computer skills.

Section 3

Part 4

(1) The advantage of inviting foreign companies to establish subsidiaries is that it would bring more job opportunities to local people.

(2) It is more convenient to arrange a trip now than in the past since people can book airplane tickets and hotel rooms online.

(3) Some travel agencies hire English-speaking guides to attract international tourists.

(4) Tourism may have adverse effect on environment as some tourists drop litter on the ground.

(5) One of the best ways to learn about the culture of a foreign country is to take a trip to that country.

(6) Some people think that public money should be spent on more important things such as education and health care rather than on the restoration of historical buildings.

(7) We should also learn a foreign country's culture when we learn its language because culture and language are inextricable.

(8) As English has become a global language, people from different countries can communicate more efficiently.

(9) Museums should also be recreational to attract visitors; otherwise people may choose other activities to pass time.

(10) Those against globalization argue that a country is likely to lose its national identity by following the trend of globalization.

(11) Local governments benefit from charging foreign visitors more money than the locals.

(12) Tourism will inevitably affect the local ecological system to some degree.

(13) Multinational companies will compete with domestic companies for market share.

(14) These days, people rarely visit museums since there are plenty of other activities they can do to kill time, such as watching movies and playing video games.

(15) Multinational companies spread latest and most advanced technologies around the world.

(16) One way to learn about a different culture is to read books written by authors from that particular culture.

Chapter 9

Section 1

Part 3

	informal	**semi-formal**	**formal**
greeting	Hi Mum	Dear Mike	Dear Sir or Madam
opening statement	Thanks for the parcel, it just arrived!	I'm afraid I won't be able to attend the meeting next week.	I'm writing in response to your advertisement.
closing statement	I can't wait to see you next week.	I'm looking forward to getting back to work.	I look forward to your reply
ending	Lots of love	Kind regards	Yours sincerely

Section 2

Part 3

句子翻译

(1) I am writing to express my dissatisfaction about the product.

(2) At the beginning, I got on well with my neighbors.

(3) I couldn't tolerate the non-stop noise they made day and night.

(4) It was inconceivable that the repairman asked me to pay such a high fee.

(5) It was completely out of my expectation that the facilities in this famous five-star hotel were so shabby.

(6) The guide was a troublemaker — he always led me to the wrong direction.

(7) I demand that you should take some remedial actions.

(8) Please send a repairman to my house as soon as possible.

文中句子翻译

(1) I am writing to complain about a tour organized by your company between the 1st and 7th of May this year.

(2) The food in the restaurant was similarly disappointing.

(3) I trust you will take my complaints seriously and make every effort to improve your service in the future.

Section 3

Part 3

句子翻译

(1) I'd like to know if it is possible for you to provide me with information regarding the performance.

(2) I take great interest in the international exchange student project.

(3) Could you tell me more details of the application for accommodation?

(4) It would be highly appreciated if you could send me a map of Greece.

(5) I am greatly concerned about whether the insurance company would cover my loss.

(6) Thank you for your time and consideration.

文中句子翻译

(1) I would like to receive some information about the forthcoming Qing Dynasty exhibition at your museum.

(2) (I) have a particular interest in this period/take great interest in this period

(3) I would also like to know if you have any written documents dating back to this period in your archives.

Section 4

Part 3

句子翻译

(1) I am writing in reply to your request.

(2) I would like to express my views concerning the project.

(3) I would like to see more improvements in your menu.

(4) You may consider redesigning the website.

(5) If I were you, I would hire a salesman.

文中句子翻译

(1) I think it would be great if you stayed with me and my family

(2) If I were you, I'd spend some days on the beach relaxing and one or two days sightseeing in the city.

(3) You ought to go to our excellent theme park, which is about an hour away by bus.

Section 5

Part 3

句子翻译

(1) I am writing in response to your advertisement in *Shanghai Daily*.

(2) I would like to apply for the position of barista.

(3) I graduated from the University of Leeds with a master's degree in architecture.

(4) I have been working in finance since my graduation and have therefore attained a fair knowledge and experience in this filed.

(5) I am experienced in engineering, which I believe qualifies me for the position of senior engineer.

文中句子翻译

(1) I am looking for a part-time job and I wonder if you could help me.

(2) I have the ability to work in a team environment.

(3) I would be ready to start immediately.

Chapter 10

Section 1

Part 3

句子翻译

(1) I am writing to show my sincere apology for not being able to attend the party you held last Sunday.

(2) The date for my interview happened to be the day when you held the party.

(3) Considering the interview was a chance in a lifetime, I had to miss your party.

(4) To remedy this unpleasant matter, my friends offered to clean up your apartment.

(5) The main reason why I was late for the interview was that I was caught in a traffic jam.

(6) I did not realise how much noise would be made by the jazz band I hired.

(7) I would also explain that I had called the landlord to explain the situation, but he never answered the phone.

(8) Please accept my apologies and I assure you that tomorrow I will be punctual.

文中句子翻译

(1) I am extremely sorry that we couldn't meet yesterday.

(2) Let me explain what happened.

(3) Unfortunately, we had to make some changes to our itinerary and consequently we were late.

Section 2

Part 3

句子翻译

(1) I sincerely appreciate your assistance during the past three months.

(2) I wouldn't have succeeded without your generous help.

(3) I must also mention the savory beef stew chef Li prepared.

(4) I am also very much grateful to you for giving me such good advice.

(5) We, in particular, were satisfied with the furniture and decorations.

(6) I was impressed with the great deal of choice on your menu, from Chinese cuisine to Japanese cooking to Italian pizza.

(7) If you hadn't reminded me to pay the electricity bill, I could have forgotten it.

文中句子翻译

(1) I am writing to express my sincere gratitude for the wonderful service that I received from your staff during my recent trip to Singapore.

(2) I also appreciate the fact that your staff members are highly knowledgeable people.

(3) Please tell them how much I appreciated their kind service.

Section 3

Part 3

句子翻译

(1) I would like to bring this matter to your immediate attention.

(2) In addition, my roommate does not use a headphone when listening to music, which is a disturbance to me.

(3) For these reasons, I hope you could refund my money as soon as possible.

(4) I am wondering how to deliver the equipment to you.

(5) I can either drive you to the airport or order a taxi for you. It's your call.

(6) It would be really helpful if you could send me a cope of the guidebook.

文中句子翻译

(1) Unfortunately, I won't be able to fetch you from the station as I have a meeting that day.

(2) Thereafter we will go to the city and have dinner in a restaurant of your choice.

(3) I can't wait to see you. Have a safe trip.

Section 4

Part 3

句子翻译

(1) As you probably already know, I am heading to Hawaii on a two-week vacation.

(2) All that you need to do is to walk my poodle every morning in order to keep it healthy.

(3) As for the lawn, you need to water it twice or three times a week.

(4) Other than that, just look after the girls and keep them safe.

(5) It would be great if you could put in a good word for me.

(6) You should have no trouble communicating with my roommate since he speaks English quite well.

(7) You could perhaps tell some bedtime stories to comfort him.

文中句子翻译

(1) As for their food habits, they are not really into veggies, but they do eat fruits and cereals.

(2) In the evenings, you could perhaps take them for a walk.

(3) I hope you don't mind doing this for me.

Section 5

Part 3

句子翻译

(1) Now that I've settled down, why don't you come and stay with me during your visit in New York?

(2) Having an international reputation and positive influence among the young, you are the ideal person to encourage young people to donate what they can afford to charity.

(3) The best thing about the trip to the Swiss Alps is that we can go skiing.

(4) Perhaps you could come with me to the gallery next Thursday to see it for yourself so that you could get some authentic details of the pictures.

(5) Your flight is scheduled at 3.00 pm on Tuesday and we will have you picked up at your residence around noon.

文中句子翻译

(1) I do hope that you can come with me.

(2) It sounds as if it should be great fun.

(3) I really hope that you are available this summer.

Section 6

Part 3

句子翻译

(1) I regret to tell you that I am not be able to pick you up at the airport since I have an appointment with my dentist that day.

(2) I am wondering if you would send my son Ian to school when I am not in town.

(3) In that case, I will need you to bring some food to the party.

(4) In case I am not at home when you arrive, you can find the key under the doormat.

(5) I suggest that you should see a doctor tomorrow.

(6) Finally, a kind reminder — as there might be a traffic jam tomorrow, you had better leave the hotel early.

文中句子翻译

(1) Now that I've finished my studies, I'm sort of free.

(2) The reason why I'm writing this letter is to ask for a small favour.

(3) I would really appreciate it if you could recommend me for the job.